ntroduction to the ITIL® Service Lifecycle

London: TSO

Published by TSO (The Stationery Office) and available from:

Online
www.tsoshop.co.uk

Mail, Telephone, Fax & E-mail
TSO
PO Box 29, Norwich, NR3 1GN
Telephone orders/General enquiries: 0870 600 5522
Fax orders: 0870 600 5533
E-mail: customer.services@tso.co.uk
Textphone 0870 240 3701

TSO@Blackwell and other Accredited Agents

© Crown Copyright 2011

This is a Crown copyright value added product, reuse of which requires a Licence from the Cabinet Office.

Applications to reuse, reproduce or republish material in this publication should be sent to
The Efficiency & Reform Group Service Desk, Cabinet Office, Rosebery Court, St Andrews Business Park, Norwich, Norfolk NR7 0HS
Tel No: (+44) (0)845 000 4999.

E-mail: servicedesk@cabinet-office.gsi.gov.uk or complete the application form on the Cabinet Office website, Licensing section.

Copyright in the typographical arrangement and design is vested in The Stationery Office Limited. Applications for reproduction should be made in writing to The Stationery Office Limited, St Crispins, Duke Street, Norwich, NR3 1PD.

The Swirl logo™ is a trade mark of the Cabinet Office

ITIL® is a registered trade mark of the Cabinet Office

PRINCE2® is a registered trade mark of the Cabinet Office

M_o_R® is a registered trade mark of the Cabinet Office

P3O® is a registered trade mark of the Cabinet Office

MSP® is a registered trade mark of the Cabinet Office

MoV™ is a trade mark of the Cabinet Office

MoP™ is a trade mark of the Cabinet Office

P3M3® is a registered trade mark of the Cabinet Office

The OGC Official Product endorsement logo™ is a trade mark of the Cabinet Office

OGC (former owner of Best Management Practice) and its functions have moved into the Cabinet Office part of HM Government –
www.cabinetoffice.gov.uk

First edition Crown Copyright 2007
Second edition Crown Copyright 2010
Third edition Crown Copyright 2011

First published 2011

ISBN 9780113313099

Printed in the United Kingdom for The Stationery Office using material containing 60% FSC post-consumer recycled fibre, 20% pre-consumer recycled fibre and 20% FSC virgin fibre.

P002459666   c10   12/11

Contents

List of figures

List of tables

Foreword

As the ITIL® portfolio manager, I am delighted to see how ITIL has grown since its inception in the late 1980s. What started life as a UK government initiative has developed into the most widely accepted approach in IT service management, and is now globally recognized as a framework of best management practice. The universal appeal of ITIL is that it provides a set of processes and procedures that are efficient, reliable and are adaptable to fit every size of organization, which in turn improves the level of services that organizations can provide.

This publication takes you on a brief tour of the ITIL service management lifecycle so that you can build a complete, if slightly out of focus, picture of service management. If you want more clarity in the picture, you will need to delve into the more comprehensive guidance within the five core publications (see Appendix B for details). The latest editions (published in 2011) provide you with the ITIL journey that many companies and individuals have already undertaken. These experiences and measurable benefits have been provided in consultation with leading experts across the globe and have enabled us to provide a top-quality product that will create value for the whole of the IT service management community.

Whether you are starting or continuing along the ITIL path, you are joining a legion of individuals and organizations that have recognized the benefits of good-quality service and have a genuine resolve to improve their service level provision. ITIL is not a panacea for all problems; it is, however, a tried and tested methodology and has been proven to work.

Written in English as the primary language, the core ITIL material is now translated into many languages and is supported by complementary books, white papers, software tools and many other helpful additions. For the individual there is training that ensures your understanding of the framework is at the level you require and a range of examinations in which you can prove to yourself, and others, that you are on your own service management journey.

I wish you luck on your chosen path.

Phil Hearsum
ITIL Portfolio Manager
Cabinet Office

Preface

Life-cycle (noun) – The various stages through which a living thing passes (Kernerman English Multilingual Dictionary)

The very term 'lifecycle' is used to describe the evolution of many living things in this world from their creation to expiration. The time between creation and expiration is the 'journey'. We need only look at our own life journey to see a living example:

■ **Creation – the first part of our journey** As an embryo develops, its life blueprint is being established through the architecture of its DNA. The embryo's genetic structure will dictate its capability, propensity for immunity or vulnerability to disease, and certain personality characteristics that it will carry throughout life.

■ **Childhood – the formative stage** We are influenced by our exposure to the world around us and can influence our life blueprint in how we manifest and integrate ourselves with our environment. Our understanding of our needs, both for growth and creativity, are our 'requirements' that allow us to create value for ourselves and those who come into contact with us.

■ **Adulthood – where we hone our skills and perform within expected societal parameters** We strive to improve our capabilities continually and define our value. By this time, we have built a complex network of relationships and dependencies on others. The world we live in has become far more complex than in childhood, and managing our lives has become more challenging.

If you replace the human metaphor above with the lifecycle of service management, you will see many similarities. This is because the ITIL service lifecycle represents the same evolution – from creation to expiration – and the stages in the ITIL service lifecycle are what happen in between.

We often forget that services are living things. They require sustenance to survive; they must continually adapt and evolve with the changing needs of the business; and they will pass through various stages in their lifetime.

Services are constrained by their genetic blueprint – risks, financial investment, culture and economics – but should evolve to influence their value through interaction, evolution, dependencies and relationships, and exploit these for positive outcomes.

This publication will accompany you on your service management journey and introduce the basic concepts of the ITIL service lifecycle and its benefits. It serves as a reference to ITIL service management practices, but should not be considered a substitute for the ITIL core publications.

Contact information

Full details of the range of material published under the ITIL banner can be found at

www.best-management-practice.com/IT-Service-Management-ITIL/

If you would like to inform us of any changes that may be required to this publication, please log them at

www.best-management-practice.com/changelog/

For further information on qualifications and training accreditation, please visit

www.itil-officialsite.com

Alternatively, please contact:

APM Group – The Accreditor Service Desk
Sword House
Totteridge Road
High Wycombe
Buckinghamshire
HP13 6DG
UK
Tel: +44 (0) 1494 458948
Email: servicedesk@apmgroupltd.com

Acknowledgements

2011 EDITION

Authors and mentors

Anthony T. Orr (BMC Software)	Author
Shirley Lacy (ConnectSphere)	Project mentor
Ashley Hanna (HP)	Technical continuity editor

Change advisory board

The change advisory board (CAB) spent considerable time and effort reviewing all the comments submitted through the change control log and their hard work was essential to this project. Members of the CAB involved in this review included:

David Cannon, Emily Egle, David Favelle, Ashley Hanna, Kevin Holland, Stuart Rance, Frances Scarff and Sharon Taylor.

Once authors and mentors were selected for the 2011 update, a revised CAB was appointed and now includes:

Emily Egle, David Favelle, Phil Hearsum, Kevin Holland and Frances Scarff.

Reviewers

Claire Agutter, IT Training Zone; Ian Clark, Pink Elephant South Africa; Jason Druebert, AT&T; Thomas Fischer, Danish Agency for Governmental IT; Stefan Gabriel, independent; Anne Goddard, Goddard Service Management Consulting; Bartosz Górczyński, itSMF Poland; Jitendera Pratap, Singh Tata Consultancy Services; Dmitry Raudin, independent; Peter Ravnholt, UXC Consulting/ Lucid IT; Brian Rowlatt, Logica; John Sansbury, Infrassistance Consulting; Dominic Schaefer, Serco Services GmbH; Vaishali Somasundaram, independent; Helen Sussex, Logica; Abbey Wiltse, SMV Inc.

Introduction

1

1 Introduction

This publication introduces IT service management and ITIL. Service management is a set of specialized organizational capabilities for providing value to customers in the form of services. These capabilities are embedded in an organization's management, processes, knowledge and people. They represent a service organization's capacity, competency and confidence for action in service provisioning.

1.1 WHAT IS ITIL?

ITIL is part of a suite of best-practice publications for IT service management (ITSM).[1] ITIL provides guidance to service providers on the provision of quality IT services, and on the processes, functions and other capabilities needed to support them. ITIL is used by many hundreds of organizations around the world and offers best-practice guidance to all types of organization that provide services. ITIL is not a standard that has to be followed; it is guidance that should be read and understood, and used to create value for the service provider and its customers. Organizations are encouraged to adopt ITIL best practices and to adapt them to work in their specific environments in ways that meet their needs.

ITIL is the most widely recognized framework for ITSM in the world. In the 20 years since it was created, ITIL has evolved and changed its breadth and depth as technologies and business practices have developed.

In 2007, the second major refresh of ITIL was published in response to significant advancements in technology and emerging challenges for IT service providers. New models and architectures such as outsourcing, shared services, utility computing, cloud computing, virtualization, web services and mobile commerce have become widespread within IT. The process-based approach of ITIL was augmented with the service lifecycle to address these additional service management challenges. In 2011, as part of its commitment to continual improvement, the Cabinet Office published this update to improve consistency across the core publications.

1.2 THE ITIL VALUE PROPOSITION

All high-performing service providers share similar characteristics. This is not coincidence. There are specific capabilities inherent in their success that they demonstrate consistently. A core capability is their strategy. If you were to ask a high-achieving service provider what makes them distinctive from their competitors, they would tell you that it is their intrinsic understanding of how they provide value to their customers. They understand the customer's business objectives and the role they play in enabling those objectives to be met. A closer look would reveal that their ability to do this does not come from reacting to customer needs, but from predicting them through preparation, analysis and examining customer usage patterns.

The next significant characteristic is the systematic use of service management practices that are

---

[1] ITSM and other concepts from this chapter are described in more detail in Chapter 2.

responsive, consistent and measurable, and define the provider's quality in the eyes of their customers. These practices provide stability and predictability, and permeate the service provider's culture.

The final characteristic is the provider's ability to continuously analyse and fine tune service provision to maintain stable, reliable yet adaptive and responsive services that allow the customer to focus on their business without concern for IT service reliability.

1.3 THE ITIL SERVICE LIFECYCLE

The ITIL framework is based on the five stages of the service lifecycle as shown in Figure 1.1, with a core publication providing best-practice guidance for each stage. This guidance includes key principles, required processes and activities, organization and roles, technology, associated challenges, critical success factors and risks. The service lifecycle uses a hub-and-spoke design, with service strategy at the hub, and service design, transition and operation as the revolving lifecycle stages or 'spokes'. Continual service improvement surrounds and supports all stages of the service lifecycle. Each stage of the lifecycle exerts influence on the others and relies on them for inputs and feedback. In this way, a constant set of checks and balances throughout the service lifecycle ensures that as business demand changes with business need, the services can adapt and respond effectively.

In addition to the core publications, there is also a complementary set of ITIL publications providing guidance specific to industry sectors, organization types, operating models and technology architectures.

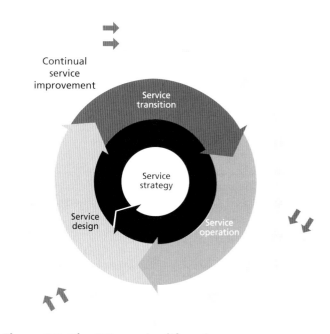

Figure 1.1 The ITIL service lifecycle

1.4 OVERVIEW

This publication provides a summary of each stage of the service lifecycle and the best practices described in the corresponding core ITIL publication. Although it can be read in isolation, it is recommended that it be used in conjunction with the other ITIL publications. This will help you to fully appreciate and understand the overall lifecycle of services and of IT service management.

In the following chapters you will learn about the key concepts within the ITIL service lifecycle. You begin by working your way from the core of the lifecycle, service strategy, then around the revolving lifecycle practices of service design, transition and operation, finishing with continual service improvement. Afterwards, you should have a clear understanding of the basic concepts of the ITIL service lifecycle and how the core practice publications can be useful to you. This will help you to further examine particular areas within any of the core guidance publications that offer detailed practice information in areas that support your day-to-day service management role.

1.4.1 Value to business

Selecting and adopting the best practices as recommended in the ITIL core publications will assist organizations in delivering significant benefits. By implementing these best practices it is possible to deliver and support quality, cost-effective services and to ensure that the business requirements are being met consistently.

Adopting and implementing standard and consistent approaches across the service lifecycle will:

- Deliver value for customers through services
- Integrate the strategy for services with the business strategy and customer needs
- Measure, monitor and optimize IT services and service provider performance
- Manage the IT investment and budget
- Manage risk
- Manage knowledge
- Manage capabilities and resources to effectively and efficiently deliver services
- Ensure a standard approach to service management across the enterprise
- Change the organizational culture to support the achievement of sustained success
- Improve the interaction and relationship with customers
- Coordinate delivery of goods and services across the value network
- Optimize and reduce cost.

1.4.2 Target audience

Service management is a generic concept and this publication is applicable to all types of organization including in-house and commercial service providers. It is relevant to any professional involved in the management of services, particularly the management of IT-enabled business services, including:

- IT steering/governance
- Chief information officers (CIOs)/IT directors
- IT service managers
- Portfolio managers
- Service desk managers/staff
- Incident managers/technical support staff
- Operations management
- Change managers/change requestors
- Solution development/design
- Testing/production assurance
- Service level managers
- Application/infrastructure
- Supplier relationship management
- Business relationship management

1.5 CONTEXT

The ITIL core consists of five lifecycle publications. Each provides part of the guidance necessary for an integrated approach as required by the ISO/IEC 20000 standard specification. The five publications are:

- *ITIL Service Strategy*
- *ITIL Service Design*
- *ITIL Service Transition*
- *ITIL Service Operation*
- *ITIL Continual Service Improvement.*

Each one addresses capabilities having direct impact on a service provider's performance. The core is expected to provide structure, stability and strength to service management capabilities, with durable principles, methods and tools. This serves to protect investments and provide the necessary basis for measurement, learning and improvement. This publication, *Introduction to the ITIL Service Lifecycle*, provides an overview of the lifecycle stages described in the ITIL core.

ITIL guidance can be adapted to support various business environments and organizational strategies. Complementary ITIL publications provide flexibility to implement the core in a diverse range of environments. Practitioners can select complementary publications as needed to provide traction for the ITIL core in a given context, in much the same way as tyres are selected based on the type of vehicle, purpose and road conditions. This is to increase the durability and portability of knowledge assets and to protect investments in service management capabilities.

1.5.1 Service strategy

At the centre of the service lifecycle is service strategy. Value creation begins here with understanding organizational objectives and customer needs. Every organizational asset including people, processes and products should support the strategy.

ITIL Service Strategy provides guidance on how to view service management not only as an organizational capability but as a strategic asset. It describes the principles underpinning the practice of service management which are useful for developing service management policies, guidelines and processes across the ITIL service lifecycle.

Topics covered in *ITIL Service Strategy* include the development of market spaces, characteristics of internal and external provider types, service assets, the service portfolio and implementation of strategy through the service lifecycle. Business relationship management, demand management, financial management, organizational development and strategic risks are among the other major topics.

Organizations should use *ITIL Service Strategy* to set objectives and expectations of performance towards serving customers and market spaces, and to identify, select and prioritize opportunities. Service strategy is about ensuring that organizations are in a position to handle the costs and risks associated with their service portfolios, and are set up not just for operational effectiveness but for distinctive performance.

Organizations already practising ITIL can use *ITIL Service Strategy* to guide a strategic review of their ITIL-based service management capabilities and to improve the alignment between those capabilities and their business strategies. *ITIL Service Strategy* will encourage readers to stop and think about why something is to be done before thinking of how.

1.5.2 Service design

For services to provide true value to the business, they must be designed with the business objectives in mind. Design encompasses the whole IT organization, for it is the organization as a whole that delivers and supports the services. Service design is the stage in the lifecycle that turns a service strategy into a plan for delivering the business objectives.

ITIL Service Design provides guidance for the design and development of services and service management practices. It covers design principles and methods for converting strategic objectives into portfolios of services and service assets. The scope of *ITIL Service Design* is not limited to new services. It includes the changes and improvements necessary to increase or maintain value to customers over the lifecycle of services, the continuity of services, achievement of service levels, and conformance to standards and regulations. It guides organizations on how to develop design capabilities for service management.

Other topics in *ITIL Service Design* include design coordination, service catalogue management, service level management, availability management, capacity management, IT service continuity management, information security management and supplier management.

1.5.3 Service transition

ITIL Service Transition provides guidance for the development and improvement of capabilities for introducing new and changed services into supported environments. It describes how to transition an organization from one state to another while controlling risk and supporting organizational knowledge for decision support. It ensures that the value(s) identified in the service strategy, and encoded in service design, are effectively transitioned so that they can be realized in service operation.

ITIL Service Transition describes best practice in transition planning and support, change management, service asset and configuration management, release and deployment management, service validation and testing, change evaluation and knowledge management. It provides guidance on managing the complexity related to changes to services and service

management processes, preventing undesired consequences while allowing for innovation.

ITIL Service Transition also introduces the service knowledge management system, which can support organizational learning and help to improve the overall efficiency and effectiveness of all stages of the service lifecycle. This will enable people to benefit from the knowledge and experience of others, support informed decision-making, and improve the management of services.

1.5.4 Service operation

ITIL Service Operation describes best practice for managing services in supported environments. It includes guidance on achieving effectiveness and efficiency in the delivery and support of services to ensure value for the customer, the users and the service provider.

Strategic objectives are ultimately realized through service operation, therefore making it a critical capability. *ITIL Service Operation* provides guidance on how to maintain stability in service operation, allowing for changes in design, scale, scope and service levels. Organizations are provided with detailed process guidelines, methods and tools for use in two major control perspectives: reactive and proactive. Managers and practitioners are provided with knowledge allowing them to make better decisions in areas such as managing the availability of services, controlling demand, optimizing capacity utilization, scheduling of operations, and avoiding or resolving service incidents and managing problems. New models and architectures such as shared services, utility computing, web services and mobile commerce to support service operation are described.

Other topics in *ITIL Service Operation* include event management, incident management, request

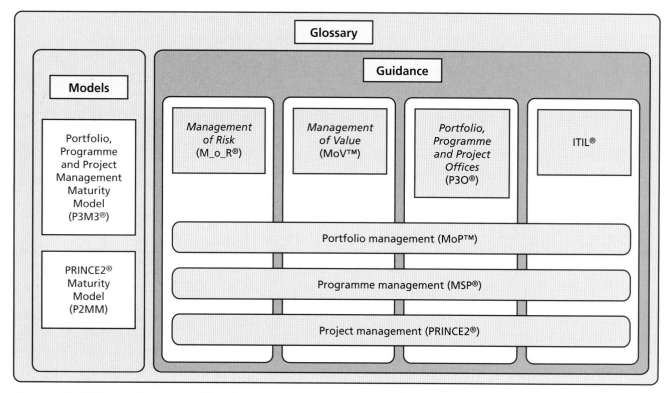

Figure 1.2 ITIL's relationship with other Best Management Practice guides

fulfilment, problem management and access management processes; as well as the service desk, technical management, IT operations management and application management functions.

1.5.5 Continual service improvement

ITIL Continual Service Improvement provides guidance on creating and maintaining value for customers through better strategy, design, transition and operation of services. It combines principles, practices and methods from quality management, change management and capability improvement.

ITIL Continual Service Improvement describes best practice for achieving incremental and large-scale improvements in service quality, operational efficiency and business continuity, and for ensuring that the service portfolio continues to be aligned to business needs. Guidance is provided for linking improvement efforts and outcomes with service strategy, design, transition and operation. A closed-loop feedback system, based on the Plan-Do-Check-Act (PDCA) cycle, is established. Feedback from any stage of the service lifecycle can be used to identify improvement opportunities for any other stage of the lifecycle.

Other topics in *ITIL Continual Service Improvement* include service measurement, demonstrating value with metrics, developing baselines and maturity assessments.

1.6 ITIL IN RELATION TO OTHER PUBLICATIONS IN THE BEST MANAGEMENT PRACTICE PORTFOLIO

ITIL is part of a portfolio of best-practice publications (known collectively as Best Management Practice or BMP) aimed at helping organizations and individuals manage projects, programmes and services consistently and effectively (see Figure 1.2). ITIL can be used in harmony with other BMP products, and international or internal organization standards. Where appropriate, BMP guidance is supported by a qualification scheme and accredited training and consultancy services. All BMP guidance is intended to be tailored for use by individual organizations.

BMP publications include:

- *Management of Portfolios* **(MoP™)**   Portfolio management concerns the twin issues of how to do the 'right' projects and programmes in the context of the organization's strategic objectives, and how to do them 'correctly' in terms of achieving delivery and benefits at a collective level. MoP encompasses consideration of the principles upon which effective portfolio management is based; the key practices in the portfolio definition and delivery cycles, including examples of how they have been applied in real life; and guidance on how to implement portfolio management and sustain progress in a wide variety of organizations.

  Office of Government Commerce (2011). *Management of Portfolios*. TSO, London.

- *Management of Risk* **(M_o_R®)**   M_o_R offers an effective framework for taking informed decisions about the risks that affect performance objectives. The framework allows organizations to assess risk accurately (selecting the correct responses to threats and opportunities created by uncertainty) and thereby improve their service delivery.

  Office of Government Commerce (2010). *Management of Risk: Guidance for Practitioners*. TSO, London.

- *Management of Value* **(MoV™)**   MoV provides a cross-sector and universally applicable guide on how to maximize value in a way that takes account of organizations' priorities, differing stakeholders' needs and, at the same time, uses resources as efficiently and effectively as possible. It will help organizations to put in place effective methods to deliver enhanced value across their portfolio, programmes, projects and operational activities to meet the challenges of ever-more competitive and resource-constrained environments.

  Office of Government Commerce (2010). *Management of Value*. TSO, London.

- *Managing Successful Programmes* **(MSP®)**   MSP provides a framework to enable the achievement of high-quality change outcomes and benefits that fundamentally affect the way in which organizations work. One of the core themes in MSP is that a programme must add more value than that provided by the sum of its constituent project and major activities.

  Cabinet Office (2011). *Managing Successful Programmes*. TSO, London.

- ***Managing Successful Projects with PRINCE2®***
PRINCE2 (PRojects IN Controlled Environments, V2) is a structured method to help effective project management via clearly defined products. Key themes that feature throughout PRINCE2 are the dependence on a viable business case confirming the delivery of measurable benefits that are aligned to an organization's objectives and strategy, while ensuring the management of risks, costs and quality.

  Office of Government Commerce (2009). *Managing Successful Projects with PRINCE2*. TSO, London.

- ***Portfolio, Programme and Project Offices (P3O®)*** P3O provides universally applicable guidance, including principles, processes and techniques, to successfully establish, develop and maintain appropriate support structures. These structures will facilitate delivery of business objectives (portfolios), programmes and projects within time, cost, quality and other organizational constraints.

  Office of Government Commerce (2008). *Portfolio, Programme and Project Offices*. TSO, London.

1.7 WHY IS ITIL SO SUCCESSFUL?

ITIL embraces a practical approach to service management – do what works. And what works is adapting a common framework of practices that unite all areas of IT service provision towards a single aim – that of delivering value to the business. The following list defines the key characteristics of ITIL that contribute to its global success:

- **Vendor-neutral** ITIL service management practices are applicable in any IT organization because they are not based on any particular technology platform or industry type. ITIL is owned by the UK government and is not tied to any commercial proprietary practice or solution.
- **Non-prescriptive** ITIL offers robust, mature and time-tested practices that have applicability to all types of service organization. It continues to be useful and relevant in public and private sectors, internal and external service providers, small, medium and large enterprises, and within any technical environment. Organizations should adopt ITIL and adapt it to meet the needs of the IT organization and their customers.
- **Best practice** ITIL represents the learning experiences and thought leadership of the world's best-in-class service providers.

ITIL is successful because it describes practices that enable organizations to deliver benefits, return on investment and sustained success. ITIL is adopted by organizations to enable them to:

- Deliver value for customers through services
- Integrate the strategy for services with the business strategy and customer needs
- Measure, monitor and optimize IT services and service provider performance
- Manage the IT investment and budget
- Manage risk
- Manage knowledge
- Manage capabilities and resources to deliver services effectively and efficiently
- Enable adoption of a standard approach to service management across the enterprise
- Change the organizational culture to support the achievement of sustained success

- Improve the interaction and relationship with customers
- Coordinate the delivery of goods and services across the value network
- Optimize and reduce costs.

1.8 A COMMON STRUCTURE ACROSS THE ITIL CORE

A common chapter structure across all five core ITIL publications makes it easier to find similar guidance within each stage of the lifecycle. The following references are to the chapters within the core publications, and not to the chapters within *Introduction to the ITIL Service Lifecycle*:

- **Service management as a practice (Chapter 2)** This chapter explains the concepts of service management and services, and describes how these can be used to create value. It also summarizes a number of generic ITIL concepts that the publication depends on.
- **Lifecycle stage principles (Chapter 3)** This chapter describes the terminology and key principles which form the building blocks of the lifecycle stage.
- **Lifecycle stage processes (Chapter 4)** This chapter sets out the processes and activities on which an effective implementation of the lifecycle depends, and how they integrate with the other stages of the lifecycle.
- **Additional lifecycle stage guidance (Chapter 5)** This chapter provides guidance on other practices and activities specific to the lifecycle stage.
- **Organizing for the lifecycle stage (Chapter 6)** This chapter identifies the organizational roles and responsibilities that are needed to manage the lifecycle stage and

its associated processes. The roles are provided as guidelines and can be combined to fit into a variety of organizational structures.

- **Technology considerations (Chapter 7)** ITIL service management practices gain momentum when the right type of technical automation is applied. This chapter provides recommendations for the use of technology in the lifecycle stage and the basic requirements a service provider will need to consider when choosing service management tools.
- **Challenges, risks and critical success factors (Chapter 8)** It is important for any organization to understand the challenges, risks and critical success factors that could influence their performance. This chapter discusses typical examples of these.
- **Related guidance (Appendix)** This appendix contains a list of some of the many external methods, practices and frameworks that align well with ITIL best practice. Notes are provided on how they integrate into the lifecycle stage, and when and how they are useful.
- **Examples and templates (Appendix)** Examples and templates are provided in various appendices to help you capitalize on the industry experience and expertise already in use. Each can be adapted within your particular organizational context.
- **Inputs and outputs across the service lifecycle (Appendix)** This contains examples of some of the major inputs and outputs between each stage of the service lifecycle.
- **Abbreviations and glossary** This contains a selected glossary of terms.

1.9 CHAPTER SUMMARY

Introduction to the ITIL Service Lifecycle comprises:

- **Chapter 2 Service management as a practice**
  This chapter explains the concepts of service management and services.

- **Chapters 3 to 7 The ITIL service lifecycle stages**
  These chapters provide an overview of the key principles and processes of each lifecycle stage.

- **Chapter 8 ITIL qualifications and credentials**
  This chapter describes service management certification and credentials.

- **Appendix A Examples of inputs and outputs across the service lifecycle**
  This appendix identifies some of the major inputs and outputs across the service lifecycle.

- **Appendix B Related guidance**
  This appendix provides a list of other sources of information that informed the writing of the core publications.

- **Abbreviations and glossary**
  The glossary is a full version of the terms used in the ITIL core publications (unlike the glossaries in the core publications which are bespoke).

Service management as a practice

2

2 Service management as a practice

2.1 SERVICES AND SERVICE MANAGEMENT

2.1.1 Services

Services are a means of delivering value to customers by facilitating the outcomes customers want to achieve without the ownership of specific costs and risks. Services facilitate outcomes by enhancing the performance of associated tasks and reducing the effect of constraints. These constraints may include regulation, lack of funding or capacity, or technology limitations. The end result is an increase in the probability of desired outcomes. While some services enhance performance of tasks, others have a more direct impact – they perform the task itself.

The preceding paragraph is not just a definition, as it is a recurring pattern found in a wide range of services. Patterns are useful for managing complexity, costs, flexibility and variety. They are generic structures useful to make an idea applicable in a wide range of environments and situations. In each instance the pattern is applied with variations that make the idea effective, economical or simply useful in that particular case.

Definition: outcome

The result of carrying out an activity, following a process, or delivering an IT service etc. The term is used to refer to intended results, as well as to actual results.

An outcome-based definition of service moves IT organizations beyond business–IT alignment towards business–IT integration. Internal dialogue and discussion on the meaning of services is an elementary step towards alignment and integration with a customer's business (Figure 2.1). Customer outcomes become the ultimate concern of business relationship managers instead of the gathering of requirements, which is necessary but not sufficient. Requirements are generated for internal coordination and control only after customer outcomes are well understood.

Customers seek outcomes but do not wish to have accountability or ownership of all the associated costs and risks. All services must have a budget when they go live and this must be managed. The service cost is reflected in financial terms such as return on investment (ROI) and total cost of ownership (TCO). The customer will only be exposed to the overall cost or price of a service, which will include all the provider's costs and risk mitigation measures (and any profit margin if appropriate). The customer can then judge the value of a service based on a comparison of cost or price and reliability with the desired outcome.

Definitions

Service: A means of delivering value to customers by facilitating outcomes customers want to achieve without the ownership of specific costs and risks.

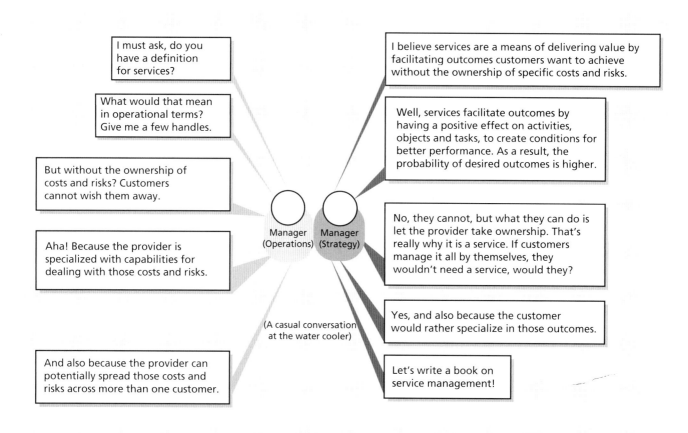

Figure 2.1 Conversation about the definition and meaning of services

IT service: A service provided by an IT service provider. An IT service is made up of a combination of information technology, people and processes. A customer-facing IT service directly supports the business processes of one or more customers and its service level targets should be defined in a service level agreement. Other IT services, called supporting services, are not directly used by the business but are required by the service provider to deliver customer-facing services.

Customer satisfaction is also important. Customers need to be satisfied with the level of service and feel confident in the ability of the service provider to continue providing that level of service – or even improving it over time. The difficulty is that customer expectations keep shifting, and a service provider that does not track this will soon find itself losing business. *ITIL Service Strategy* is helpful in understanding how this happens, and how a service provider can adapt its services to meet the changing customer environment.

Services can be discussed in terms of how they relate to one another and their customers, and can be classified as core, enabling or enhancing.

Core services deliver the basic outcomes desired by one or more customers. They represent the value that the customer wants and for which they are willing to pay. Core services anchor the value proposition for the customer and provide the basis for their continued utilization and satisfaction.

Enabling services are services that are needed in order for a core service to be delivered. Enabling services may or may not be visible to the customer, but the customer does not perceive them as services in their own right. They are 'basic factors' which enable the customer to receive the 'real' (core) service.

Enhancing services are services that are added to a core service to make it more exciting or enticing to the customer. Enhancing services are not essential to the delivery of a core service, and are added to a core service as 'excitement' factors, which will encourage customers to use the core service more (or to choose the core service provided by one company over those of its competitors).

Services may be as simple as allowing a user to complete a single transaction, but most services are complex. They consist of a range of deliverables and functionality. If each individual aspect of these complex services were defined independently, the service provider would soon find it impossible to track and record all services.

Most service providers will follow a strategy where they can deliver a set of more generic services to a broad range of customers, thus achieving economies of scale and competing on the basis of price and a certain amount of flexibility. One way of achieving this is by using service packages.

A service package is a collection of two or more services that have been combined to offer a solution to a specific type of customer need or to underpin specific business outcomes. A service package can consist of a combination of core services, enabling services and enhancing services.

Where a service or service package needs to be differentiated for different types of customer, one or more components of the package can be changed, or offered at different levels of utility and warranty, to create service options. These different service options can then be offered to customers and are sometimes called service level packages.

2.1.2 Service management

When we turn on a water tap, we expect to see water flow from it. When we turn on a light switch, we expect to see light fill the room. Not so many years ago, these very basic things were not as reliable as they are today. We know instinctively that the advances in technology have made them reliable enough to be considered a utility. But it isn't just the technology that makes the services reliable. It is how they are managed.

The use of IT today has become the utility of business. Business today wants IT services that behave like other utilities such as water, electricity or the telephone. Simply having the best technology will not ensure that IT provides utility-like reliability. Professional, responsive, value-driven service management is what brings this quality of service to the business.

Service management is a set of specialized organizational capabilities for providing value to customers in the form of services. The more mature a service provider's capabilities are, the greater is their ability to consistently produce quality services that meet the needs of the customer in a timely and cost-effective manner. The act of transforming capabilities and resources into valuable services is at the core of service management. Without these capabilities, a service organization is merely a bundle of resources that by itself has relatively low intrinsic value for customers.

> **Definitions**
>
> *Service management*: A set of specialized organizational capabilities for providing value to customers in the form of services.
>
> *Service provider*: An organization supplying services to one or more internal or external customers.

Organizational capabilities are shaped by the challenges they are expected to overcome. An example of this is provided by Toyota in the 1950s when it developed unique capabilities to overcome the challenge of smaller scale and financial capital compared to its American rivals. Toyota developed new capabilities in production engineering, operations management and managing suppliers to compensate for its inability to afford large inventories, make components, produce raw materials or own the companies that produced them (Magretta, 2002).[2]

Service management capabilities are similarly influenced by the following challenges that distinguish services from other systems of value creation, such as manufacturing, mining and agriculture:

■ Intangible nature of the output and intermediate products of service processes: they are difficult to measure, control and validate (or prove).

■ Demand is tightly coupled with the customer's assets: users and other customer assets such as processes, applications, documents and transactions arrive with demand and stimulate service production.

■ High level of contact for producers and consumers of services: there is little or no buffer between the service provider's creation of the service and the customer's consumption of that service.

■ The perishable nature of service output and service capacity: there is value for the customer from assurance on the continued supply of consistent quality. Providers need to secure a steady supply of demand from customers.

Service management is more than just a set of capabilities. It is also a professional practice supported by an extensive body of knowledge, experience and skills. A global community of individuals and organizations in the public and private sectors fosters its growth and maturity. Formal schemes exist for the education, training and certification of practising organizations, and individuals influence its quality. Industry best practices, academic research and formal standards contribute to and draw from its intellectual capital.

The origins of service management are in traditional service businesses such as airlines, banks, hotels and phone companies. Its practice has grown with the adoption by IT organizations of a service-oriented approach to managing IT applications, infrastructure and processes. Solutions to business problems and support for business models, strategies and operations are increasingly in the form of services. The popularity of shared services and outsourcing has contributed to the increase in

---

[2] Magretta, J. (2002). *What Management Is: How it Works and Why it's Everyone's Business*. The Free Press, New York.

the number of organizations that behave as service providers, including internal IT organizations. This in turn has strengthened the practice of service management while at the same time imposed greater challenges.

2.1.3 IT service management

Information technology (IT) is a commonly used term that changes meaning depending on the different perspectives that a business organization or people may have of it. A key challenge is to recognize and balance these perspectives when communicating the value of IT service management (ITSM) and understanding the context for how the business sees the IT organization. Some of these meanings are:

■ IT is a collection of systems, applications and infrastructures which are components or sub-assemblies of a larger product. They enable or are embedded in processes and services.

■ IT is an organization with its own set of capabilities and resources. IT organizations can be of various types such as business functions, shared services units and enterprise-level core units.

■ IT is a category of services utilized by business. The services are typically IT applications and infrastructure that are packaged and offered by internal IT organizations or external service providers. IT costs are treated as business expenses.

■ IT is a category of business assets that provide a stream of benefits for their owners, including, but not limited to, revenue, income and profit. IT costs are treated as investments.

Every IT organization should act as a service provider, using the principles of service management to ensure that they deliver the outcomes required by their customers.

> **Definitions**
>
> *IT service management (ITSM)*: The implementation and management of quality IT services that meet the needs of the business. IT service management is performed by IT service providers through an appropriate mix of people, process and information technology.
>
> *IT service provider*: A service provider that provides IT services to internal or external customers.

ITSM must be carried out effectively and efficiently. Managing IT from the business perspective enables organizational high performance and value creation.

A good relationship between an IT service provider and its customers relies on the customer receiving an IT service that meets its needs, at an acceptable level of performance and at a cost that the customer can afford. The IT service provider needs to work out how to achieve a balance between these three areas, and communicate with the customer if there is anything which prevents it from being able to deliver the required IT service at the agreed level of performance or price.

A service level agreement (SLA) is used to document agreements between an IT service provider and a customer. An SLA describes the IT service, documents service level targets, and specifies the responsibilities of the IT service provider and the customer. A single agreement may cover multiple IT services or multiple customers.

2.1.4 Service providers

There are three main types of service provider. While most aspects of service management apply equally to all types of service provider, other aspects such as customers, contracts, competition, market spaces, revenue and strategy take on different meanings depending on the specific type. The three types are:

- **Type I – internal service provider** An internal service provider that is embedded within a business unit. There may be several Type I service providers within an organization.
- **Type II – shared services unit** An internal service provider that provides shared IT services to more than one business unit.
- **Type III – external service provider** A service provider that provides IT services to external customers.

ITSM concepts are often described in the context of only one of these types and as if only one type of IT service provider exists or is used by a given organization. In reality most organizations have a combination of IT service providers. In a single organization it is possible that some IT units are dedicated to a single business unit, others provide shared services, and yet others have been outsourced or depend on external service providers.

Many IT organizations who traditionally provide services to internal customers find that they are dealing directly with external users because of the online services that they provide. *ITIL Service Strategy* provides guidance on how the IT organization interacts with these users, and who owns and manages the relationship with them.

2.1.5 Stakeholders in service management

Stakeholders have an interest in an organization, project or service etc. and may be interested in the activities, targets, resources or deliverables from service management. Examples include organizations, service providers, customers, consumers, users, partners, employees, shareholders, owners and suppliers. The term 'organization' is used to define a company, legal entity or other institution. It is also used to refer to any entity that has people, resources and budgets – for example, a project or business.

Within the service provider organization there are many different stakeholders including the functions, groups and teams that deliver the services. There are also many stakeholders external to the service provider organization, for example:

- **Customers** Those who buy goods or services. The customer of an IT service provider is the person or group who defines and agrees the service level targets. This term is also sometimes used informally to mean user – for example, 'This is a customer-focused organization.'
- **Users** Those who use the service on a day-to-day basis. Users are distinct from customers, as some customers do not use the IT service directly.
- **Suppliers** Third parties responsible for supplying goods or services that are required to deliver IT services. Examples of suppliers include commodity hardware and software vendors, network and telecom providers, and outsourcing organizations.

There is a difference between customers who work in the same organization as the IT service provider, and customers who work for other organizations. They are distinguished as follows:

■ **Internal customers**   These are customers who work for the same business as the IT service provider. For example, the marketing department is an internal customer of the IT organization because it uses IT services. The head of marketing and the chief information officer both report to the chief executive officer. If IT charges for its services, the money paid is an internal transaction in the organization's accounting system, not real revenue.

■ **External customers**   These are customers who work for a different business from the IT service provider. External customers typically purchase services from the service provider by means of a legally binding contract or agreement.

2.1.6 Utility and warranty

The value of a service can be considered to be the level to which that service meets a customer's expectations. It is often measured by how much the customer is willing to pay for the service, rather than the cost to the service provider of providing the service or any other intrinsic attribute of the service itself.

Unlike products, services do not have much intrinsic value. The value of a service comes from what it enables someone to do. The value of a service is not determined by the provider, but by the person who receives it – because they decide what they will do with the service, and what type of return they will achieve by using the service. Services contribute value to an organization only when their value is perceived to be higher than the cost of obtaining the service.

From the customer's perspective, value consists of achieving business objectives. The value of a service is created by combining two primary elements: utility (fitness for purpose) and warranty (fitness

for use). These two elements work together to achieve the desired outcomes upon which the customer and the business base their perceptions of a service.

Utility is the functionality offered by a product or service to meet a particular need. Utility can be summarized as 'what the service does', and can be used to determine whether a service is able to meet its required outcomes, or is 'fit for purpose'. Utility refers to those aspects of a service that contribute to tasks associated with achieving outcomes. For example, a service that enables a business unit to process orders should allow sales people to access customer details, stock availability, shipping information etc. Any aspect of the service that improves the ability of sales people to improve the performance of the task of processing sales orders would be considered utility. Utility can therefore represent any attribute of a service that removes, or reduces the effect of, constraints on the performance of a task.

Warranty is an assurance that a product or service will meet its agreed requirements. This may be a formal agreement such as a service level agreement or contract, or a marketing message or brand image. Warranty refers to the ability of a service to be available when needed, to provide the required capacity, and to provide the required reliability in terms of continuity and security. Warranty can be summarized as 'how the service is delivered', and can be used to determine whether a service is 'fit for use'. For example, any aspect of the service that increases the availability or speed of the service would be considered warranty. Warranty can therefore represent any attribute of a service that increases the potential of the business to be able to perform a task. Warranty refers to any means by which utility is made available to the users.

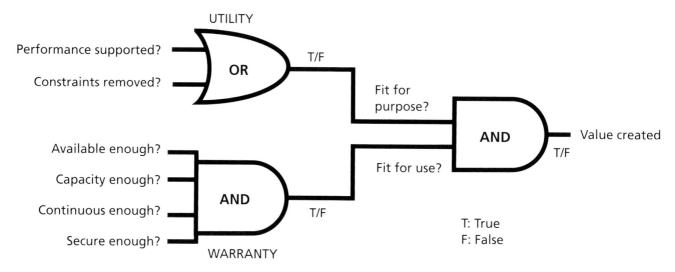

Figure 2.2 Services are designed, built and delivered with both utility and warranty

Utility is *what* the service does, and warranty is *how* it is delivered.

Customers cannot benefit from something that is fit for purpose but not fit for use, and vice versa. The value of a service is therefore only delivered when both utility and warranty are designed and delivered. Figure 2.2 illustrates the logic that a service has to have both utility and warranty to create value. Utility is used to improve the performance of the tasks required to achieve an outcome, or to remove constraints that prevent the task from being performed adequately (or both). Warranty requires the service to be available, continuous and secure and to have sufficient capacity for the service to perform at the required level. If the service is both fit for purpose and fit for use, it will create value.

It should be noted that the elements of warranty in Figure 2.2 are not exclusive. It is possible to define other components of warranty, such as usability, which refers to how easy it is for the user to access

and use the features of the service to achieve the desired outcomes.

The warranty aspect of the service needs to be designed at the same time as the utility aspect in order to deliver the required value to the business. Attempts to design warranty aspects after a service has been deployed can be expensive and disruptive.

Information about the desired business outcomes, opportunities, customers, utility and warranty of the service is used to develop the definition of a service. Using an outcome-based definition helps to ensure that managers plan and execute all aspects of service management from the perspective of what is valuable to the customer.

2.1.7 Best practices in the public domain

Organizations benchmark themselves against peers and seek to close gaps in capabilities. This enables them to become more competitive by improving their ability to deliver quality services that meet

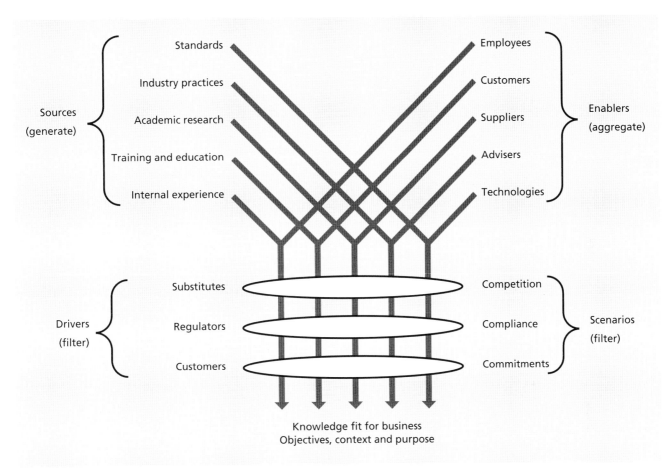

Figure 2.3 Sources of service management best practice

the needs of their customers at a price their customers can afford. One way to close such gaps is the adoption of best practices in wide industry use. There are several sources for best practice including public frameworks, standards and the proprietary knowledge of organizations and individuals (Figure 2.3). ITIL is the most widely recognized and trusted source of best-practice guidance in the area of ITSM.

Public frameworks and standards are attractive when compared with proprietary knowledge for the following reasons:

■ Proprietary knowledge is deeply embedded in organizations and therefore difficult to adopt, replicate or even transfer with the cooperation of the owners. Such knowledge is often in the form of tacit knowledge which is inextricable and poorly documented.

- Proprietary knowledge is customized for the local context and the specific needs of the business to the point of being idiosyncratic. Unless the recipients of such knowledge have matching circumstances, the knowledge may not be as effective in use.

- Owners of proprietary knowledge expect to be rewarded for their investments. They may make such knowledge available only under commercial terms through purchases and licensing agreements.

- Publicly available frameworks and standards such as ITIL, LEAN, Six Sigma, COBIT, CMMI, PRINCE2, PMBOK®, ISO 9000, ISO/IEC 20000 and ISO/IEC 27001 are validated across a diverse set of environments and situations rather than the limited experience of a single organization. They are subject to broad review across multiple organizations and disciplines, and vetted by diverse sets of partners, suppliers and competitors.

- The knowledge of public frameworks is more likely to be widely distributed among a large community of professionals through publicly available training and certification. It is easier for organizations to acquire such knowledge through the labour market.

Ignoring public frameworks and standards can needlessly place an organization at a disadvantage. Organizations should cultivate their own proprietary knowledge on top of a body of knowledge based on public frameworks and standards. Collaboration and coordination across organizations become easier on the basis of shared practices and standards. Further information on best practice in the public domain is provided in Appendix B.

2.2 BASIC CONCEPTS

2.2.1 Assets, resources and capabilities

The service relationship between service providers and their customers revolves around the use of assets – both those of the service provider and those of the customer. Each relationship involves an interaction between the assets of each party.

Many customers use the service they receive from a service provider to build and deliver services or products of their own and then deliver them on to their own customers. In these cases, what the service provider considers to be the customer asset would be considered to be a service asset by their customer.

Without customer assets, there is no basis for defining the value of a service. The performance of customer assets is therefore a primary concern for service management.

Definitions

Asset: Any resource or capability.

Customer asset: Any resource or capability used by a customer to achieve a business outcome.

Service asset: Any resource or capability used by a service provider to deliver services to a customer.

There are two types of asset used by both service providers and customers – resources and capabilities. Organizations use them to create value in the form of goods and services. Resources are direct inputs for production. Capabilities represent an organization's ability to coordinate, control and deploy resources to produce value. Capabilities are typically experience-driven, knowledge-intensive, information-based and firmly embedded within an organization's people, systems, processes and technologies. It is relatively easy to acquire resources compared to capabilities (see Figure 2.4 for examples of capabilities and resources).

Service providers need to develop distinctive capabilities to retain customers with value propositions that are hard for competitors to duplicate. For example, two service providers may have similar resources such as applications, infrastructure and access to finance. Their capabilities, however, differ in terms of management systems, organization structure, processes and knowledge assets. This difference is reflected in actual performance.

Capabilities by themselves cannot produce value without adequate and appropriate resources. The productive capacity of a service provider is dependent on the resources under its control. Capabilities are used to develop, deploy and coordinate this productive capacity. For example, capabilities such as capacity management and availability management are used to manage the performance and utilization of processes, applications and infrastructure, ensuring service levels are effectively delivered.

2.2.2 Processes

> **Definition: process**
>
> A process is a structured set of activities designed to accomplish a specific objective. A process takes one or more defined inputs and turns them into defined outputs.

Processes define actions, dependencies and sequence. Well-defined processes can improve

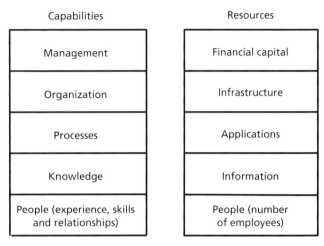

Figure 2.4 Examples of capabilities and resources

productivity within and across organizations and functions. Process characteristics include:

- **Measurability**   We are able to measure the process in a relevant manner. It is performance-driven. Managers want to measure cost, quality and other variables while practitioners are concerned with duration and productivity.
- **Specific results**   The reason a process exists is to deliver a specific result. This result must be individually identifiable and countable.
- **Customers**   Every process delivers its primary results to a customer or stakeholder. Customers may be internal or external to the organization, but the process must meet their expectations.
- **Responsiveness to specific triggers**   While a process may be ongoing or iterative, it should be traceable to a specific trigger.

A process is organized around a set of objectives. The main outputs from the process should be driven by the objectives and should include process measurements (metrics), reports and process improvement.

The output produced by a process has to conform to operational norms that are derived from business objectives. If products conform to the set norm, the process can be considered effective (because it can be repeated, measured and managed, and achieves the required outcome). If the activities of the process are carried out with a minimum use of resources, the process can also be considered efficient.

Inputs are data or information used by the process and may be the output from another process.

A process, or an activity within a process, is initiated by a trigger. A trigger may be the arrival of an input or other event. For example, the failure of a server may trigger the event management and incident management processes.

A process may include any of the roles, responsibilities, tools and management controls required to deliver the outputs reliably. A process may define policies, standards, guidelines, activities and work instructions if they are needed.

Processes, once defined, should be documented and controlled. Once under control, they can be repeated and managed. Process measurement and metrics can be built into the process to control and improve the process as illustrated in Figure 2.5. Process analysis, results and metrics should be incorporated in regular management reports and process improvements.

2.2.3 Organizing for service management

There is no single best way to organize, and best practices described in ITIL need to be tailored to suit individual organizations and situations. Any changes made will need to take into account resource constraints and the size, nature and needs of the business and customers.

The starting point for organizational design is strategy. Organizational development for service management is described in more detail in Chapter 6 of each core publication.

2.2.3.1 Functions

A function is a team or group of people and the tools or other resources they use to carry out one or more processes or activities. In larger organizations, a function may be broken out and performed by several departments, teams and groups, or it may be embodied within a single organizational unit (e.g. the service desk). In smaller organizations, one person or group can perform multiple functions – for example, a technical management department could also incorporate the service desk function.

For the service lifecycle to be successful, an organization will need to clearly define the roles and responsibilities required to undertake the processes and activities involved in each lifecycle stage. These roles will need to be assigned to individuals, and an appropriate organization structure of teams, groups or functions will need to be established and managed. These are defined as follows:

■ **Group** A group is a number of people who are similar in some way. In ITIL, groups refer to people who perform similar activities – even though they may work on different technologies or report into different organizational structures or even different companies. Groups are usually not formal organizational structures, but are very useful in defining common processes across the organization – for example, ensuring that all people who resolve incidents complete the incident record in the same way.

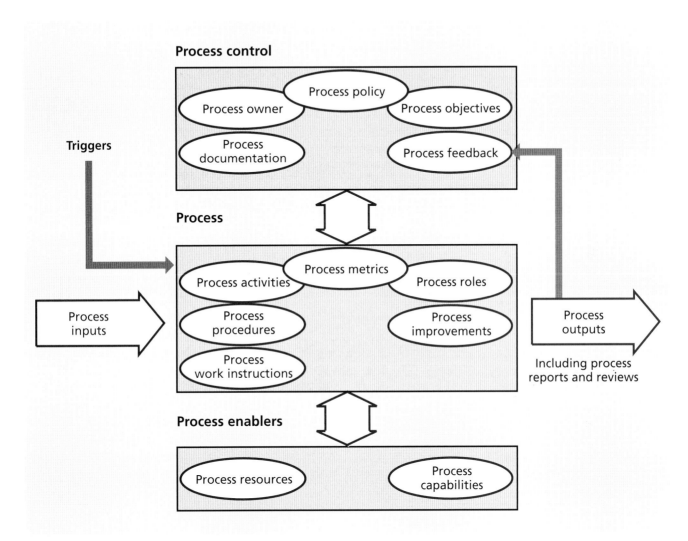

Figure 2.5 Process model

■ **Team** A team is a more formal type of group. These are people who work together to achieve a common objective, but not necessarily in the same organizational structure. Team members can be co-located, or work in multiple locations and operate virtually. Teams are useful for collaboration, or for dealing with a situation of a temporary or transitional nature. Examples of teams include project teams, application development teams (often consisting of people from several different business units) and incident or problem resolution teams.

- **Department** Departments are formal organizational structures which exist to perform a specific set of defined activities on an ongoing basis. Departments have a hierarchical reporting structure with managers who are usually responsible for the execution of the activities and also for day-to-day management of the staff in the department.
- **Division** A division refers to a number of departments that have been grouped together, often by geography or product line. A division is normally self-contained.

ITIL Service Operation describes the following functions in detail:

- **Service desk** The single point of contact for users when there is a service disruption, for service requests, or even for some categories of request for change. The service desk provides a point of communication to the users and a point of coordination for several IT groups and processes.
- **Technical management** Provides detailed technical skills and resources needed to support the ongoing operation of IT services and the management of the IT infrastructure. Technical management also plays an important role in the design, testing, release and improvement of IT services.
- **IT operations management** Executes the daily operational activities needed to manage IT services and the supporting IT infrastructure. This is done according to the performance standards defined during service design. IT operations management has two sub-functions that are generally organizationally distinct. These are IT operations control and facilities management.

- **Application management** Is responsible for managing applications throughout their lifecycle. The application management function supports and maintains operational applications and also plays an important role in the design, testing and improvement of applications that form part of IT services.

The other core ITIL publications do not define any functions in detail, but they do rely on the technical and application management functions described in *ITIL Service Operation*. Technical and application management provide the technical resources and expertise to manage the whole service lifecycle, and practitioner roles within a particular lifecycle stage may be performed by members of these functions.

2.2.3.2 Roles

A number of roles need to be performed during the service lifecycle. The core ITIL publications provide guidelines and examples of role descriptions. These are not exhaustive or prescriptive, and in many cases roles will need to be combined or separated. Organizations should take care to apply this guidance in a way that suits their own structure and objectives.

> **Definition: role**
>
> A role is a set of responsibilities, activities and authorities granted to a person or team. A role is defined in a process or function. One person or team may have multiple roles – for example, the roles of configuration manager and change manager may be carried out by a single person.

Roles are often confused with job titles but it is important to realize that they are not the same.

Each organization will define appropriate job titles and job descriptions which suit their needs, and individuals holding these job titles can perform one or more of the required roles.

It should also be recognized that a person may, as part of their job assignment, perform a single task that represents participation in more than one process. For example, a technical analyst who submits a request for change (RFC) to add memory to a server to resolve a performance problem is participating in activities of the change management process at the same time as taking part in activities of the capacity management and problem management processes.

See Chapter 6 in each core publication for more details about the roles and responsibilities associated with each stage of the lifecycle.

2.2.3.3 Organizational culture and behaviour

Organizational culture is the set of shared values and norms that control the service provider's interactions with all stakeholders, including customers, users, suppliers, internal staff etc. An organization's values are desired modes of behaviour that affect its culture. Examples of organizational values include high standards, customer care, respecting tradition and authority, acting cautiously and conservatively, and being frugal.

High-performing service providers continually align the value network for efficiency and effectiveness. Culture through the value network is transmitted to staff through socialization, training programmes, stories, ceremonies and language.

Constraints such as governance, capabilities, standards, resources, values and ethics play a significant role in organization culture and

behaviour. Organizational culture can also be affected by structure or management styles resulting in a positive or negative impact on performance. Organizational structures and management styles contribute to the behaviour of people, process, technology and partners. These are important aspects in adopting service management practices and ITIL.

Change related to service management programmes will affect organizational culture and it is important to prepare people with effective communication plans, training, policies and procedures to achieve the desired performance outcomes. Establishing cultural change is also an important factor for collaborative working between the many different people involved in service management. Managing people through service transitions is discussed at more length in Chapter 5 of *ITIL Service Transition*.

2.2.4 The service portfolio

The service portfolio is the complete set of services that is managed by a service provider and it represents the service provider's commitments and investments across all customers and market spaces. It also represents present contractual commitments, new service development, and ongoing service improvement plans initiated by continual service improvement. The portfolio may include third-party services, which are an integral part of service offerings to customers.

The service portfolio represents all the resources presently engaged or being released in various stages of the service lifecycle. It is a database or structured document in three parts:

■ **Service pipeline** All services that are under consideration or development, but are not yet available to customers. It includes major investment opportunities that have to be traced to the delivery of services, and the value that will be realized. The service pipeline provides a business view of possible future services and is part of the service portfolio that is not normally published to customers.

■ **Service catalogue**   All live IT services, including those available for deployment. It is the only part of the service portfolio published to customers, and is used to support the sale and delivery of IT services. It includes a customer-facing view (or views) of the IT services in use, how they are intended to be used, the business processes they enable, and the levels and quality of service the customer can expect for each service. The service catalogue also includes information about supporting services required by the service provider to deliver customer-facing services. Information about services can only enter the service catalogue after due diligence has been performed on related costs and risks.

■ **Retired services**   All services that have been phased out or retired. Retired services are not available to new customers or contracts unless a special business case is made.

Service providers often find it useful to distinguish customer-facing services from supporting services:

■ **Customer-facing services**   IT services that are visible to the customer. These are normally services that support the customer's business processes and facilitate one or more outcomes desired by the customer.

■ **Supporting services**   IT services that support or 'underpin' the customer-facing services. These are typically invisible to the customer, but are essential to the delivery of customer-facing IT services.

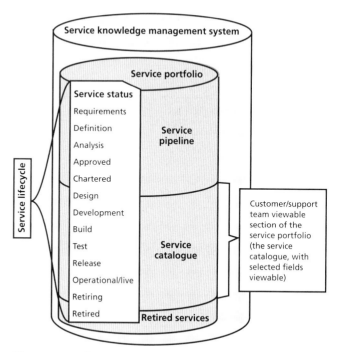

Figure 2.6 The service portfolio and its contents

Figure 2.6 illustrates the components of the service portfolio, which are discussed in detail in *ITIL Service Strategy*. These are important components of the service knowledge management system (SKMS) described in section 2.2.5.

2.2.5 Knowledge management and the SKMS

Quality knowledge and information enable people to perform process activities and support the flow of information between service lifecycle stages and processes. Understanding, defining, establishing and maintaining information is a responsibility of the knowledge management process.

Implementing an SKMS enables effective decision support and reduces the risks that arise from a lack of proper mechanisms. However, implementing an SKMS can involve a large investment in tools to store and manage data, information and knowledge. Every organization will start this work in a different place, and have their own vision of where they want to be, so there is no simple answer to the question 'What tools and systems are needed to support knowledge management?' Data, information and knowledge need to be interrelated across the organization. A document management system and/or a configuration management system (CMS) can be used as a foundation for implementation of the SKMS.

Figure 2.7 illustrates an architecture for service knowledge management that has four layers including examples of possible content at each layer. These are:

■ **Presentation layer**   Enables searching, browsing, retrieving, updating, subscribing and collaboration. The different views onto the other layers are suitable for different audiences. Each view should be protected to ensure that only authorized people can see or modify the underlying knowledge, information and data.

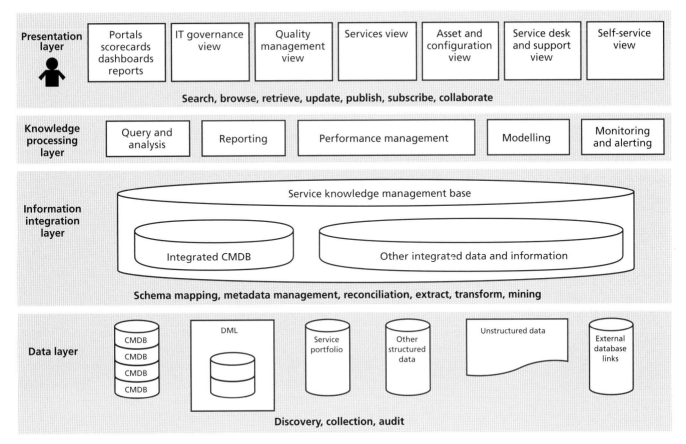

Figure 2.7 Architectural layers of an SKMS

- **Knowledge processing layer**   Is where the information is converted into useful knowledge which enables decision-making.
- **Information integration layer**   Provides integrated information that may be gathered from data in multiple sources in the data layer.
- **Data layer**   Includes tools for data discovery and data collection, and data items in unstructured and structured forms.

In practice, an SKMS is likely to consist of multiple tools and repositories. For example, there may be a tool that provides all four layers for the support of different processes or combinations of processes. Various tools providing a range of perspectives will be used by different stakeholders to access this common repository for collaborative decision support.

This architecture is applicable for many of the management information systems in ITIL. A primary component of the SKMS is the service portfolio, covered in section 2.2.4. Other examples include the CMS, the availability management information system (AMIS) and the capacity management information system (CMIS).

2.3   GOVERNANCE AND MANAGEMENT SYSTEMS

2.3.1 Governance

Governance is the single overarching area that ties IT and the business together, and services are one way of ensuring that the organization is able to execute that governance. Governance is what defines the common directions, policies and rules that both the business and IT use to conduct business.

Many ITSM strategies fail because they try to build a structure or processes according to how they would like the organization to work instead of working within the existing governance structures.

Definition: governance

Ensures that policies and strategy are actually implemented, and that required processes are correctly followed. Governance includes defining roles and responsibilities, measuring and reporting, and taking actions to resolve any issues identified.

Governance works to apply a consistently managed approach at all levels of the organization – first by ensuring a clear strategy is set, then by defining the policies whereby the strategy will be achieved. The policies also define boundaries, or what the organization may not do as part of its operations.

Governance needs to be able to evaluate, direct and monitor the strategy, policies and plans. Further information on governance and service management is provided in Chapter 5 of *ITIL Service Strategy*. The international standard for corporate governance of IT is ISO/IEC 38500, described in the appendix on related guidance in each of the core publications.

2.3.2 Management systems

A system is a number of related things that work together to achieve an overall objective. Systems should be self-regulating for agility and timeliness. In order to accomplish this, the relationships within the system must influence one another for the sake of the whole. Key components of the system are the structure and processes that work together.

A systems approach to service management ensures learning and improvement through a big-picture view of services and service management. It extends the management horizon and provides a sustainable long-term approach.

By understanding the system structure, the interconnections between all the assets and service components, and how changes in any area will affect the whole system and its constituent parts over time, a service provider can deliver benefits such as:

- Ability to adapt to the changing needs of customers and markets
- Sustainable performance
- Better approach to managing services, risks, costs and value delivery
- Effective and efficient service management
- Simplified approach that is easier for people to use
- Less conflict between processes
- Reduced duplication and bureaucracy.

Many businesses have adopted management system standards for competitive advantage and to ensure a consistent approach in implementing service management across their value network. Implementation of a management system also provides support for governance (see section 2.3.1).

> **Definition: management system (ISO 9001)**
>
> The framework of policy, processes, functions, standards, guidelines and tools that ensures an organization or part of an organization can achieve its objectives.

A management system of an organization can adopt multiple management system standards, such as:

- A quality management system (ISO 9001)
- An environmental management system (ISO 14000)
- A service management system (ISO/IEC 20000)
- An information security management system (ISO/IEC 27001)
- A management system for software asset management (ISO/IEC 19770).

Service providers are increasingly adopting these standards to be able to demonstrate their service management capability. As there are common elements between such management systems, they should be managed in an integrated way rather than having separate management systems. To meet the requirements of a specific management system standard, an organization needs to analyse the requirements of the relevant standard in detail and compare them with those that have already been incorporated in the existing integrated management system. The appendix on related guidance in each of the core publications provides further information on these standards.

ISO management system standards use the Plan-Do-Check-Act (PDCA) cycle shown in Figure 2.8. The ITIL service lifecycle approach embraces and enhances the interpretation of the PDCA cycle. You will see the PDCA cycle used in the structure of the guidance provided in each of the core ITIL publications. This guidance recognizes the need to drive governance, organizational design and management systems from the business strategy, service strategy and service requirements.

> **Definition: ISO/IEC 20000**
>
> An international standard for IT service management.

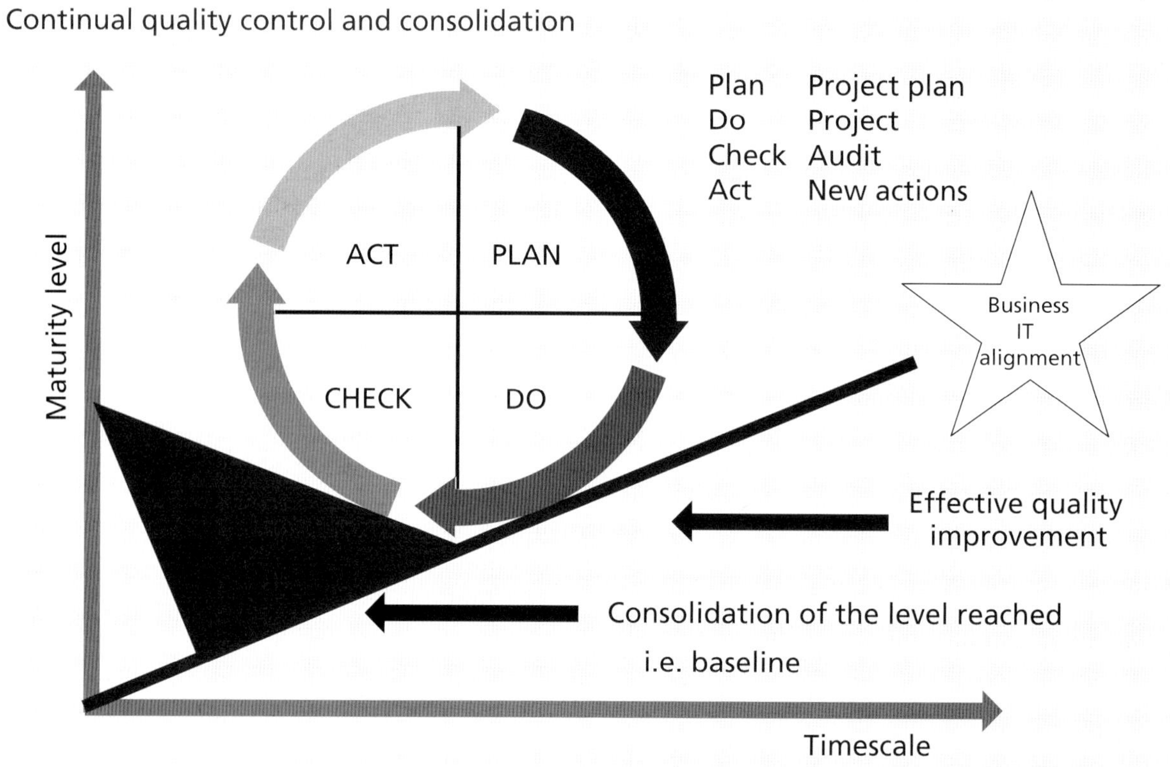

Continual quality control and consolidation

Plan   Project plan
Do   Project
Check   Audit
Act   New actions

ACT   PLAN

CHECK   DO

Business IT alignment

Effective quality improvement

Consolidation of the level reached
i.e. baseline

Maturity level

Timescale

Figure 2.8 Plan-Do-Check-Act cycle

ISO/IEC 20000 is an internationally recognized standard that allows organizations to demonstrate excellence and prove best practice in ITSM. Part 1 specifies requirements for the service provider to plan, establish, implement, operate, monitor, review, maintain and improve a service management system (SMS). Coordinated integration and implementation of an SMS, to meet the Part 1 requirements, provides ongoing control, greater effectiveness, efficiency and opportunities for continual improvement. It ensures that the service provider:

- Understands and fulfils the service requirements to achieve customer satisfaction
- Establishes the policy and objectives for service management
- Designs and delivers changes and services that add value for the customer
- Monitors, measures and reviews performance of the SMS and the services
- Continually improves the SMS and the services based on objective measurements.

Service providers across the world have successfully established an SMS to direct and control their service management activities. The adoption of an SMS should be a strategic decision for an organization.

One of the most common routes for an organization to achieve the requirements of ISO/IEC 20000 is by adopting ITIL service management best practices and using the ITIL qualification scheme for professional development.

Certification to ISO/IEC 20000-1 by an accredited certification body shows that a service provider is committed to delivering value to its customers and continual service improvement. It demonstrates the existence of an effective SMS that satisfies the requirements of an independent external audit. Certification gives a service provider a competitive edge in marketing. Many organizations specify a requirement to comply with ISO/IEC 20000 in their contracts and agreements.

2.4 THE SERVICE LIFECYCLE

Services and processes describe how things change, whereas structure describes how they are connected. Structure helps to determine the correct behaviours required for service management.

Structure describes how process, people, technology and partners are connected. Structure is essential for organizing information. Without structure, our service management knowledge is merely a collection of observations, practices and conflicting goals. The structure of the service lifecycle is an organizing framework, supported by the organizational structure, service portfolio and service models within an organization. Structure can influence or determine the behaviour of the organization and people. Altering the structure of

service management can be more effective than simply controlling discrete events.

Without structure, it is difficult to learn from experience. It is difficult to use the past to educate for the future. We can learn from experience but we also need to confront directly many of the most important consequences of our actions.

See Chapter 1 for an introduction to each ITIL service lifecycle stage.

2.4.1 Specialization and coordination across the lifecycle

Organizations need a collaborative approach for the management of assets which are used to deliver and support services for their customers.

Organizations should function in the same manner as a high-performing sports team. Each player in a team and each member of the team's organization who are not players position themselves to support the goal of the team. Each player and team member has a different specialization that contributes to the whole. The team matures over time taking into account feedback from experience, best practice and current processes and procedures to become an agile high-performing team.

Specialization and coordination are necessary in the lifecycle approach. Specialization allows for expert focus on components of the service but components of the service also need to work together for value. Specialization combined with coordination helps to manage expertise, improve focus and reduce overlaps and gaps in processes. Specialization and coordination together help to create a collaborative and agile organizational architecture that maximizes utilization of assets.

Coordination across the lifecycle creates an environment focused on business and customer outcomes instead of just IT objectives and projects. Coordination is also essential between functional groups, across the value network, and between processes and technology.

Feedback and control between organizational assets helps to enable operational efficiency, organizational effectiveness and economies of scale.

2.4.2 Processes through the service lifecycle

Each core ITIL lifecycle publication includes guidance on service management processes as shown in Table 2.1.

Service management is more effective if people have a clear understanding of how processes interact throughout the service lifecycle, within the organization and with other parties (users, customers, suppliers).

Process integration across the service lifecycle depends on the service owner, process owners, process practitioners and other stakeholders understanding:

■ The context of use, scope, purpose and limits of each process
■ The strategies, policies and standards that apply to the processes and to the management of interfaces between processes
■ Authorities and responsibilities of those involved in each process
■ The information provided by each process that flows from one process to another; who produces it; and how it is used by integrated processes.

Integrating service management processes depends on the flow of information across process and organizational boundaries. This in turn depends on implementing supporting technology and management information systems across organizational boundaries, rather than in silos. If service management processes are implemented, followed or changed in isolation, they can become a bureaucratic overhead that does not deliver value for money. They could also damage or negate the operation or value of other processes and services.

As discussed in section 2.2.2, each process has a clear scope with a structured set of activities that transform inputs to deliver the outputs reliably. A process interface is the boundary of the process. Process integration is the linking of processes by ensuring that information flows from one process to another effectively and efficiently. If there is management commitment to process integration, processes are generally easier to implement and there will be fewer conflicts between processes.

Stages of the lifecycle work together as an integrated system to support the ultimate objective of service management for business value realization. Every stage is interdependent as shown in Figure 2.9. See Appendix A for examples of inputs and outputs across the service lifecycle.

The SKMS, described in section 2.2.5, enables integration across the service lifecycle stages. It provides secure and controlled access to the knowledge, information and data that are needed to manage and deliver services. The service portfolio represents all the assets presently engaged or being released in various stages of the lifecycle.

Table 2.1 The processes described in each core ITIL publication

Core ITIL lifecycle publication	Processes described in the publication
ITIL Service Strategy	Strategy management for IT services
	Service portfolio management
	Financial management for IT services
	Demand management
	Business relationship management
ITIL Service Design	Design coordination
	Service catalogue management
	Service level management
	Availability management
	Capacity management
	IT service continuity management
	Information security management
	Supplier management
ITIL Service Transition	Transition planning and support
	Change management
	Service asset and configuration management
	Release and deployment management
	Service validation and testing
	Change evaluation
	Knowledge management
ITIL Service Operation	Event management
	Incident management
	Request fulfilment
	Problem management
	Access management
ITIL Continual Service Improvement	Seven-step improvement process

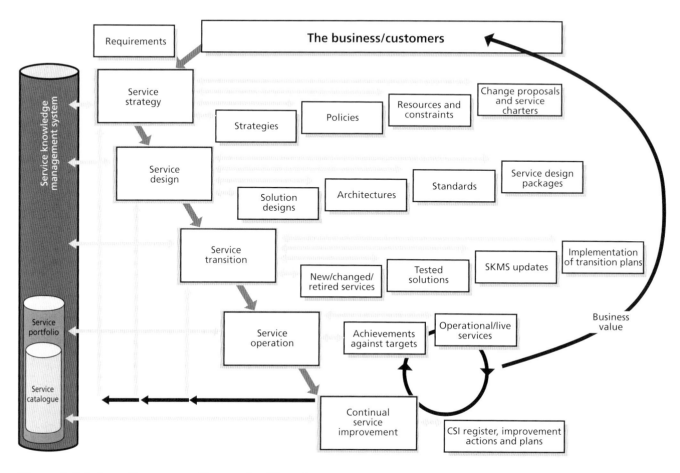

Figure 2.9 Integration across the service lifecycle

Chapter 1 provides a summary of each stage in the service lifecycle but it is also important to understand how the lifecycle stages work together.

Service strategy establishes policies and principles that provide guidance for the whole service lifecycle. The service portfolio is defined in this lifecycle stage, and new or changed services are chartered.

During the service design stage of the lifecycle, everything needed to transition and operate the new or changed service is documented in a service design package. This lifecycle stage also designs everything needed to create, transition and operate the services, including management information systems and tools, architectures, processes, measurement methods and metrics.

The activities of the service transition and service operation stages of the lifecycle are defined during service design. Service transition ensures that the requirements of the service strategy, developed in service design, are effectively realized in service operation while controlling the risks of failure and disruption.

The service operation stage of the service lifecycle carries out the activities and processes required to deliver the agreed services. During this stage of the lifecycle, the value defined in the service strategy is realized.

Continual service improvement acts in tandem with all the other lifecycle stages. All processes, activities, roles, services and technology should be measured and subjected to continual improvement.

Most ITIL processes and functions have activities that take place across multiple stages of the service lifecycle. For example:

- The service validation and testing process may design tests during the service design stage and perform these tests during service transition.
- The technical management function may provide input to strategic decisions about technology, as well as assisting in the design and transition of infrastructure components.
- Business relationship managers may assist in gathering detailed requirements during the service design stage of the lifecycle, or take part in the management of major incidents during the service operation stage.
- All service lifecycle stages contribute to the seven-step improvement process.

Appendix A identifies some of the major inputs and outputs between each stage of the service lifecycle. Chapter 3 of each core ITIL publication provides more detail on the inputs and outputs of the specific lifecycle stage it describes.

The strength of the service lifecycle rests upon continual feedback throughout each stage of the lifecycle. This feedback ensures that service optimization is managed from a business perspective and is measured in terms of the value the business derives from services at any point in time during the service lifecycle. The service lifecycle is non-linear in design. At every point in the service lifecycle, the process of monitoring, assessment and feedback between each stage drives decisions about the need for minor course corrections or major service improvement initiatives.

Figure 2.10 illustrates some examples of the continual feedback system built into the service lifecycle.

Adopting appropriate technology to automate the processes and provide management with the information that supports the processes is also important for effective and efficient service management.

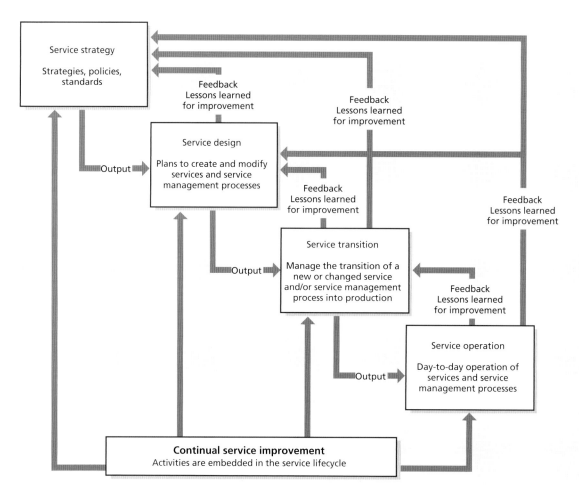

Figure 2.10 Continual service improvement and the service lifecycle

Service strategy

3

3 Service strategy

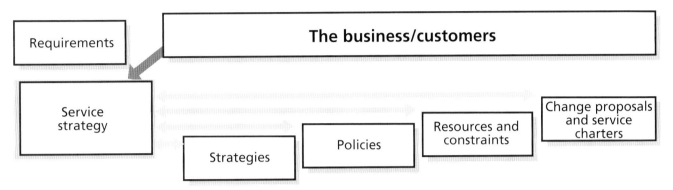

Figure 3.1 Service strategy is at the core of the service lifecycle

As the core of the ITIL service lifecycle, service strategy sets the stage for developing a service provider's capabilities and services to achieve the strategy (see Figure 3.1). This chapter will discuss a selection of the key concepts from *ITIL Service Strategy* to help aid the understanding of the role of service strategy in the ITIL service lifecycle.

3.1 SERVICE STRATEGY OVERVIEW

Imagine you have been given responsibility for an IT organization. This organization could be internal or external, commercial or not-for-profit. How would you go about deciding on a strategy to serve customers? What if you have a variety of customers, all with specific needs and demands? How do you define your service strategy to meet all of them?

Service strategy provides guidance to help answer that key question. It comprises the following key concepts and processes in addition to the concepts outlined in Chapter 2:

- Strategy to deliver value
- Market spaces
- How to define services
- Service models
- Strategy for customer satisfaction
- Increasing service potential
- Increasing performance potential
- Service economics
- Sourcing strategy
- Value chains and value networks
- Organizational development
- Strategy management for IT services
- Service portfolio management
- Financial management
- Demand management
- Business relationship management.

3.1.1 Purpose and objectives of service strategy

The purpose of the service strategy stage of the service lifecycle is to define the perspective, position, plans and patterns that a service provider needs to be able to execute to meet an organization's business outcomes.

The objectives of service strategy include providing:

■ An understanding of what strategy is

■ A clear identification of the definition of services and the customers who use them

■ The ability to define how value is created and delivered

■ A means to identify opportunities to provide services and how to exploit them

■ A clear service provision model, that articulates how services will be delivered and funded, and to whom they will be delivered and for what purpose

■ The means to understand the organizational capability required to deliver the strategy

■ Documentation and coordination of how service assets are used to deliver services, and how to optimize their performance

■ Processes that define the strategy of the organization, which services will achieve the strategy, what level of investment will be required, at what levels of demand, and the means to ensure a working relationship exists between the customer and service provider.

3.1.2 Scope

The scope of service strategy includes:

■ Defining a strategy whereby a service provider will deliver services to meet a customer's business outcomes

■ Defining a strategy for how to manage those services.

3.1.3 Value to business

Selecting and adopting the best practice as recommended in *ITIL Service Strategy* will assist organizations in delivering significant benefits. Adopting and implementing standard and consistent approaches for service strategy will:

■ Support the ability to link activities performed by the service provider to outcomes that are critical to internal or external customers

■ Enable the service provider to have a clear understanding of what types and levels of service will make its customers successful and then organize itself optimally to deliver and support those services

■ Enable the service provider to respond quickly and effectively to changes in the business environment, ensuring increased competitive advantage over time

■ Support the creation and maintenance of a portfolio of quantified services that will enable the business to achieve positive return on its investment in services.

3.2 SERVICE STRATEGY PRINCIPLES

3.2.1 Strategy must enable service providers to deliver value

A good business model describes the means of fulfilling an organization's objectives. However, without a strategy that in some way makes a service provider uniquely valuable to the customer, there is little to prevent alternatives from displacing the provider, degrading its mission or entering its market space. A service strategy therefore defines a unique approach for delivering better value. The need for having a service strategy is not limited to service providers who are commercial enterprises. Internal service providers need just as much to have a clear perspective, positioning and plans to ensure they remain relevant to the business strategies of their enterprises.

Customers continually seek to improve their business models and strategies. They want solutions that break through performance barriers – and achieve higher quality of outcomes in business processes with little or no increase in cost. Such solutions are usually made available through innovative products and services. If such solutions are not available within a customer's existing span of control, service contracts or value network, they are compelled to look elsewhere.

Service providers should not take for granted their position and role within their customer's plans even though they have the advantage of being incumbents. The value of services from a customer's perspective may change over time due to conditions, events and factors outside a provider's control. A strategic view of service management means a carefully considered approach to the relationships with customers and a state of readiness in dealing with the uncertainties in the value that defines that relationship.

3.2.2 Market spaces

Each customer has a number of requirements, and each service provider has a number of competencies. How does the service provider understand where its competencies will be able to meet the customer's requirements? These intersections between the service provider's competencies and the customer's requirements are called market spaces.

More formally, market spaces are the opportunities that an IT service provider could exploit to meet the business needs of customers. Market spaces identify the possible IT services that an IT service provider may wish to consider delivering.

A market space is defined by a set of business outcomes, which can be facilitated by a service. The opportunity to facilitate those outcomes defines a market space. The following are examples of business outcomes that can be the bases of one or more market spaces:

- Sales teams are productive with the sales management system on wireless computers.
- E-commerce website is linked to the warehouse management system.
- Key business applications are monitored and secure.
- Loan officers have faster access to information required on loan applicants.
- Online bill payment service offers more options for shoppers to pay.
- Business continuity is assured.

Each of the outcomes is related to one or more categories of customer assets, such as people, infrastructure, information, accounts receivable and purchase orders, and can then be linked to the services that make them possible. Each outcome can be met in multiple ways, although customers normally prefer those with lower costs and risks. Service providers create the conditions under which outcomes can be met through the services they deliver.

3.2.3 How to define services

In Chapter 2, services, customers, value and service providers are described. Understanding these concepts and how the organization relates to them helps to define which services will be delivered, and to which customers.

The following steps will typically happen as part of service portfolio management (discussed in section 4.2 in *ITIL Service Strategy*), but are listed here to illustrate the application of the principles:

- Step 1 – Define the market and identify customers
- Step 2 – Understand the customer
- Step 3 – Quantify the outcomes
- Step 4 – Classify and visualize the service
- Step 5 – Understand the opportunities (market spaces)
- Step 6 – Define services based on outcomes
- Step 7 – Service models
- Step 8 – Define service units and packages.

Steps 6 and 7 are worth exploring here in more detail.

3.2.3.1 Define services based on outcomes (Step 6)

An outcome-based definition of services ensures that managers plan and execute all aspects of service management entirely from the perspective of what is valuable to the customer. Such an approach ensures that services not only create value for customers but also capture value for the service provider.

Solutions that enable or enhance the performance of the customer assets indirectly support the achievement of the outcomes generated by those assets. Such solutions and propositions hold utility for the business. When that utility is backed by a suitable warranty, customers are ready to buy.

Customers can express dissatisfaction with a service provider even when terms and conditions of service level agreements (SLAs) are fulfilled. Often this is because it is not clear how services create value for customers. In these cases, services are often defined in the terms of resources made available for use by customers. Service definitions lack clarity on the context in which such resources are useful, and the business outcomes that justify the expense of a service from a customer's perspective. This problem leads to poor designs, ineffective operation and lacklustre performance in service contracts. Service improvements are difficult when it is not clear where improvements are truly required. Customers can understand and appreciate improvements only within the context of their own business assets, performances and outcomes. A proper definition of services takes into account the context in which customers perceive value from the services.

3.2.3.2 Service models (Step 7)

The definition of a service model is 'a model that shows how service assets interact with customer assets to create value. Service models describe the structure of a service (how the configuration items fit together) and the dynamics of the service (activities, flow of resources and interactions). A service model can be used as a template or blueprint for multiple services.'

Service models can take many forms, from a simple logical chart showing the different components and their dependencies, to a complex analytical model analysing the dynamics of a service under different configurations and demand patterns.

Service models have a number of uses, especially in service portfolio management (see section 4.2 in *ITIL Service Strategy*), including:

- Understanding what it will take to deliver a new service
- Identifying critical service components, customer assets or service assets – and then ensuring that they are designed to cope with the required demand
- Illustrating how value is created
- Mapping the teams and assets that are involved in delivering a service, and ensuring that they understand their impact on the customer's ability to achieve their business outcomes
- As a starting point for designing new services
- As an assessment tool for understanding the impact of changes to existing services
- As a means of identifying whether new services can be delivered using existing assets
- If not, then assessing what type of investment would be required to deliver the service
- Identifying the interface between technology, people and processes required to develop and deliver the service.

> **Key message**
>
> A service model is not a design. A service model is a list or diagram of items that will be needed in order to be able to deliver the service. The service model shows how these items are related and how they are used by the service.

Service models are the blueprints for service management processes and functions to communicate and collaborate on value creation. Service models describe how service assets interact with customer assets and create value for a given portfolio of contracts. Interaction means demand connects with the capacity to serve. Service level agreements specify the terms and conditions in which such interaction occurs with commitments and expectations on each side. The outcomes define the value to be created for the customer, which itself rests on the utility provided to customers and the warranty.

Service models also represent the structure and dynamics of services, which in turn are influenced by the customer's utility and warranty requirements. The structure and dynamics are influenced by factors of utility and warranty to be delivered to customers. Structure is defined in terms of particular service assets needed and the patterns in which they are configured. Dynamics are defined in terms of activities, flow of resources, coordination and interactions. This includes the cooperation and communication between users and service providers. The dynamics of a service include patterns of business activity, demand patterns, exceptions and variations.

3.2.4 Strategies for customer satisfaction

It is often not enough for a service to meet a customer's business outcome. Especially in a competitive environment, it is necessary for customers to feel satisfied with the level of service they have received. They also need to feel confident in the ability of the service provider to continue providing that level of service – or even improving it over time.

The only difficulty is that customer expectations keep shifting, and a service provider that does not track this will soon lose business. The following discussion on service attributes and the Kano model is helpful in understanding how this happens, and how a service provider can

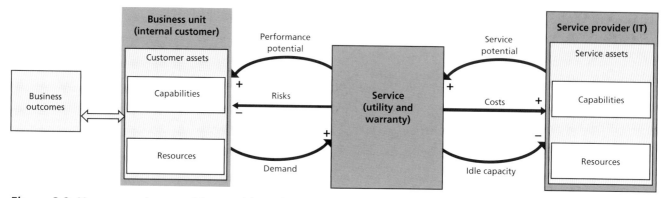

Figure 3.2 How a service provider enables a business unit's outcomes

adapt its services to meet the changing customer environment.

Attributes of a service are the characteristics that provide form and function to the service from a utilization perspective. The attributes are traced from business outcomes to be supported by the service. Certain attributes must be present for value creation to begin. Others add value on a sliding scale determined by how customers evaluate increments in utility and warranty. Service level agreements commonly provide for differentiated levels of service quality for different sets of users.

Some attributes are more important to customers than others. They have a direct impact on the performance of customer assets and therefore the realization of basic outcomes. Such attributes are 'must-have' attributes.[3]

3.2.4.1 Increasing the service potential

In Figure 3.2 the capabilities and resources (service assets) of a service provider represent the service

potential or the productive capacity available to customers through a set of services. Projects that develop or improve capabilities and resources increase the service potential. There is greater efficiency in the utilization of those assets and therefore service potential because of capability improvements in configuration management. Similar examples are given in Table 3.8 of *ITIL Service Strategy*. One of the key objectives of service management is to improve the service potential of its capabilities and resources.

Through configuration management, all service assets should be tagged with the name of the services to which they add service potential. This helps decisions related to service improvement and asset management. Clear relationships make it easier to ascertain the impact of changes, make business cases for investments in service assets and identify opportunities for scale and scope economies. IT identifies critical service assets across the service portfolio for a given customer or market space.

---

[3] Kano, N., Seraku, N., Tsuji, S. and Takahashi, F. (1984). Attractive Quality and Must-be Quality. *Hinshitsu* (*Quality, The Journal of Japanese Society for Quality Control*), 14(2), 39–48.

3.2.4.2 Increasing performance potential

Figure 3.2 shows that the services offered by a service provider represent the potential to increase the performance of customer assets. Without this potential there is no justification for customers to procure the services. Visualize and define the performance potential of services so that all decisions made by managers are rooted in the creation of value for customers. This approach avoids many of the problems of service businesses where value for customers is created in intangible forms and is therefore harder to define and control. Working backwards from the performance potential of customers ensures that service providers are always aligned with business needs regardless of how often those needs change.

The performance potential of services is increased primarily by having the right mix of services to offer to customers, and designing those services to have an impact on the customer's business. The key questions to be asked are:

- Who are our customers?
- What do those customers want?
- Can we offer anything unique to those customers?
- Are the opportunities already saturated with good solutions?
- Do we have the right portfolio of services developed for given opportunities?
- Do we have the right catalogue of services offered to a given customer?
- Is every service designed to support the required outcomes?
- Is every service operated to support the required outcomes?
- Do we have the right models and structures to be a service provider?

The productive capacity of service assets is transformed into the productive capacity of customer assets. An important aspect of delivering

value for customers through services is the reduction of risks for customers. By deciding to utilize a service, customers are often seeking to avoid owning certain risks and costs. Therefore the performance potential of services also arises from the removal of costs and risks from the customer's businesses.

For example, a service that securely processes payments or the transfer of funds for the customer reduces the risks of financial losses through error and fraud and at the same time reduces the cost per transaction by leveraging economies of scale and scope on behalf of the customer. The service provider can deploy the same set of service assets to process a large volume of transactions and free the customer from having to own and operate such assets. For certain business functions such as payroll, finance and administration, the customer may face the financial risk of under-utilized or over-utilized assets and may therefore prefer a service offered by a separate service provider.

3.2.5 Service economics

Service economics relate to the balance between the cost of providing services, the value of the outcomes achieved and the returns that the services enable the service provider to achieve.

The dynamics of service economics for external service providers are different from those for internal service providers. This is because the returns of internal service providers are mainly measured by their internal customers and do not accrue directly to the service provider.

Service economics relies on four main areas:

- **Service portfolio management** The process that defines the outcomes the business desires to achieve, and the services that will be used to achieve them. This is covered in detail in section 4.2 in *ITIL Service Strategy*.

- **Financial management for IT services**   The process by which service providers (and other business units) calculate, forecast and track costs and income related to services. This is covered in detail in section 4.3 in *ITIL Service Strategy*.

- **Return on investment** (ROI)   A measurement of the expected or actual benefit of an investment. Section 3.6. in *ITIL Service Strategy* focuses on how ROI is used, together with service portfolio management and financial management for IT services to build healthy service economics for the service provider's organization.

- **Business impact analysis** (BIA)   This allows an organization to establish the relative priorities of services based on their effect on the business if they are not available for a period of time. This is a key method used in IT service continuity management and is discussed in detail in *ITIL Service Design*. An overview is provided in *ITIL Service Strategy* to explain the role of BIA in service strategy.

3.2.6 Sourcing strategy

'The next layers of value creation – whether in technology, marketing, biomedicine or manufacturing – are becoming so complex that no single firm or department is going to be able to master them alone.' Thomas L. Friedman

Sourcing is about analysing how to most effectively source and deploy the resources and capabilities required to deliver outcomes to customers. It is about deciding on the best combination of supplier types to support the objectives of the organization and the effective and efficient delivery of services.

A service strategy should enhance an organization's special strengths and core competencies. Each component should reinforce the other. Change any one and the whole model changes. As organizations seek to improve their performance, they should consider which competencies are essential and know when to extend their capabilities by partnering in areas both inside and outside their enterprise.

Outsourcing moves a value-creating activity that was performed inside the organization to outside the organization where it is performed by another company. What prompts an organization to outsource an activity is the same logic that determines whether an organization makes or buys inputs. Namely, does the extra value generated from performing an activity inside the organization outweigh the costs of managing it internally? This decision can change over time.

IT services are increasingly delivered by service providers outside the enterprise. Making an informed service-sourcing decision requires finding a balance between thorough qualitative and quantitative considerations.

Historically, the financial business case is the primary basis for most sourcing decisions. These analyses include pure cost savings, lower capital investments, investment redirections and long-term cost containment. Unfortunately, most financial analyses do not include all the costs related to sourcing options, leading to difficult relationships with service providers, involving unexpected costs and service issues. If costs are a primary driver for a sourcing decision, include financials for service transition, relationship management, legal support, incentives, training, tools licensing implications and process rationalization, among others.

3.2.7 From value chains to value networks

Business executives have long described the process of creating value as links in a value chain. This model is based on the industrial-age production line: a series of value-adding activities connecting an organization's supply side with its demand side. Each service provides value through a sequence of events leading to the delivery, consumption and maintenance of that particular service. By analysing each stage in the chain, senior executives presumably find opportunities for improvements.

Much of the value of service management, however, is intangible and complex. It includes knowledge and benefits such as technical expertise, strategic information, process knowledge and collaborative design. Often the value lies in how these intangibles are combined, packaged and exchanged. Linear models have shown themselves to be inadequate for describing and understanding the complexities of value for service management, often treating information as a supporting element rather than as a source of value. Information is used to monitor and control rather than to create new value.

Value chains remain an important tool. They provide a strategy for vertically integrating and coordinating the dedicated assets required for product development. They do not, however, reflect the dynamic situation of services.

It is important to understand that the most powerful force to disrupt conventional value chains is the low cost of information. Information was the glue that held the vertical integration together. Getting the necessary information to suppliers and service providers has historically been expensive, requiring dedicated assets and proprietary systems. These barriers to entry gave value chains their competitive advantage. Through the exchange of open and inexpensive information, however, businesses can now make use of resources and capabilities without owning them.

Lower transaction costs allow organizations to control and track information that would have been too costly to capture and process just years ago. Transaction costs still exist, but are increasingly more burdensome within the organization than without. This in turn has created new opportunities for collaboration between service providers and suppliers. The end result is a flexible mix of mechanisms that undermine the rigid vertical integration.

New strategies are now available to service providers:

- **Marshal external talent** No single organization can organically produce all the resources and capabilities required within an industry. Most innovation occurs outside the organization.
- **Reduce costs** Produce more robust services in less time and for less expense than possible through conventional value-chain approaches. If it is less expensive to perform a transaction within the organization, keep it there. If it is cheaper to source externally, take a second look. An organization should contract until the cost of an internal transaction no longer exceeds the cost of performing the transaction externally. This is a corollary to 'Coase's law': a firm tends to expand until the costs of organizing an extra transaction within the firm become equal to the costs of carrying out the

same transaction on the open market. The concept of Coase's law was first developed by Tapscott *et al.* (2000).[4]

■ **Change the focal point of distinctiveness** By harnessing external talent, an organization can redeploy its own resources and capabilities to enhance services better suited to its customer or market space. Take the case of a popular North American sports league and its Type I service provider. By harnessing the capabilities of Type III infrastructure service providers, the Type I is free to redeploy its capabilities to enhance its new media services, namely web-based services with state-of-the-art streaming video, ticket sales, statistics, fantasy leagues and promotions.

■ **Increase demand for complementary services** An organization, particularly a Type I, may lack the breadth of services offered by Type II and Type III service providers. By acting as a service integrator, such organizations not only remedy the gap but also boost demand through complementary offerings.

■ **Collaborate** As transaction costs drop, collaboration is less optional. There are always more smart people outside an organization than inside.

An effective service provider will view service management as patterns of collaborative exchanges, rather than an assembly line. From a systems-thinking perspective it is more useful to think of service management as a value network or net.

A value network is a web of relationships that generates tangible and intangible value via complex dynamic exchanges through two or more

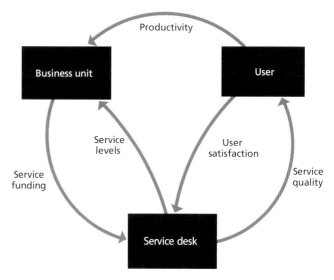

Figure 3.3 Example of a value network

organizations. A simple example of this is shown in Figure 3.3.

In a value net diagram, an arrow designates a transaction. The direction of the arrow denotes the direction of the transaction or impact on a participant: service provider or customer. Transactions can be temporary. They may include deliverables, tangible or intangible. Dotted arrows can be used to distinguish intangible transactions. Figure 3.48 in *ITIL Service Strategy* shows that the traditional model of supplier–service provider–business unit is not adequate to show the complexity of real transactions in a service management situation.

3.2.8 Organizational development
When senior managers adopt a service management orientation, they are adopting a vision for the organization. Such a vision provides a model toward which staff can work. Organizational change, however, is not instantaneous. Senior

---
[4] Tapscott, Don, Ticoll, David and Lowy, Alex (2000). *Digital Capital: Harnessing the Power of Business Webs*. Harvard Business School Press.

managers often make the mistake of thinking that announcing the organizational change is the same as making it happen.

There is no one best way to organize. Elements of an organizational design, such as scale, scope and structure, are highly dependent on strategic objectives. Over time, an organization is likely to outgrow its design. There is the underlying problem of structural fit. Certain organizational designs fit while others do not. The design challenge is to identify and select among often distinct choices. Thus the problem becomes much more solvable when there is an understanding of the factors that influence fit and the trade-offs involved, such as control and coordination.

When the organization performs well, the structure tends to drift towards a decentralized model where local managers possess greater autonomy. When problems persist, the tendency is to shift to a centralized model. This pendulum swing represents a lack of confidence in local decision-making. Despite the extreme difficulties, there is a persistent belief that an organization is controlled from the top. But giving orders is not the same as being in control. There are no guarantees, however, that local managers will appreciate the impact of their decisions on the larger organization. Their decisions can be short-term and short-sighted. This wavering between centralized and decentralized management is attributed as the source of long-term organizational problems and has been described as 'the illusion of being in control'. How then does an organization decide how best to manage its current organization and where to land along the design spectrum?

The process for major organizational change involves many events and can be a matter of

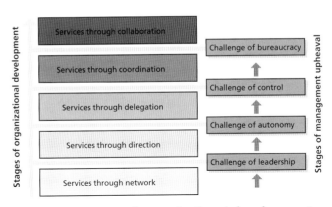

Figure 3.4 Stages of organizational development

years rather than months. Leading this change is difficult and should not be reduced to quick or simple fixes. The ability to lead this change is an important competence for senior executives and managers. Understanding when a service strategy is too complicated and rigid is as important as any support process.

Figure 3.4 illustrates the dominant management styles which serve the needs of an organization as it evolves over time.

3.3 SERVICE STRATEGY PROCESSES

3.3.1 Strategy management for IT services

Strategy management for IT services is the process of defining and maintaining an organization's perspective, position, plans and patterns with regard to its services and the management of those services. The purpose of a service strategy is to articulate how a service provider will enable an organization to achieve its business outcomes; it establishes the criteria and mechanisms to decide which services will be best suited to meet the business outcomes and the most effective and efficient way to manage these services. Strategy

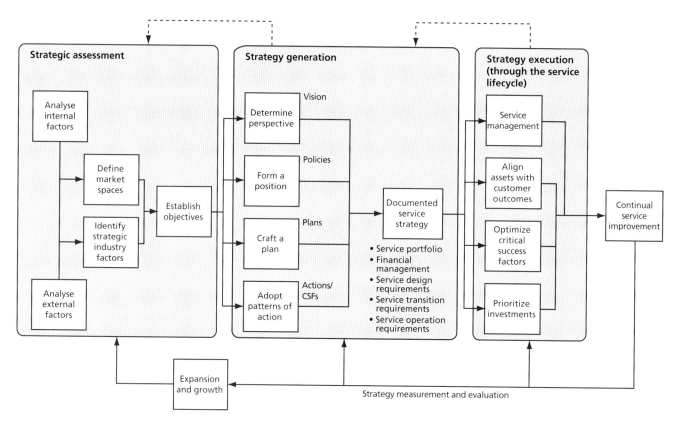

Figure 3.5 The strategy management process

management for IT services is the process that ensures that the strategy is defined, maintained and achieves its purpose. Figure 3.5 represents the strategy management process.

3.3.1.1 Strategic assessment

No organization exists in isolation, and every organization is defined by how it interacts with its ever-changing environment. The purpose of the strategic assessment is to determine the service provider's current situation and what changes are likely to impact it in the foreseeable future. The assessment will also highlight constraints that will limit or prevent the service provider from being able to progress its current goals, or to adapt to change.

The strategic assessment analyses both the internal environment (the service provider's own organization) and the external environment (the world with which the service provider's organization interacts), and then arrives at a set of objectives which will be used to define the actual strategy.

In crafting a service strategy, a provider should first take a careful look at what it does already. The starting point is to identify the service provider's strengths and weaknesses through an internal analysis. This information will help to define the strategy by identifying which strengths can be leveraged, and which weaknesses need to be strengthened. Although internal analysis has sometimes been reduced to a brainstorming session between senior managers, it should be a conscious activity based on careful assessment of the organization over a period of time.

The questions in Table 3.1 can help expose a service provider's distinctive capabilities.

3.3.1.2 Strategy generation, evaluation and selection

Once the assessment has been completed and the service provider has defined the objectives of the strategy, it is possible to generate the actual strategy in terms of the 'four Ps' (perspective, positions, plans and patterns) of strategy described in section 3.1.2 of *ITIL Service Strategy*.

Table 3.1 Questions to assess existing services as differentiators

Which of our services or service varieties are the most distinctive? Are there services that the business or customer cannot easily substitute?	Are there barriers to entry which prevent other service providers from offering the same services? Barriers to entry could be the service provider's knowledge of the customer's business or the broadness of service offerings.
	Would it be expensive to switch to another service provider for the same services? The service provider might have lower cost structures because of specialization or service sourcing.
	Do we offer a particular attribute not readily found elsewhere? This could include product knowledge, regulatory compliance, provisioning speeds, technical capabilities or global support structures.
Which of our services are the most profitable?	The form of value may be monetary, as in higher profits or lower expenses, or social, as in saving lives or collecting taxes. For non-profit organizations, are there services that allow the organization to perform its mission better? Substitute 'profit' with 'benefits realized'.
Which of our customers and stakeholders are the most satisfied?	The answer to this question will indicate services that are high quality, low cost, unique to a specific customer's requirements, or some combination of the three.
Which customers, channels or purchase occasions are the most profitable?	Again, the form of value can be monetary, social or other.
Which of our activities in our value chain or value network are the most different and effective?	These activities will be viewed by the business as a core competency, and therefore will ensure that the service provider is seen as strategic.

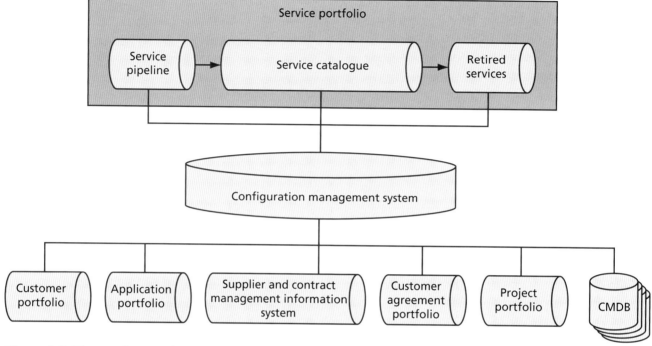

Figure 3.6 The service portfolio

3.3.1.3 Strategy execution

Once a strategy has been agreed, it needs to be put into action. The question of how to execute the strategy is answered in a set of more detailed tactical plans. Tactical plans describe what approaches and methods will be used to achieve the strategy. If a strategy answers the question 'Where are we going?' then tactics answer the question 'How will we get there?'

All service management processes have a role to play in executing a strategy since they are all about achieving the vision, objectives and plans defined in strategy management. In a very real sense, the other stages of the service lifecycle all have to do with strategy execution. In addition, all services and business outcomes should be in line with the strategy. If they are not then the strategy management process was ineffectual, was not updated regularly enough or was simply bypassed by parts of the organization.

3.3.2 Service portfolio management

The service portfolio is the complete set of services that is managed by a service provider. The service portfolio is used to manage the entire lifecycle of all services. It includes three categories of service: service pipeline (proposed or in development), service catalogue (live or available for deployment) and retired services. The service portfolio represents the investment made in an organization's services, and also articulates the value that services help it to realize.

Service portfolio management is responsible for managing the service portfolio. It is therefore also the process that is responsible for defining which services will be entered into the service portfolio and how those services are tracked and progressed through their lifecycle. In other words, service portfolio management acts as a gatekeeper for the service provider, ensuring that it only provides services that contribute to strategic objectives and meet the agreed business outcomes.

Some of the objectives of service portfolio management include:

■ Provide a process and mechanisms to enable an organization to investigate and decide on which services to provide, based on an analysis of the potential return and acceptable level of risk

■ Provide a mechanism for the organization to evaluate how services enable it to achieve its strategy, and to respond to changes in its internal or external environments

■ Control which services are offered, under what conditions and at what level of investment

■ Track the investment in services throughout their lifecycle, thus enabling the organization to evaluate its strategy, as well as its ability to execute against that strategy.

Figure 3.6 illustrates the components of the service portfolio.

3.3.2.1 Service pipeline

The service pipeline is a database or structured document listing all services that are under consideration or development, but are not yet available to customers. It also includes any major investment opportunities, such as a data centre relocation or virtualization project. This is because these investments have to be traced to the delivery of services and the value that is realized. The service pipeline provides a business view of possible future services and is part of the service portfolio that is not normally published to customers.

3.3.2.2 Service catalogue

The service catalogue is a database or structured document with information about all live IT services, including those available for deployment. The service catalogue is the only part of the service portfolio published to customers, and is used to support the sale and delivery of IT services. The service catalogue includes information about deliverables, prices, contact points, ordering and request processes.

3.3.2.3 Retired services

Some services in the service portfolio are phased out or retired. There is a decision to be made by each organization, following a service review, on when to move a service from catalogue to retired. Some organizations will do this when the service is no longer available to new customers, even though the service is still being delivered to existing customers. Other organizations will only move the service out of the catalogue when it is no longer delivered to any customers.

The process of retiring services is managed through service transition. This is to ensure that all commitments made to customers are duly fulfilled and service assets are released from contracts. When services are retired the related knowledge and information are stored in a knowledge base for future use. Retired services are not available to new or existing customers or contracts unless a special business case is made. Such services may be reactivated into operation under special conditions and SLAs that are to be approved by senior management. This is necessary because such services may cost a lot more to support and may disrupt economies of scale and scope.

3.3.2.4 Prioritizing service investments

Service portfolio management works with financial management for IT services to quantify the investment and value of each service. This requires an understanding of the business outcomes to be achieved, how the service will be used to achieve those outcomes, any supporting services that will be used, and how these are linked to the achievement of the business outcomes.

Executives will need to decide which services will take priority. Services will be classified in one of three strategic categories:

- **Run the business** (RTB)   RTB investments are centred on maintaining service operations.
- **Grow the business** (GTB)   GTB investments are intended to grow the organization's scope of services.
- **Transform the business** (TTB)   TTB investments are moves into new market spaces.

Each of these categories is further classified in terms of the type of budget that will be available for this category of service. Since some types of investment are more risky than others, executives allocate funding so that that there is a balance between higher-risk categories of spending and lower-risk categories. These categories are:

- **Venture**   This is the portion of the budget that is available to create services in a new market space.
- **Growth**   This is the portion of the budget that has been allocated to create new services in existing market space.

- **Discretionary**   This is money in the budget that is available if needed, but which does not have to be spent. This portion of the budget is often used to provide enhancements to existing services.
- **Non-discretionary**   This represents money that has to be spent in order to operate and maintain existing services.
- **Core**   This is the portion of the budget that takes the highest priority, since it is used to operate and maintain business-critical services.

3.3.3 Financial management for IT services

Financial management enables the organization to manage its resources, and to ensure that these resources are being used to achieve the organization's objectives.

The IT organization, along with all other departments in the organization, is involved in the organization's financial management process. They apply the organization's financial management procedures and practices to ensure that they are aligned with the organization's objectives and financial policies. In doing so, these departments often create their own financial management processes.

ITIL Service Strategy recognizes that these two layers of financial management exist within most organizations, and refers to financial management as a general process used by the organization, as well as to financial management as it is applied by an IT service provider. In *ITIL Service Strategy*, the text therefore uses the term 'financial management' as follows:

- **Financial management**   This refers to the generic use of the term.

- **Enterprise financial management** This refers specifically to the process as it is used by the 'corporate' financial department.
- **Financial management for IT services** This refers to the way in which the IT service provider has applied the process.

Finance is the common language which allows the service provider to communicate effectively with its customers and other business units. Financial management enables the service provider to develop the capabilities of operational visibility, insight and superior decision-making. Just as business units are able to generate value by analysing product mix and margin data, or customer profiles and product behaviour, financial data continues to increase the importance of financial management for IT and the business as well.

More than any other process, financial management enables an IT service provider to play a strategic role in the business. It helps to quantify IT's value and contributions, and quantifies the business opportunities that IT services enable.

Financial management as a strategic tool is equally applicable to all three service provider types. Internal service providers are increasingly asked to operate with the same levels of financial visibility and accountability as their business units and external counterparts. Moreover, technology and innovation have become the core revenue-generating capabilities of many companies.

Financial management provides the business and IT with the quantification, in financial terms, of the value of IT services, the value of the assets used to provide those services, and the qualification of operational forecasting. Talking about IT in terms of services is a crucial aspect of changing the perception of IT and its value to the business. Therefore, a significant portion of financial management is working in tandem with IT and the business to help identify, document and agree on the value of the services being received, and the enablement of service demand modelling and management.

Financial management consists of three main processes:

- **Budgeting** This is the process of predicting and controlling the income and expenditure of money within the organization. Budgeting consists of a periodic negotiation cycle to set budgets (usually annual) and the monthly monitoring of the current budgets.
- **Accounting** This is the process that enables the IT organization to account fully for the way its money is spent (particularly the ability to identify costs by customer, by service and by activity). It usually involves accounting systems, including ledgers, charts of accounts, journals etc. and should be overseen by someone trained in accountancy.
- **Charging** This is the process required to bill customers for the services supplied to them. This requires sound IT accounting practices and systems.

3.3.4 Demand management

The purpose of demand management is to understand, anticipate and influence customer demand for services and to work with capacity management to ensure the service provider has capacity to meet this demand. Demand management works at every stage of the lifecycle to ensure that services are designed, tested and delivered to support the achievement of business outcomes at the appropriate levels of activity.

This is where the service provider has the opportunity to understand the customer needs and feed these into the service strategies to realize the service potential of the customer and to differentiate the services to the customers.

The objectives of demand management are to:

■ Identify and analyse patterns of business activity to understand the levels of demand that will be placed on a service

■ Define and analyse user profiles to understand the typical profiles of demand for services from different types of user

■ Ensure that services are designed to meet the patterns of business activity and the ability to meet business outcomes

■ Work with capacity management to ensure that adequate resources are available at the appropriate levels of capacity to meet the demand for services, thus maintaining a balance between the cost of service and the value that it achieves

■ Anticipate and prevent or manage situations where demand for a service exceeds the capacity to deliver it

■ Gear the utilization of resources that deliver services to meet the fluctuating levels of demand for those services.

Demand management is a critical aspect of service management. Poorly managed demand is a source of risk for service providers because of uncertainty in demand. Excess capacity generates cost without creating value that provides a basis for cost recovery. Customers are reluctant to pay for idle capacity unless it has value for them.

In some cases a certain amount of unused capacity is necessary to deliver service levels. This capacity creates value because it enables a higher level of assurance. This capacity cannot be considered idle capacity because it has been designed into the service on purpose.

Insufficient capacity has impact on the quality of services delivered and limits the growth of the service. Service level agreements, forecasting, planning and tight coordination with the customer can reduce the uncertainty in demand but cannot entirely eliminate it.

3.3.5 Business relationship management

Business relationship management is the process that enables business relationship managers (BRMs) to provide links between the service provider and customers at the strategic and tactical levels. The purpose of these links is to ensure that the service provider understands the business requirements of the customer and is able to provide services that meet these needs. The primary measure of whether this purpose is being achieved is the level of customer satisfaction.

The purpose of the business relationship management process is two-fold:

■ To establish and maintain a business relationship between the service provider and the customer based on understanding the customer and their business needs.

■ To identify customer needs and ensure that the service provider is able to meet these needs as business needs change over time and between circumstances. Business relationship management ensures that the service provider understands these changing needs. Business relationship management also assists the business in articulating the value of a service. Put another way, business relationship management ensures that customer expectations do not exceed what they are willing to pay for, and that the service provider is able to meet the customer's expectations before agreeing to deliver the service.

For internal service providers, business relationship management is typically executed between a senior representative from IT (larger organizations may have dedicated BRMs) and senior managers (customers) from the business units. Here the emphasis is on aligning the objectives of the business with the activity of the service provider.

In external service providers, business relationship management is often executed by a separate and dedicated function of BRMs or account managers – each one dedicated to a customer, or group of smaller customers. The emphasis here is on maximizing contract value through customer satisfaction.

Business relationship management and service level management both have activities that interact with customers. It is useful to understand the differences between the processes and these are summarized in Table 3.2.

3.4 SERVICE STRATEGY INPUTS AND OUTPUTS

The main outputs from service strategy are the vision and mission, strategies and strategic plans, the service portfolio, change proposals and financial information. Table 3.3 shows the major service strategy inputs and outputs, by lifecycle stage. Appendix A provides a summary of the major inputs and outputs between each stage of the service lifecycle.

Table 3.2 Differences between business relationship management and service level management

	Business relationship management	Service level management
Purpose	To establish and maintain a business relationship between the service provider and the customer based on understanding the customer and their business needs. To identify customer needs (utility and warranty) and ensure that the service provider is able to meet these needs.	To negotiate service level agreements (warranty terms) with customers and ensure that all service management processes, operational level agreements and underpinning contracts are appropriate for the agreed service level targets.
Focus	Strategic and tactical – the focus is on the overall relationship between the service provider and its customer, and which services the service provider will deliver to meet customer needs.	Tactical and operational – the focus is on reaching agreement on the level of service that will be delivered for new and existing services, and whether the service provider was able to meet those agreements.
Primary measure	Customer satisfaction, also an improvement in the customer's intention to better use and pay for the service. Another metric is whether customers are willing to recommend the service to other (potential) customers.	Achieving agreed levels of service (which leads to customer satisfaction).

Table 3.3 Service strategy inputs and outputs by lifecycle stage

Lifecycle stage	Service strategy inputs (from the lifecycle stages in the first column)	Service strategy outputs (to the lifecycle stages in the first column)
Service design	Input to business cases and the service portfolio	Vision and mission
	Service design packages	Service portfolio
	Updated service models	Policies
	Service portfolio updates including the service catalogue	Strategies and strategic plans
		Priorities
	Financial estimates and reports	Service charters including service packages and details of utility and warranty
	Design-related knowledge and information in the service knowledge management system (SKMS)	Financial information and budgets
		Documented patterns of business activity and user profiles
	Designs for service strategy processes and procedures	Service models
Service transition	Transitioned services	Vision and mission
	Information and feedback for business cases and service portfolio	Service portfolio
		Policies
	Response to change proposals	Strategies and strategic plans
	Service portfolio updates	Priorities
	Change schedule	Change proposals, including utility and warranty requirements and expected timescales
	Feedback on strategies and policies	
	Financial information for input to budgets	
	Financial reports	Financial information and budgets
	Knowledge and information in the SKMS	Input to change evaluation and change advisory board (CAB) meetings

Table 3.3 – *continued*

Lifecycle stage	Service strategy inputs (from the lifecycle stages in the first column)	Service strategy outputs (to the lifecycle stages in the first column)
Service operation	Operating risks	Vision and mission
	Operating cost information for total cost of ownership (TCO) calculations	Service portfolio
		Policies
	Actual performance data	Strategies and strategic plans
		Priorities
		Financial information and budgets
		Demand forecasts and strategies
		Strategic risks
Continual service improvement	Results of customer and user satisfaction surveys	Vision and mission
		Service portfolio
	Input to business cases and the service portfolio	Policies
	Feedback on strategies and policies	Strategies and strategic plans
		Priorities
	Financial information regarding improvement initiatives for input to budgets	Financial information and budgets
		Patterns of business activity
	Data required for metrics, key performance indicators (KPIs) and critical success factors (CSFs)	Achievements against metrics, KPIs and CSFs
	Service reports	Improvement opportunities logged in the continual service improvement (CSI) register
	Requests for change (RFCs) for implementing improvements	

4

Service design

4   Service design

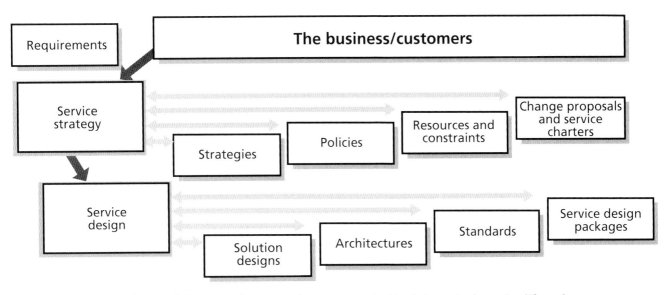

Figure 4.1 Service design follows on from service strategy in the integrated service lifecycle

Following on from service strategy, service design is the next stage in the ITIL service lifecycle (Figure 4.1). *ITIL Service Design* provides best-practice guidance for the service design stage of the ITIL service lifecycle. While the lifecycle is not entirely linear, we will portray each stage from a logical progression.

4.1   SERVICE DESIGN OVERVIEW

4.1.1   Purpose and objective of service design

The purpose of the service design stage of the lifecycle is to design IT services, together with the governing IT practices, processes and policies, to realize the service provider's strategy and to facilitate the introduction of these services into supported environments ensuring quality service delivery, customer satisfaction and cost-effective service provision.

The objective of service design is to design IT services so effectively that minimal improvement during their lifecycle will be required. However, continual improvement should be embedded in all service design activities to ensure that the solutions and designs become even more effective over time, and to identify changing trends in the business that may offer improvement opportunities. Service design activities can be periodic or exception-based when they may be triggered by a specific business need or event.

4.1.2 Scope

ITIL Service Design provides guidance for the design of appropriate and innovative IT services to meet current and future agreed business requirements. It describes the principles of service design and looks at identifying, defining and aligning the IT solution with the business requirement. It also introduces the concept of the service design package (SDP) and looks at selecting the appropriate service design model. It covers the methods, practices and tools to achieve excellence in service design. It discusses the fundamentals of the design processes and attends to what are called the 'five aspects of service design'.

ITIL Service Design enforces the principle that the initial service design should be driven by a number of factors, including the functional requirements, the requirements within service level agreements (SLAs), the business benefits and the overall design constraints.

The processes considered important to successful service design are design coordination, service catalogue management, service level management, availability management, capacity management, IT service continuity management, information security management and supplier management. Almost all of these processes are also active throughout the other stages of the service lifecycle. All processes within the service lifecycle must be linked closely together for managing, designing, supporting and maintaining the services, the IT infrastructure, the environment, the applications and the data. Other processes are described in detail in the other core ITIL publications. The interfaces between processes need to be clearly defined when designing a service or improving or implementing a process.

The appendices in *ITIL Service Design* give examples of important service design documents and templates such as the SDP and SLA.

4.1.3 Usage

ITIL Service Design provides access to proven best practice based on the skill and knowledge of experienced industry practitioners in adopting a standardized and controlled approach to service management. Although *ITIL Service Design* can be used and applied in isolation, it is recommended that it is used in conjunction with the other core ITIL publications. All of the core publications need to be read to fully appreciate and understand the overall lifecycle of services and IT service management.

4.1.4 Value to business

Selecting and adopting the best practice as recommended in *ITIL Service Design* will assist organizations in delivering significant benefits. With good service design, it is possible to deliver quality, cost-effective services and to ensure that the business requirements are being met consistently.

Adopting and implementing standard and consistent approaches for service design will:

- **Reduce total cost of ownership (TCO)** Cost of ownership can only be minimized if all aspects of services, processes and technology are designed properly and implemented against the design.
- **Improve quality of service** Both service and operational quality will be enhanced through services that are better designed to meet the required outcomes of the customer.
- **Improve consistency of service** This will be achieved by designing services within

the corporate strategy, architectures and constraints.

- **Ease the implementation of new or changed services** Integrated and full service designs and the production of comprehensive SDPs will support effective and efficient transitions.

- **Improve service alignment** Involvement of service design from the conception of the service will ensure that new or changed services match business needs, with services designed to meet service level requirements.

- **Improve service performance** Performance will be enhanced if services are designed to meet specific performance criteria and if capacity, availability, IT service continuity and financial plans are recognized and incorporated.

- **Improve IT governance** By building controls into designs, service design can contribute towards the effective governance of IT.

- **Improve effectiveness of service management and IT processes** Processes will be designed with optimal quality and cost effectiveness.

- **Improve information and decision-making** Comprehensive and effective measurements and metrics will enable better decision-making and continual improvement of services and service management practices throughout the service lifecycle.

- **Improve alignment with customer values and strategies** For organizations with commitments to concepts such as green IT or that establish strategies such as the use of cloud technologies, service design will ensure that all areas of services and service management are aligned with these values and strategies.

4.2 SERVICE DESIGN PRINCIPLES

4.2.1 Holistic service design

There are five aspects of service design that are discussed in more detail in *ITIL Service Design*. These aspects are the design of:

- **Service solutions for new or changed services** The requirements for new or changed services are extracted from the service portfolio. Each requirement is analysed, documented and agreed, and a solution design is produced that is then compared with the strategies and constraints from service strategy to ensure that it conforms to corporate and IT policies. The design must ensure that this new or changed service is consistent with all other services, and that all other services that interface with, underpin or depend on the new or changed service are consistent with the new service. If not, either the design of the new service or the other existing services will need to be adapted.

  Each individual service solution design is also considered in conjunction with each of the other four aspects of service design.

- **The management information systems and tools, especially the service portfolio** The management information systems and tools should be reviewed to ensure they are capable of supporting the new or changed service.

- **The technology architectures and management architectures** These are reviewed to ensure that all the technology architectures and management architectures are consistent with the new or changed service and have the capability to operate and maintain the new service. If not, then either the architectures will need to be amended or the design of the new service will need to be revised.

- **The processes required**   These are reviewed to ensure that the processes, roles, responsibilities and skills have the capability to operate, support and maintain the new or changed service. If not, the design of the new service will need to be revised or the existing process capabilities will need to be enhanced. This includes all IT and service management processes, not just the processes involved in the service design stage itself.

- **The measurement methods and metrics**   These are reviewed to ensure that the existing measurement methods can provide the required metrics on the new or changed service. If not, then the measurement methods will need to be enhanced or the service metrics will need to be revised.

It is important that a holistic, results-driven approach to all aspects of design is adopted, and that when changing or amending any of the individual elements of design all other aspects are considered. When designing and developing a new application, this should not be done in isolation, but should also consider the impact on the overall service, the management information systems and tools (e.g. service portfolio and service catalogue), the architectures, the technology, the service management processes and the necessary measurements and metrics. This will ensure not only that the functional elements are addressed by the design, but also that all of the management and operational requirements are addressed as a fundamental part of the design and are not added as an afterthought.

This holistic approach and the five aspects of design identified above are important parts of

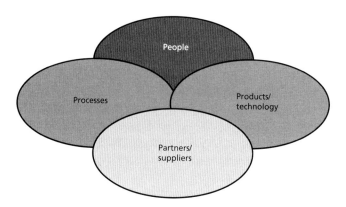

Figure 4.2 The four Ps of design

the service provider's overall service management system. This approach should also be used when the change to the service is its retirement. Unless the retirement of a service or any aspect of a service is carefully planned, the retirement could cause unexpected negative effects on the customer or business which might otherwise have been avoided.

Many designs, plans and projects fail through a lack of preparation and management. The implementation of ITSM as a practice is about preparing and planning the effective and efficient use of the four Ps of design: the people, the processes, the products (services, technology and tools) and the partners (suppliers, manufacturers and vendors), as illustrated in Figure 4.2.

The composition of a service and its constituent parts is illustrated in Figure 4.3.

Service design must consider all these aspects when designing service solutions to meet new and evolving business needs:

- **Business process**   To define the functional needs of the service being provided – for

Business service management

Business service A (delivered to business customers)

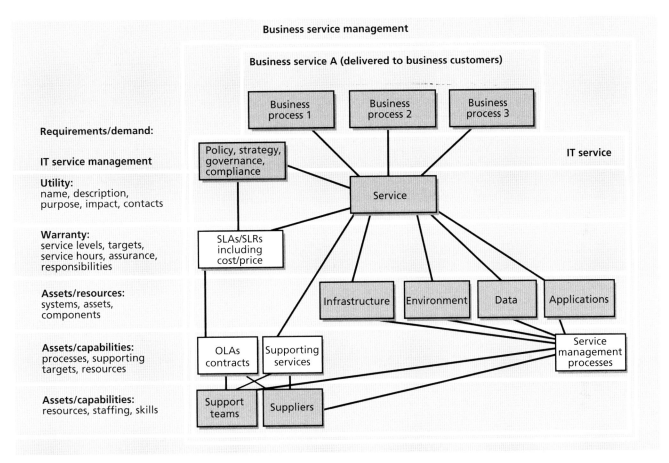

Figure 4.3 Service composition

example, telesales, invoicing, orders, credit checking
- **Service**   The service itself that is being delivered to the customers and business by the service provider – for example, email, billing
- **Policy, strategy, governance, compliance**   The elements defined by the organization to direct activity and thereby ensure adherence to organizational goals and objectives
- **SLAs/SLRs**   The documents agreed with the customers that specify the level, scope and

quality of service to be provided, either now for an existing service (SLAs) or in the future for a new service (SLRs)
- **Infrastructure**   All of the IT equipment necessary to deliver the service to the customers and users, including servers, network circuits, switches, personal computers (PCs), telephones
- **Environment**   The environment required to secure and operate the infrastructure – for example, data centres, power, air conditioning

- **Data** The data necessary to support the service and provide the information required by the business processes – for example, customer records, accounts ledger
- **Applications** All of the software applications required to manipulate the data and provide the functional requirements of the business processes – for example, enterprise resource management, financial or customer relationship management applications
- **Supporting services** Any services that are necessary to support the operation of the delivered service – for example, a shared service, a managed network service
- **Operational level agreements (OLAs) and underpinning contracts** Any underpinning agreements necessary to deliver the quality of service agreed within the SLA
- **Support teams** Any internal teams providing support for any of the components required to provide the service – for example, Unix, mainframe, networks
- **Suppliers** Any external third parties necessary to provide support for any of the components required to provide the service – for example, networks, hardware, software
- **Service management processes** Any processes needed by the service provider to ensure the successful provision of the service.

The design activities must not just consider each of the components above in isolation, but also must consider the relationships between each of the components and their interactions and dependencies on any other components and services, in order to provide an effective and comprehensive solution that meets the business needs.

4.2.2 Identifying service requirements

Service design must consider all elements of the service by taking a holistic approach to the design of a new service. This approach should consider the service and its constituent components and their inter-relationships, ensuring that the services delivered meet the requirements of the business in all of the following areas:

- The scalability of the service to meet future requirements, in support of the long-term business objectives
- The business processes and business units supported by the service
- The IT service and the agreed business requirements for functionality (i.e. utility)
- The service itself and its SLR or SLA (addressing warranty)
- The technology components used to deploy and deliver the service, including the infrastructure, the environment, the data and the applications
- The internally delivered supporting services and components and their associated OLAs
- The externally supplied supporting services and components and their associated underpinning contracts, which will often have their own related agreements and/or schedules
- The performance measurements and metrics required
- The legislated or required security levels
- Sustainability requirements.

Design activities are also affected by external influences, many of which arise from the need for good corporate and IT governance, and from the requirement for compliance with regulations, legislation and international standards. It is essential, therefore, that all designers recognize these and ensure that the designs and solutions they produce have all of the necessary controls and capability within them. For more information on some of these external influences, see *ITIL Service Design*.

4.2.3 Service design models

The model selected for the design of IT services will depend mainly on the model selected for the delivery of IT services. Before adopting a design model for a major new service, a review of the current capability and provisions with respect to all aspects of the delivery of IT services should be conducted. This review should consider all aspects of the new service, including the:

■ Business drivers and requirements
■ Demands, targets and requirements of the new service
■ Scope and capability of the existing service provider unit
■ Scope and capability of external suppliers
■ Maturity of the organizations currently involved and their processes
■ Culture of the organizations involved
■ IT infrastructure, applications, data, services and other components involved
■ Degree of corporate and IT governance and the level of ownership and control required
■ Budgets and other resources available
■ Staff levels and skills.

4.2.4 Delivery model options

Although the readiness assessment determines the gap between the current and desired capabilities, an IT organization should not necessarily try to bridge that gap by itself. There are many different delivery strategies or models that can be used, reflecting how and to what degree the service provider will rely on suppliers. Each strategy has its own set of advantages and disadvantages, but all require some level of adaptation and customization for the situation at hand. Table 4.1 lists the main categories of sourcing structure (delivery strategy) with a short abstract for each. Delivery practices tend to fall into one of these categories or some variant of them.

4.3 SERVICE DESIGN PROCESSES

4.3.1 Design coordination

The purpose of the design coordination process is to ensure the goals and objectives of the service design stage are met by providing and maintaining a single point of coordination and control for all activities and processes within this stage of the service lifecycle.

The main value of the design coordination process to the business is the production of a set of consistent quality solution designs and SDPs that will provide the desired business outcomes.

Through the work of design coordination, organizations can:

■ Achieve the intended business value of services through design at acceptable risk and cost levels
■ Minimize rework and unplanned labour costs associated with reworking design issues during later service lifecycle stages
■ Support the achievement of higher customer and user satisfaction and improved confidence in IT and in the services received
■ Ensure that all services conform to a consistent architecture, allowing integration and data exchange between services and systems

Table 4.1 Main sourcing structures (delivery strategies)

Sourcing structure	Description
Insourcing	This approach relies on utilizing internal organizational resources in the design, development, transition, maintenance, operation and/or support of new, changed or revised services.
Outsourcing	This approach utilizes the resources of an external organization or organizations in a formal arrangement to provide a well-defined portion of a service's design, development, maintenance, operations and/or support. This includes the consumption of services from application service providers (ASPs).
Co-sourcing or multi-sourcing	Often a combination of insourcing and outsourcing, using a number of organizations working together to co-source key elements within the lifecycle. This generally involves using a number of external organizations working together to design, develop, transition, maintain, operate and/or support a portion of a service.
Partnership	Formal arrangements between two or more organizations to work together to design, develop, transition, maintain, operate and/or support IT service(s). The focus here tends to be on strategic partnerships that leverage critical expertise or market opportunities.
Business process outsourcing (BPO)	The increasing trend of relocating entire business functions using formal arrangements between organizations where one organization provides and manages the other organization's entire business process(es) or function(s) in a low-cost location. Common examples are accounting, payroll and call centre operations.
Application service provision	Involves formal arrangements with an ASP organization that will provide shared computer-based services to customer organizations over a network from the service provider's premises. Applications offered in this way are also sometimes referred to as on-demand software/applications. Through ASPs, the complexities and costs of such shared software can be reduced and provided to organizations that could otherwise not justify the investment.
Knowledge process outsourcing (KPO)	KPO is a step ahead of BPO in one respect. KPO organizations provide domain-based processes and business expertise rather than just process expertise. In other words the organization is not only required to execute a process, but also to make certain low-level decisions based on knowledge of local conditions or industry-specific information. One example is the outsourcing of credit risk assessment, where the outsourcing organization has historical information that they have analysed to create knowledge, which in turn enables them to provide a service. For every credit card company to collect and analyse this data for itself would not be as cost-effective as using KPO.
'Cloud'	Cloud service providers offer specific predefined services, usually on demand. Services are usually standard, but can be customized to a specific organization if there is enough demand for the service. Cloud services can be offered internally, but generally refer to outsourced service provision.
Multi-vendor sourcing	This type of sourcing involves sourcing different services from different vendors, often using multiple options from the above.

- Provide improved focus on service value as well as business and customer outcomes
- Develop improved efficiency and effectiveness of all service design activities and processes, thereby supporting higher volumes of successful change delivered in a timely and cost-effective manner
- Achieve greater agility and better quality in the design of service solutions, within projects and major changes.

4.3.2 Service catalogue management

The service catalogue provides a central source of information on the IT services delivered by the service provider organization. This ensures that all areas of the business can view an accurate, consistent picture of the IT services, their details and their status. It includes a customer-facing view (or views) of the IT services in use, how they are intended to be used, the business processes they enable, and the levels and quality of service the customer can expect for each service.

Through the work of service catalogue management, organizations can:

- Ensure a common understanding of IT services and improved relationships between the customer and service provider by utilizing the service catalogue as a marketing and communication tool
- Improve service provider focus on customer outcomes by correlating internal service provider activities and service assets to business processes and outcomes
- Improve efficiency and effectiveness of other service management processes by leveraging the information contained in or connected to the service catalogue

- Improve knowledge, alignment and focus on the 'business value' of each service throughout the service provider organization and its activities.

To avoid confusion, it may be useful to define a hierarchy of services within the service catalogue, by qualifying exactly what type of service is recorded. The most valuable distinction is between:

- **Customer-facing services** IT services that are seen by the customer. These are typically services that support the customer's business units/business processes, directly facilitating some outcome or outcomes desired by the customer.
- **Supporting services** IT services that support or 'underpin' the customer-facing services. These are typically invisible to the customer, but essential to the delivery of customer-facing IT services.

Supporting services may be of many different types or go by many different names, such as infrastructure services, network services, application services or technical services. Whatever terms are used by a service provider to describe the different types of supporting service they may choose to recognize, the use and scope of each term should be clearly defined and agreed within the organization to avoid confusion. (In this context, the type of service has to do with relevance of a service to a particular group or audience or its role in the service chain. For a discussion of the different types of service relating to service packaging and value creation, see *ITIL Service Strategy*, section 3.2.2.)

It is advisable to present more than one view of the information in the service catalogue to accommodate the different needs of those who will use it. In order to ensure that both the customer and IT have a clear understanding of the relationship between the outcome-based, customer-facing services (see section 2.1.1 as well as section 3.4.3 in *ITIL Service Strategy*) and the business processes they support, it is recommended that a service provider, at the minimum, defines two different views, each one focusing on one type of service: a view for customers that shows the customer-facing services, and a second view for the IT service provider showing all the supporting services. The data stored in the service catalogue regarding relationships and dependencies between items would allow information in one view to be accessed from another, when deemed appropriate.

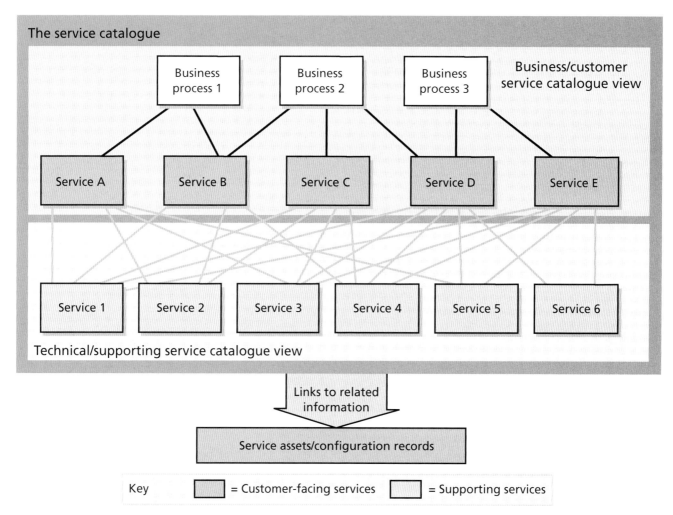

Figure 4.4 A two-view service catalogue

4.3.2.1 Sample service catalogue presentations

Figure 4.4 shows a service catalogue with two views:

■ **The business/customer service catalogue view**   This contains details of all the IT services delivered to the customers (customer-facing services), together with relationships to the business units and the business processes that rely on the IT services. This is the customer view of the service catalogue. In other words, this is the service catalogue for the business to see and use.

■ **The technical/supporting service catalogue view**   This contains details of all the supporting IT services, together with relationships to the customer-facing services they underpin and the components, configuration items (CIs) and other supporting services necessary to support the provision of the service to the customers.

Some organizations maintain a service catalogue that includes only the customer-facing services, while others maintain information only on the supporting services. The preferred situation adopted by the more mature organizations maintains both types of service within a single service catalogue, which is in turn part of a totally integrated service portfolio. (More information on the design and contents of a service catalogue is contained in *ITIL Service Design*.) Some organizations project more than two views. There is no correct or suggested number of views an organization should project. The number of views projected will depend upon the audiences to be addressed and the uses to which the catalogue will be put.

There is no single correct way to structure and deploy a service catalogue. Each service provider organization will consider its goals, objectives and uses for the service catalogue and create a structure that will meet its current and evolving needs appropriately.

4.3.3 Service level management

The purpose of the service level management (SLM) process is to ensure that all current and planned IT services are delivered to agreed achievable targets. This is accomplished through a constant cycle of negotiating, agreeing, monitoring, reporting on and reviewing IT service targets and achievements, and through instigation of actions to correct or improve the level of service delivered.

The objectives of SLM are to:

■ Define, document, agree, monitor, measure, report and review the level of IT services provided and instigate corrective measures whenever appropriate

■ Provide and improve the relationship and communication with the business and customers in conjunction with business relationship management

■ Ensure that specific and measurable targets are developed for all IT services

■ Monitor and improve customer satisfaction with the quality of service delivered

■ Ensure that IT and the customers have a clear and unambiguous expectation of the level of service to be delivered

■ Ensure that even when all agreed targets are met, the levels of service delivered are subject to proactive, cost-effective continual improvement.

The key activities within the SLM process should include:

■ Determining, negotiating, documenting and agreeing requirements for new or changed services in SLRs, and managing and reviewing them through the service lifecycle into SLAs for operational services

■ Monitoring and measuring service performance achievements of all operational services against targets within SLAs

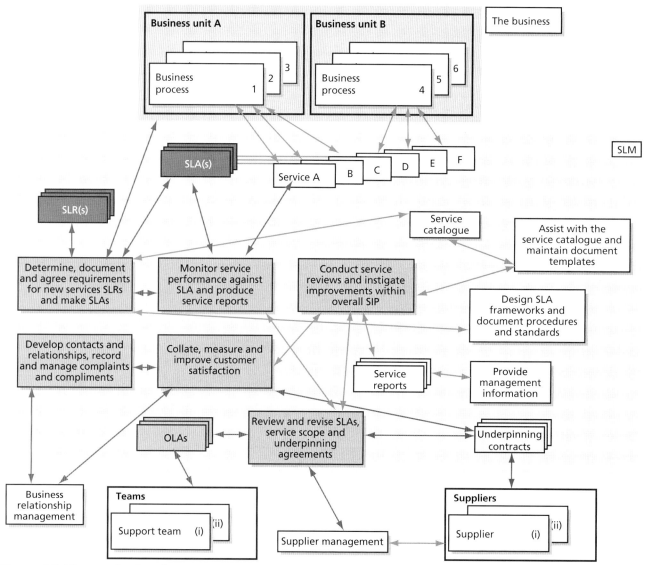

Figure 4.5 The service level management process

- Producing service reports
- Conducting service reviews, identifying improvement opportunities for inclusion in the CSI register, and managing appropriate SIPs
- Collating, measuring and improving customer satisfaction, in cooperation with business relationship management
- Reviewing and revising SLAs, service scope and OLAs
- Assisting supplier management to review and revise underpinning contracts or agreements
- Developing and documenting contacts and relationships with the business, customers and other stakeholders, in cooperation with the business relationship management process
- Logging and managing complaints and compliments, in cooperation with business relationship management
- Providing appropriate management information to aid performance management and demonstrating service achievement.

Figure 4.5 illustrates many of the interfaces between the main activities of SLM.

Using the service catalogue as an aid, SLM must design the most appropriate SLA structure to ensure that all services and all customers are covered in a manner best suited to the organization's needs. There are a number of potential options, including the following.

4.3.3.1 Service-based SLA

This is where an SLA covers one service, for all the customers of that service – for example, an SLA may be established for an organization's email service, covering all the customers of that service.

4.3.3.2 Customer-based SLA

This is an agreement with an individual customer group, covering all the services they use.

4.3.3.3 Multi-level SLAs

Some organizations have chosen to adopt a multi-level SLA structure. For example, a three-layer structure might look as follows:

- **Corporate level** This will cover all the generic SLM issues appropriate to every customer throughout the organization. These issues are likely to be less volatile, so updates are less frequently required.
- **Customer level** This will cover all SLM issues relevant to the particular customer group or business unit, regardless of the service being used.

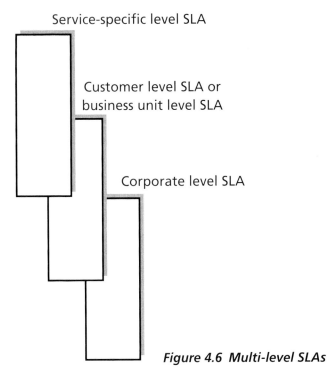

Figure 4.6 Multi-level SLAs

- **Service level**   This will cover all SLM issues relevant to the specific service, in relation to a specific customer group (one for each service covered by the SLA).

As shown in Figure 4.6, such a structure allows SLAs to be kept to a manageable size, avoids unnecessary duplication, and reduces the need for frequent updates. However, it does mean that extra effort is required to maintain the necessary relationships and links within the service catalogue and the CMS.

Many organizations have found it valuable to produce standards and a set of pro-formas or templates that can be used as a starting point for all SLAs, SLRs and OLAs. The pro-forma can often be developed alongside the draft SLA. Creating standards and templates will ensure that all agreements are developed in a consistent manner, and this will ease their subsequent use, operation and management.

> **Hints and tips**
>
> Make roles and responsibilities a part of the SLA. Consider three perspectives – the IT provider, the IT customer and the actual users.

The wording of SLAs should be clear and concise and leave no room for ambiguity. There is usually no need for agreements to be written in legal terminology, and plain language aids a common understanding. It is often helpful to have an independent person, who has not been involved with the drafting, to do a final read-through. This often identifies potential ambiguities and difficulties that can then be addressed and clarified. For this reason alone, it is recommended that all SLAs contain a glossary, defining any terms and providing clarity for any areas of ambiguity.

4.3.4 Availability management

The purpose of the availability management process is to ensure that the level of availability delivered in all IT services meets the agreed availability needs and/or service level targets in a cost-effective and timely manner. Availability management is concerned with meeting both the current and future availability needs of the business.

Availability management defines, analyses, plans, measures and improves all aspects of the availability of IT services, ensuring that all IT infrastructure, processes, tools, roles etc. are appropriate for the agreed availability service level targets. It provides a point of focus and management for all availability-related issues, with regard to both services and resources, ensuring that availability targets in all areas are measured and achieved.

The objectives of availability management are to:

- Produce and maintain an appropriate and up-to-date availability plan that reflects the current and future needs of the business
- Provide advice and guidance to all other areas of the business and IT on all availability-related issues
- Ensure that service availability achievements meet all their agreed targets by managing services and resources-related availability performance
- Assist with the diagnosis and resolution of availability-related incidents and problems
- Assess the impact of all changes on the availability plan and the availability of all services and resources
- Ensure that proactive measures to improve the availability of services are implemented wherever it is cost-justifiable to do so.

The measurement and monitoring of IT availability is a key activity to ensure that availability levels are being met consistently. Availability management should look to continually optimize and proactively improve the availability of the IT infrastructure, the services and the supporting organization, in order to provide cost-effective availability improvements that can deliver business and customer benefits.

The availability management process should include:

■ Monitoring of all aspects of availability, reliability and maintainability of IT services and the supporting components, with appropriate events, alarms and escalation, with automated scripts for recovery

■ Maintaining a set of methods, techniques and calculations for all availability measurements, metrics and reporting

■ Actively participating in risk assessment and management activities

■ Collecting measurements and the analysis and production of regular and ad hoc reports on service and component availability

■ Understanding the agreed current and future demands of the business for IT services and their availability

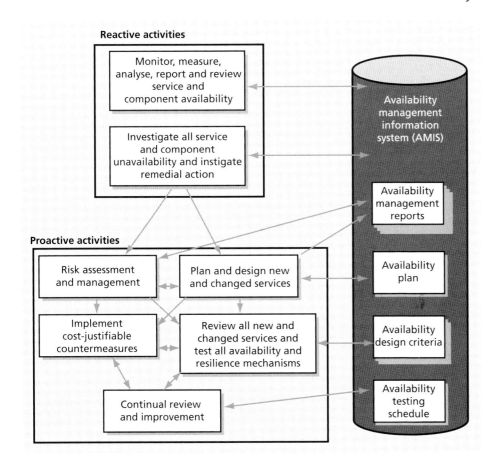

Figure 4.7 The availability management process

- Influencing the design of services and components to align with business availability needs
- Producing an availability plan that enables the service provider to continue to provide and improve services in line with availability targets defined in SLAs, and to plan and forecast future availability levels required, as defined in SLRs
- Maintaining a schedule of tests for all resilience and fail-over components and mechanisms
- Assisting with the identification and resolution of any incidents and problems associated with service or component unavailability
- Proactively improving service or component availability wherever it is cost-justifiable and meets the needs of the business.

The availability management process includes two key elements (see Figure 4.7):

- **Reactive activities**   These involve the monitoring, measuring, analysis and management of all events, incidents and problems involving unavailability. These activities are principally performed as part of the operational roles.
- **Proactive activities**   These involve the proactive planning, design and improvement of availability. These activities are principally performed as part of the design and planning roles.

Availability management is completed at two inter-connected levels:

- **Service availability**   This involves all aspects of service availability and unavailability and the impact of component availability, or the potential impact of component unavailability on service availability.

- **Component availability**   This involves all aspects of component availability and unavailability.

A guiding principle of availability management is to recognize that it is still possible to gain customer satisfaction even when things go wrong. One approach to help achieve this requires availability management to ensure that the duration of any incident is minimized to enable normal business operations to resume as quickly as possible. An aim of availability management is to ensure that the duration and impact from incidents affecting IT services are minimized, to enable business operations to resume as quickly as possible. The analysis of the 'expanded incident lifecycle' enables the total IT service downtime for any given incident to be broken down and mapped against the major stages through which all incidents progress (the lifecycle). Availability management should work closely with incident management and problem management in the analysis of all incidents causing unavailability.

4.3.4.1 Designing for availability

The level of availability required by the business influences the overall cost of the IT service provided. In general, the higher the level of availability required by the business, the higher the cost. These costs are not just the procurement of the base IT technology and services required to underpin the IT infrastructure. Additional costs are incurred in providing the appropriate service management processes, systems management tools and high-availability solutions required to meet the more stringent availability requirements. The greatest level of availability should be included in the design of those services supporting the most critical of the vital business functions (VBFs).

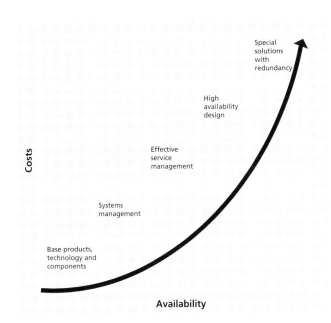

Figure 4.8 Relationship between levels of availability and overall costs

When considering how the availability requirements of the business are to be met, it is important to ensure that the level of availability to be provided for an IT service is at the level actually required, and is affordable and cost-justifiable to the business. Figure 4.8 indicates the products and processes required to provide varying levels of availability and the cost implications.

4.3.5 Capacity management

Capacity management is a process that extends across the service lifecycle. A key success factor in managing capacity is ensuring that it is considered during the design stage. It is for this reason that the capacity management process is included here. Capacity management is supported initially in service strategy where the decisions and analysis of business requirements and customer outcomes

influence the development of patterns of business activity, lines of service (LOS) and service options. This provides the predictive and ongoing capacity indicators needed to align capacity to demand. Capacity management provides a point of focus and management for all capacity- and performance-related issues, with regard to both services and resources.

Capacity management ensures that the capacity and performance of the IT services and systems match the evolving agreed demands of the business in the most cost-effective and timely manner. Capacity management is essentially a balancing act:

- **Balancing costs against resources needed** The requirement to ensure that processing capacity that is purchased is cost-justifiable in terms of business need, and the requirement to make the most efficient use of those resources.
- **Balancing supply against demand** The need to ensure that the available supply of IT processing power matches the demands made on it by the business, both now and in the future. It may also be necessary to manage or influence the demand for a particular resource.

The objectives of capacity management are to:

- Produce and maintain an appropriate and up-to-date capacity plan, which reflects the current and future needs of the business
- Provide advice and guidance to all other areas of the business and IT on all capacity- and performance-related issues
- Ensure that service performance achievements meet all of their agreed targets by managing the performance and capacity of both services and resources

- Assist with the diagnosis and resolution of performance- and capacity-related incidents and problems
- Assess the impact of all changes on the capacity plan, and the performance and capacity of all services and resources
- Ensure that proactive measures to improve the performance of services are implemented wherever it is cost-justifiable to do so.

The capacity management process should include:

- Monitoring patterns of business activity through performance, utilization and throughput of IT services and the supporting infrastructure, environmental, data and applications components, and the production of regular and ad hoc reports on service and component capacity and performance
- Undertaking tuning activities to make the most efficient use of existing IT resources
- Understanding the agreed current and future demands being made by the customer for IT resources, and producing forecasts for future requirements
- Influencing demand in conjunction with the financial management for IT services and demand management processes
- Producing a capacity plan that enables the service provider to continue to provide services of the quality defined in SLAs and that covers a sufficient planning timeframe to meet future service levels required as defined in the service portfolio and SLRs
- Assisting with the identification and resolution of any incidents and problems associated with service or component capacity or performance

- The proactive improvement of service or component performance, wherever it is cost-justifiable and meets the needs of the business.

Capacity management consists of three sub-processes (see Figure 4.9): business capacity management, service capacity management and component capacity management. There are many similar activities that are performed by business, service and component capacity management, but each of these sub-processes has a very different focus. Business capacity management is focused on the current and future business requirements, while service capacity management concentrates on the delivery of the existing services that support the business, and component capacity management deals with the IT infrastructure that underpins service provision.

4.3.5.1 Business capacity management

The business capacity management sub-process translates business needs and plans into requirements for service and IT infrastructure, ensuring that the future business requirements for IT services are quantified, designed, planned and implemented in a timely fashion. This can be achieved by using the existing data on the current resource utilization by the various services and resources to trend, forecast, model or predict future requirements. These future requirements come from the service strategy and service portfolio detailing new processes and service requirements, changes, improvements, and also the growth in the existing services.

4.3.5.2 Service capacity management

The service capacity management sub-process focuses on the management, control and prediction of the end-to-end performance and

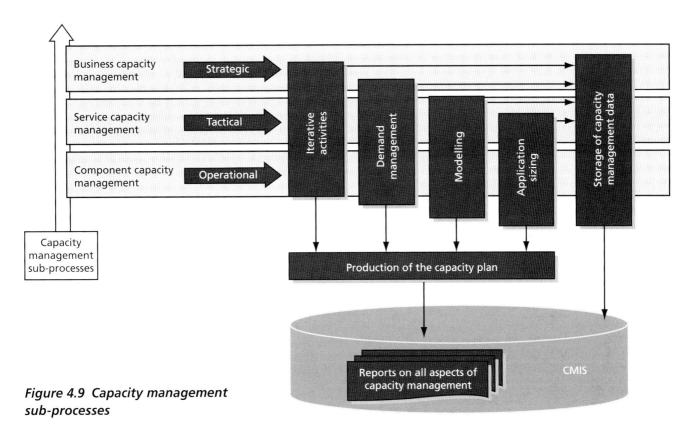

Figure 4.9 Capacity management sub-processes

capacity of the live, operational IT services usage and workloads. It ensures that the performance of all services, as detailed in service targets within SLAs and SLRs, is monitored and measured, and that the collected data is recorded, analysed and reported. Wherever necessary, proactive and reactive action should be instigated, to ensure that the performance of all services meets their agreed business targets. This is performed by staff with knowledge of all the areas of technology used in the delivery of end-to-end service, and often involves seeking advice from the specialists involved in component capacity management. Wherever possible, automated thresholds should be used to manage all operational services, to

ensure that situations where service targets are breached or threatened are rapidly identified and cost-effective actions to reduce or avoid their potential impact are implemented.

4.3.5.3 Component capacity management

The component capacity management sub-process focuses on the management, control and prediction of the performance, utilization and capacity of individual IT technology components. It ensures that all components within the IT infrastructure that have finite resource are monitored and measured, and that the collected data is recorded, analysed and reported. Again, wherever possible, automated thresholds should be implemented to manage all components, to ensure that situations where service targets are breached or threatened by component usage or performance are rapidly identified, and cost-effective actions to reduce or avoid their potential impact are implemented.

4.3.6 IT service continuity management

Service failures of extreme magnitude are not something any business or service provider wants to experience. Even the best-planned and managed services however, can be the victim of catastrophic failure through events that are not in the direct control of a service provider.

Most of us purchase insurance to protect us in the event that something of great value, such as our home, becomes the victim of a catastrophic event. Insurance gives us peace of mind that if the unplanned happens, we have the means to recover from such disasters. The amount of insurance we purchase is gauged on the predicted replacement value of our possessions, the likelihood such a disaster could happen and how quickly we can restore our losses. This is a form of risk management.

Service continuity is an essential part of the warranty of a service. If a service's continuity cannot be maintained and/or restored in accordance with the requirements of the business, then the business will not experience the value that has been promised. Without continuity the utility of the service cannot be accessed.

The purpose of the IT service continuity management (ITSCM) process is to support the overall business continuity management (BCM) process by ensuring that, by managing the risks that could seriously affect IT services, the IT service provider can always provide minimum agreed business continuity-related service levels.

In support of and alignment with the BCM process, ITSCM uses formal risk assessment and management techniques to:

- Reduce risks to IT services to agreed acceptable levels
- Plan and prepare for the recovery of IT services.

The objectives of ITSCM are to:

- Produce and maintain a set of IT service continuity plans that support the overall business continuity plans of the organization
- Complete regular BIA exercises to ensure that all continuity plans are maintained in line with changing business impacts and requirements
- Conduct regular risk assessment and management exercises to manage IT services within an agreed level of business risk in conjunction with the business and the availability management and information security management processes
- Provide advice and guidance to all other areas of the business and IT on all continuity-related issues
- Ensure that appropriate continuity mechanisms are put in place to meet or exceed the agreed business continuity targets
- Assess the impact of all changes on the IT service continuity plans and supporting methods and procedures
- Ensure that proactive measures to improve the availability of services are implemented wherever it is cost-justifiable to do so
- Negotiate and agree contracts with suppliers for the provision of the necessary recovery capability to support all continuity plans in

conjunction with the supplier management process.

The ITSCM process includes:

- The agreement of the scope of the ITSCM process and the policies adopted
- BIA to quantify the impact that loss of IT service would have on the business
- Risk assessment and management – the risk identification and risk assessment to identify potential threats to continuity and the likelihood of the threats becoming reality. This also includes taking measures to manage the identified threats where this can be cost-justified. The approach to managing these threats will form the core of the ITSCM strategy and plans
- Production of an overall ITSCM strategy that must be integrated into the BCM strategy. This can be produced following the BIA and the development of the risk assessment, and is likely to include elements of risk reduction as well as selection of appropriate and comprehensive recovery options
- Production of an ITSCM plan, which again must be integrated with the overall BCM plans
- Testing of the plans
- Ongoing operation and maintenance of the plans.

Service continuity is implemented and managed in four stages (see Figure 4.10):

- **Initiation**   Policy setting, defining scope and terms of reference, project planning and resource allocation
- **Requirements and strategy**   Business impact analysis, risk assessment

- **Implementation**   Executing risk reduction measures, recovery option arrangements, testing the plans
- **Ongoing operation**   Education and awareness, change control of ITSCM plans, ongoing testing.

A good place to start is by assessing the threats and risks to VBFs. This will help reveal vulnerabilities to vital business operations and ensure that preventative and recovery plans and mechanisms are in place. Consistent with the ITSCM process, this should be continually evaluated to ensure that changes to services or business requirements have not affected the ability of the ITSCM process to be effective when needed.

4.3.7 Information security management

Across the world, organizations create value through the intellectual property they own and use to deliver products and services. Protecting personal information and intellectual capital is a primary need for business and is subject to an increasing amount of legislation. The technology today offers us unlimited potential to create, gather and amass vast quantities of information. A service provider is responsible for ensuring that it can guarantee that the business information is protected from intrusion, theft, loss and unauthorized access.

Information security is a management process within the corporate governance framework, which provides the strategic direction for security activities and ensures that objectives are achieved. It further ensures that the information security risks are appropriately managed and that enterprise information resources are used responsibly. Information security management provides a focus for all aspects of IT security and manages all IT security activities.

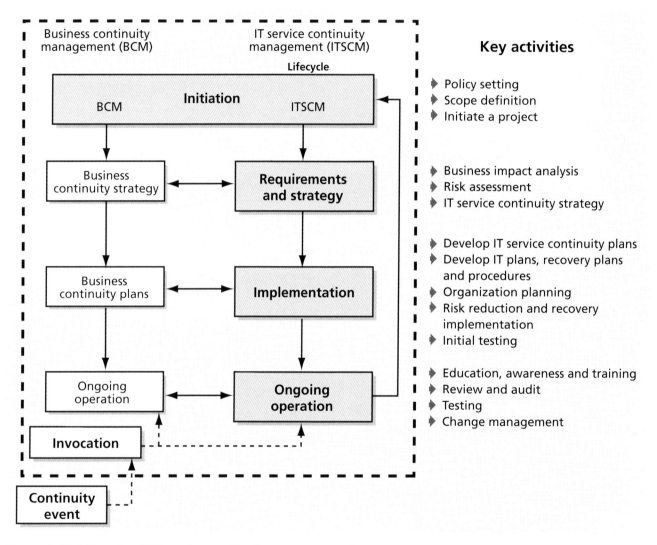

Figure 4.10 Lifecycle of IT service continuity management

In this context, the term 'information' is used as a general term and includes data stores, databases and metadata. The objective of information security management is to protect the interests of those relying on information, and the systems and communications that deliver the information, from harm resulting from failures of confidentiality, integrity and availability.

For most organizations, the security objective is met when:

- Information is observed by or disclosed to only those who have a right to know (confidentiality)
- Information is complete, accurate and protected against unauthorized modification (integrity)
- Information is available and usable when required, and the systems that provide it can appropriately resist attacks and recover from or prevent failures (availability)
- Business transactions, as well as information exchanges between enterprises, or with partners, can be trusted (authenticity and non-repudiation).

Prioritization of confidentiality, integrity and availability must be considered in the context of business and business processes. The primary guide to defining what must be protected and the level of protection has to come from the business. To be effective, security must address entire business processes from end to end and cover the physical and technical aspects. Only within the context of business needs and risks can management define security.

Information security management activities should be focused on and driven by an overall information security policy and a set of underpinning specific security policies. The information security policy should have the full support of top executive IT management and ideally the support and commitment of top executive business management. The policy should cover all areas of security, be appropriate, meet the needs of the business and should include:

- An overall information security policy
- Use and misuse of IT assets policy
- An access control policy
- A password control policy
- An email policy
- An internet policy
- An anti-virus policy
- An information classification policy
- A document classification policy
- A remote access policy
- A policy with regard to supplier access to IT service, information and components
- A copyright infringement policy for electronic material
- An asset disposal policy
- A records retention policy.

ISO/IEC 27001 is the formal standard against which organizations may seek independent certification of their information security management systems (ISMS) (meaning their frameworks to design, implement, manage, maintain and enforce information security processes and controls systematically and consistently throughout their organizations). The following five elements show an approach that is widely used and is based on the advice and guidance described in many sources, including ISO/IEC 27001:

- **Control** The objectives of the control element are to:
  - Establish a management framework to initiate and manage information security in the organization
  - Establish an organizational structure to prepare, approve and implement the information security policy
  - Allocate responsibilities
  - Establish and control documentation.
- **Plan** The objective of the plan element is to devise and recommend the appropriate security measures, based on an understanding of the requirements of the organization.

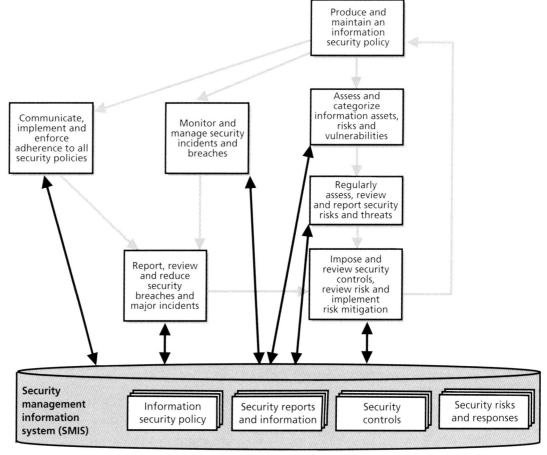

Figure 4.11 Information security management process

■ **Implement** The objective of the implementation element is to ensure that appropriate procedures, tools and controls are in place to underpin the information security policy.

■ **Evaluate** The objectives of the evaluate element are to:

● Supervise and check compliance with the security policy and security requirements in SLAs and OLAs, and in underpinning contracts in conjunction with supplier management

● Carry out regular audits of the technical security of IT systems

● Provide information to external auditors and regulators, if required.

■ **Maintain** The objectives of the maintain element are to:

● Improve security agreements as specified in, for example, SLAs and OLAs

● Improve the implementation of security measures and controls.

The key activities within the information security management process are illustrated in Figure 4.11.

Security measures can be used at a specific stage in the prevention and handling of security incidents. Security incidents are not solely caused by technical threats – statistics show that, for example, the large majority stem from human errors (intended or not) or procedural errors, and often have implications in other fields such as safety, legality or health.

The following stages can be identified. At the start there is a risk that a threat will materialize. A threat can be anything that disrupts the business process or has negative impact on the business. When a threat materializes, we speak of a security incident. This security incident may result in damage (to information or to assets) that has to be repaired or otherwise corrected. Suitable measures can be selected for each of these stages. The choice of measures will depend on the importance attached to the information.

- **Preventive** Security measures are used to prevent a security incident from occurring
- **Reductive** Further measures can be taken in advance to minimize any possible damage that may occur
- **Detective** If a security incident occurs, it is important to discover it as soon as possible – detection
- **Repressive** Measures are then used to counteract any continuation or repetition of the security incident
- **Corrective** The damage is repaired as far as possible using corrective measures.

The documentation of all controls should be maintained to reflect accurately their operation, maintenance and method of operation.

Information security management faces many challenges in establishing an appropriate information security policy with an effective supporting process and controls. One of the biggest challenges is to ensure that there is adequate support from the business, business security and senior management. If these are not available, it will be impossible to establish an effective information security management process. If there is senior IT management support, but there is no support from the business, IT security controls and risk assessment and management will be severely limited in what they can achieve. It is pointless implementing security policies, procedures and controls in IT if these cannot be enforced throughout the business. The major use of IT services and assets is outside of IT, and so are the majority of security threats and risks.

In some organizations the business perception is that security is an IT responsibility, and therefore the business assumes that IT will be responsible for all aspects of IT security and that IT services will be adequately protected. However, without the commitment and support of the business and business personnel, money invested in expensive security controls and procedures will be largely wasted and they will mostly be ineffective.

4.3.8 Supplier management

The supplier management process ensures that suppliers and the services they provide are managed to support IT service targets and business expectations. The aim of this section is to raise awareness of the business context of working with partners and suppliers, and how this work can best be directed towards realizing business benefit for the organization.

It is essential that supplier management processes and planning are involved in all stages of the service lifecycle, from strategy and design, through transition and operation, to improvement. Complex business demands require the complete breadth of skills and capability to support provision of a comprehensive set of IT services to a business; therefore the use of value networks and the suppliers and the services they provide are an integral part of any end-to-end solution. Suppliers and the management of suppliers and partners are essential to the provision of quality IT services (see Figure 4.12).

The main objectives of the supplier management process are to:

■ Obtain value for money from suppliers and contracts

■ Ensure that contracts with suppliers are aligned to business needs, and support and align with agreed targets in SLRs and SLAs, in conjunction with SLM

■ Manage relationships with suppliers

■ Manage supplier performance

■ Negotiate and agree contracts with suppliers and manage them through their lifecycle

■ Maintain a supplier policy and a supporting supplier and contract management information system (SCMIS).

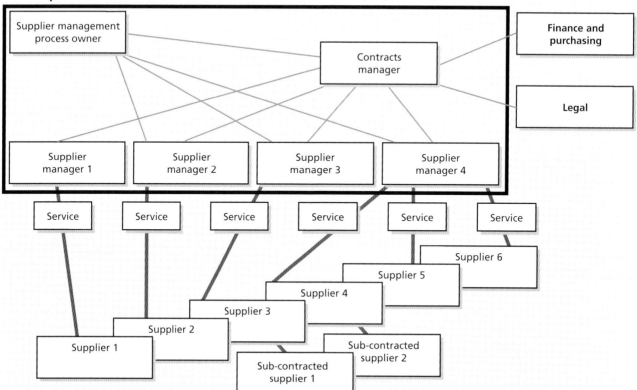

Figure 4.12 Supplier management – roles and interfaces

The supplier management process should include:

- Implementation and enforcement of the supplier policy
- Maintenance of an SCMIS
- Supplier and contract categorization and risk assessment
- Supplier and contract evaluation and selection
- Development, negotiation and agreement of contracts
- Contract review, renewal and termination
- Management of suppliers and supplier performance
- Identification of improvement opportunities for inclusion in the CSI register, and the implementation of service and supplier improvement plans
- Maintenance of standard contracts, terms and conditions
- Management of contractual dispute resolution
- Management of sub-contracted suppliers.

IT supplier management often has to comply with organizational or corporate standards, guidelines and requirements, particularly those of corporate legal, finance and purchasing, as illustrated in Figure 4.12.

Satisfaction surveys also play an important role in revealing how well supplier service levels are aligned to business needs. If the customer does not have visibility into what is being delivered by the supplier versus what is being done by internal support groups, the service provider will need to structure satisfaction surveys carefully to be able to differentiate between the two contributions. A survey may reveal instances where there is dissatisfaction with the service, yet the supplier is apparently performing well against its targets (and vice versa). This may happen where service levels are inappropriately defined and should result in a review of the contracts, agreements and targets. Some service providers publish supplier league tables based on their survey results, stimulating competition between suppliers.

For those significant supplier relationships in which the business has a direct interest, both the business (in conjunction with the procurement department) and IT will have established their objectives for the relationship, and defined the benefits they expect to realize. This forms a major part of the business case for entering into the relationship.

These benefits must be linked and complementary, and must be measured and managed. Where the business is seeking improvements in customer service, IT supplier relationships contributing to those customer services must be able to demonstrate improved service in their own domain, and how much this has contributed to improved customer service.

Strong, trusted relationships with suppliers are an integral element of successful service management and enhance the value of any service provider to the business.

4.4 SERVICE DESIGN INPUTS AND OUTPUTS

The main inputs to service design are requirements for new or changed services. The main output of service design is the service design package, which includes all of the information needed to manage the entire lifecycle of a new or changed service. Table 4.2 shows the major service design inputs and outputs, by lifecycle stage. Appendix A provides a summary of the major inputs and outputs between each stage of the service lifecycle.

Table 4.2 Service design inputs and outputs by lifecycle stage

Lifecycle stage	Service design inputs (from the lifecycle stage in the first column)	Service design outputs (to the lifecycle stage in the first column)
Service strategy	Vision and mission	Input to business cases and the service portfolio
	Service portfolio	Service design packages
	Policies	Updated service models
	Strategies and strategic plans	Service portfolio updates including the service catalogue
	Priorities	
	Service charters including service packages and details of utility and warranty	Financial estimates and reports
	Financial information and budgets	Design-related knowledge and information in the SKMS
	Documented patterns of business activity and user profiles	Designs for service strategy processes and procedures
	Service models	
Service transition	Service catalogue updates	Service catalogue
	Feedback on all aspects of service design and service design packages	Service design packages, including:
	Input and feedback to transition plans	■ Details of utility and warranty
	Response to requests for change (RFCs)	■ Acceptance criteria
	Knowledge and information in the SKMS (including the CMS)	■ Service models
		■ Designs and interface specifications
	Design errors identified in transition for re-design	■ Transition plans
	Evaluation reports	■ Operational plans and procedures
		RFCs to transition or deploy new or changed services
		Input to change evaluation and CAB meetings
		Designs for service transition processes and procedures
		SLAs, OLAs and underpinning contracts

Table 4.2 – *continued*

Lifecycle stage	Service design inputs (from the lifecycle stage in the first column)	Service design outputs (to the lifecycle stage in the first column)
Service operation	Operational requirements	Service catalogue
	Actual performance information	Service design package, including:
	RFCs to resolve operational issues	■ Details of utility and warranty
	Historical incident and problem records	■ Operational plans and procedures
		■ Recovery procedures
		Knowledge and information in the SKMS
		Vital business functions
		HW/SW maintenance requirements
		Designs for service operation processes and procedures
		SLAs, OLAs and underpinning contracts
		Security policies
Continual service improvement	Results of customer and user satisfaction surveys	Service catalogue
	Input to design requirements	Service design packages including details of utility and warranty
	Data required for metrics, KPIs and CSFs	Knowledge and information in the SKMS
	Service reports	Achievements against metrics, KPIs and CSFs
	Feedback on service design packages	Design of services; measurements; processes; infrastructure; systems
	RFCs for implementing improvements	Design for the seven-step improvement process and procedures
		Improvement opportunities logged in the CSI register

Service transition

5

5 Service transition

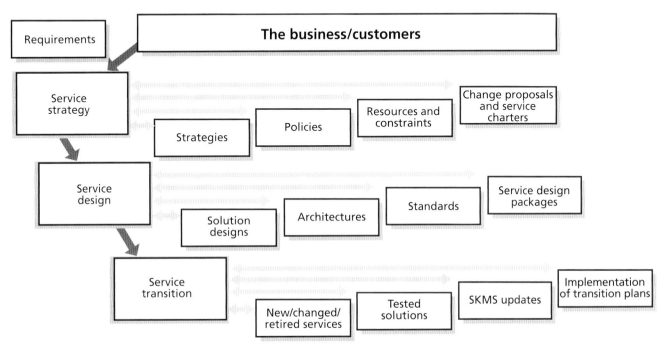

Figure 5.1 Service transition must ensure that what is planned to be implemented will achieve the defined objectives

Many business innovations are achieved through project initiatives that involve IT. In the end, whether these are minor operational improvements or major transformational events, they all produce change. In the preceding chapter we looked at creating and improving services through the design stage of the lifecycle. Now we must ensure that the knowledge that has been generated and that will be needed to manage services when in the live environment is shared across the organization. This is done through service transition (see Figure 5.1).

5.1 SERVICE TRANSITION OVERVIEW

5.1.1 Purpose and objectives of service transition

The purpose of the service transition stage of the service lifecycle is to ensure that new, modified or retired services meet the expectations of the business as documented in the service strategy and service design stages of the lifecycle.

The objectives of service transition are to:

- Plan and manage service changes efficiently and effectively
- Manage risks relating to new, changed or retired services
- Successfully deploy service releases into supported environments
- Set correct expectations on the performance and use of new or changed services
- Ensure that service changes create the expected business value
- Provide good-quality knowledge and information about services and service assets.

In order to achieve these objectives, there are many things that need to happen during the service transition lifecycle stage. These include:

- Planning and managing the capacity and resources required to manage service transitions
- Implementing a rigorous framework for evaluating service capabilities and risk profiles before new or changed services are deployed
- Establishing and maintaining the integrity of service assets
- Providing efficient repeatable mechanisms for building, testing and deploying services and releases
- Ensuring that services can be managed, operated and supported in accordance with constraints specified during the service design stage of the service lifecycle.

5.1.2 Scope

ITIL Service Transition provides guidance for the development and improvement of capabilities for transitioning new and changed services into supported environments, including release planning, building, testing, evaluation and deployment. The publication also considers service retirement and transfer of services between service providers. The guidance focuses on how to ensure that the requirements from service strategy, developed in service design, are effectively realized in service operation while controlling the risks of failure and subsequent disruption.

Consideration is given to:

- Managing the complexity associated with changes to services and service management processes
- Allowing for innovation while minimizing the unintended consequences of change
- Introducing new services
- Changes to existing services, e.g. expansion, reduction, change of supplier, acquisition or disposal of sections of user base or suppliers, change of requirements or skills availability
- Decommissioning and discontinuation of services, applications or other service components
- Transferring services to and from other service providers.

Guidance on transferring the control of services includes transfer in the following circumstances:

- Out to a new supplier, e.g. outsourcing
- From one supplier to another
- Back in from a supplier, e.g. insourcing
- Moving to a partnership or co-sourcing arrangement (e.g. partial outsourcing of some processes)
- Multiple suppliers, e.g. co-sourcing or multi-sourcing
- Joint venture
- Down-sizing, up-sizing (right-sizing) and offshoring
- Merger and acquisition.

In reality, circumstances generate a combination of several of the above options at any one time and in any one situation.

The scope also includes the transition of changes in the service provider's service management capabilities that will impact on the ways of working, the organization, people, projects and third parties involved in service management.

5.1.3 Usage

ITIL Service Transition provides access to proven best practice based on the skill and knowledge of experienced industry practitioners in adopting a standardized and controlled approach to service management. Although this publication can be used and applied in isolation, it is recommended that it is used in conjunction with the other core ITIL publications. All of the core publications need to be read to fully appreciate and understand the overall lifecycle of services and IT service management.

5.1.4 Value to business

Selecting and adopting the best practice as recommended in this publication will assist organizations in delivering significant benefits. It will help readers to set up service transition and the processes that support it, and to make effective use of those processes to facilitate the effective transitioning of new, changed or decommissioned services.

Adopting and implementing standard and consistent approaches for service transition will:

■ Enable projects to estimate the cost, timing, resource requirement and risks associated with the service transition stage more accurately
■ Result in higher volumes of successful change

■ Be easier for people to adopt and follow
■ Enable service transition assets to be shared and re-used across projects and services
■ Reduce delays from unexpected clashes and dependencies – for example, if multiple projects need to use the same test environment at the same time
■ Reduce the effort spent on managing the service transition test and pilot environments
■ Improve expectation setting for all stakeholders involved in service transition including customers, users, suppliers, partners and projects
■ Increase confidence that the new or changed service can be delivered to specification without unexpectedly affecting other services or stakeholders
■ Ensure that new or changed services will be maintainable and cost-effective
■ Improve control of service assets and configurations.

5.2 SERVICE TRANSITION PRINCIPLES

5.2.1 Managing change across the lifecycle

Change can be defined in many ways. The ITIL definition of a change is 'the addition, modification or removal of anything that could have an effect on IT services'. The scope should include changes to all architectures, processes, tools, metrics and documentation, as well as changes to IT services and other configuration items.

All changes must be recorded and managed in a controlled way. The scope of change management covers changes to all configuration items (CIs) across the whole service lifecycle, whether these

CIs are physical assets such as servers or networks, virtual assets such as virtual servers or virtual storage, or other types of asset such as agreements or contracts. It also covers all changes to any of the five aspects of service design:

- Service solutions for new or changed services, including all of the functional requirements, resources and capabilities needed and agreed
- Management information systems and tools, especially the service portfolio, for the management and control of services through their lifecycle
- Technology architectures and management architectures required to provide the services

- Processes needed to design, transition, operate and improve the services
- Measurement systems, methods and metrics for the services, the architectures, their constituent components and the processes.

Each organization should define the changes that lie outside the scope of its change management process. Typically these might include:

- Changes with significantly wider impacts than service changes, e.g. departmental organization, policies and business operations – these changes would produce RFCs to generate consequential service changes.

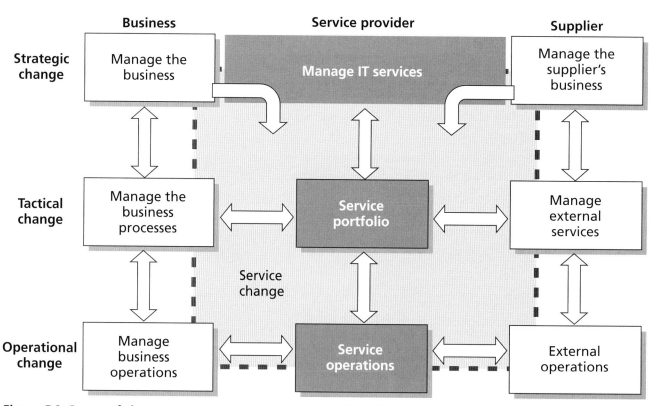

Figure 5.2 Scope of change management and release and deployment management for services

■ Changes at an operational level such as repair to printers or other routine service components.

Figure 5.2 shows the typical scope of a change management process for an IT organization and how it interfaces with the business and suppliers at strategic, tactical and operational levels. It covers interfaces to internal and external service providers where there are shared assets and configuration items that need to be under change management. Change management must interface with business change management (to the left in Figure 5.2) and with the supplier's change management (to the right in the figure). This may be an external supplier within a formal change management system, or the project change mechanisms within an internal development project.

The service portfolio provides a clear definition of all current, planned and retired services. Understanding the service portfolio helps all parties involved in the service transition to understand the potential impact of the new or changed service on current services and other new or changed services.

Strategic changes are brought in via service strategy and the service portfolio management process in the form of change proposals. Changes to a service will be brought in via service design, continual service improvement, service level management and service catalogue management. Corrective change, resolving errors detected in services, will be initiated from service operation and may route via support or external suppliers into a formal RFC.

5.2.2 Managing organization and stakeholder change

Service transition's basic role is, on the basis of agreed design, to implement a new or changed service, effectively making the organization different from the way that it was previously. For a change of any significance, this is delivering an organizational change, ranging from moving a few staff to work from new premises through to major alterations in the nature of business working, e.g. from face-to-face retail to web-based trading.

Change is an inevitable and important part of organizational development and growth. Change can occur in incremental phases or suddenly, affecting part or the whole of an organization, its people and its culture. Without change, progress does not happen. Organizational change is an essential part of continual improvement and must be built into all transitions to enable them to deliver value to the business.

Organizational change efforts fail or fall short of their goals because changes and transitions are not led, managed and monitored efficiently across the organization and throughout the change process. These gaps in key organizational activities often result in resistance, dissatisfaction and increased costs. Change is never easy; it usually takes longer than planned and creates barriers and resistance along the way. Effective leaders and managers understand the change process and plan and lead accordingly. Major negative impact can come from losing staff – disillusioned people leaving – which brings risks to the organization, e.g. loss of knowledge and lack of handover.

5.2.3 Adopting programme and project management best practice

It is best practice to manage several releases and deployments as a programme, with each significant deployment run as a project. This will typically be based on PRINCE2 or PMBOK. The actual deployment may be carried out by dedicated staff as part of broader responsibilities such as operations or through a team brought together for the purpose. Elements of the deployment may be delivered through external suppliers, and suppliers may deliver the bulk of the deployment effort, for example in the implementation of a commercial off-the-shelf system such as an ITSM support tool.

Significant deployments will be complex projects in their own right. The steps to consider in planning include the range of elements comprising that service, e.g. people, application, hardware, software, documentation and knowledge. This means that the deployment will contain sub-deployments for each type of element comprising the service.

5.3   SERVICE TRANSITION PROCESSES

5.3.1 Transition planning and support

The purpose of the transition planning and support process is to provide overall planning for service transitions and to coordinate the resources that they require.

The objectives of transition planning and support are to:

- Plan and coordinate the resources to ensure that the requirements of service strategy encoded in service design are effectively realized in service operation.

- Coordinate activities across projects, suppliers and service teams where required.
- Establish new or changed services into supported environments within the predicted cost, quality and time estimates.
- Establish new or modified management information systems and tools, technology and management architectures, service management processes, and measurement methods and metrics to meet requirements established during the service design stage of the lifecycle.
- Ensure that all parties adopt the common framework of standard re-usable processes and supporting systems in order to improve the effectiveness and efficiency of the integrated planning and coordination activities.
- Provide clear and comprehensive plans that enable customer and business change projects to align their activities with the service transition plans.
- Identify, manage and control risks, to minimize the chance of failure and disruption across transition activities; and ensure that service transition issues, risks and deviations are reported to the appropriate stakeholders and decision makers.
- Monitor and improve the performance of the service transition lifecycle stage.

Service design coordination will – in collaboration with customers, external and internal suppliers and other relevant stakeholders – develop the service design and document it in a service design package (SDP). The SDP includes the following information that is required by the service transition teams:

- The service charter, which includes a description of the expected utility and warranty, as well as outline budgets and timescales

- The service specifications
- The service models
- The architectural design required to deliver the new or changed service, including constraints
- The definition and design of each release
- The detailed design of how the service components will be assembled and integrated into a release package
- Release and deployment management plans
- The service acceptance criteria.

Service design packages will be created (or updated) for all major changes. This could include implementation of new service management processes or tools, or replacement of old infrastructure components, as well as release of new or changed services and decommissioning or retiring assets or services.

5.3.2 Change management

The purpose of the change management process is to control the lifecycle of all changes, enabling beneficial changes to be made with minimum disruption to IT services.

The objectives of change management are to:

- Respond to the customer's changing business requirements while maximizing value and reducing incidents, disruption and re-work.
- Respond to the business and IT requests for change that will align the services with the business needs.
- Ensure that changes are recorded and evaluated, and that authorized changes are prioritized, planned, tested, implemented, documented and reviewed in a controlled manner.

- Ensure that all changes to configuration items are recorded in the configuration management system (CMS).
- Optimize overall business risk – it is often correct to minimize business risk, but sometimes it is appropriate to knowingly accept a risk because of the potential benefit.

Reliability and business continuity are essential for the success and survival of any organization. Service and infrastructure changes can have a negative impact on the business through service disruption and delay in identifying business requirements, but change management enables the service provider to add value to the business by:

- Protecting the business, and other services, while making required changes
- Implementing changes that meet the customers' agreed service requirements while optimizing costs
- Contributing to meet governance, legal, contractual and regulatory requirements by providing auditable evidence of change management activity. This includes better alignment with ISO/IEC 20000, ISO/IEC 38500 and COBIT where these have been adopted
- Reducing failed changes and therefore service disruption, defects and re-work
- Reducing the number of unauthorized changes, leading to reduced service disruption and reduced time to resolve change-related incidents
- Delivering change promptly to meet business timescales
- Tracking changes through the service lifecycle and to the assets of its customers
- Contributing to better estimates of the quality, time and cost of change

- Assessing the risks associated with the transition of services (introduction or disposal)
- Improving productivity of staff by minimizing disruptions caused by high levels of unplanned or 'emergency' change and hence maximizing service availability
- Reducing the mean time to restore service (MTRS), via quicker and more successful implementations of corrective changes
- Liaising with the business change process to identify opportunities for business improvement.

Policies that support change management include:

- Creating a culture of change management across the organization where there is zero tolerance for unauthorized change
- Aligning the change management process with business, project and stakeholder change management processes
- Ensuring that changes create business value and that the benefits for the business created by each change are measured and reported
- Prioritization of change, e.g. innovation versus preventive versus detective versus corrective change
- Establishing accountability and responsibilities for changes through the service lifecycle
- Segregation of duty controls
- Establishing a single focal point for changes in order to minimize the likelihood of conflicting changes and potential disruption to supported environments
- Preventing people who are not authorized to make a change from having access to supported environments
- Integration with other service management processes to establish traceability of change,

detect unauthorized change and identify change-related incidents
- Change windows – enforcement and authorization for exceptions
- Performance and risk evaluation of all changes that impact service capability
- Performance measures for the process, e.g. efficiency and effectiveness.

5.3.2.1 The seven Rs of change management

The following questions must be answered for all changes. Without this information, the impact assessment cannot be completed, and the balance of risk and benefit to the live service will not be understood. This could result in the change not delivering all the possible or expected business benefits or even in it having a detrimental, unexpected effect on the live service. The questions are:

- Who **raised** the change?
- What is the **reason** for the change?
- What is the **return** required from the change?
- What are the **risks** involved in the change?
- What **resources** are required to deliver the change?
- Who is **responsible** for the build, test and implementation of the change?
- What is the **relationship** between this change and other changes?

5.3.2.2 Types of change request

A change request is a formal communication seeking an alteration to one or more configuration items. This could take several forms, e.g. a 'request for change' document, service desk call or project initiation document. Different types of change may require different types of change request. For example, a major change may require a change proposal, which is usually created by the service portfolio management process. An organization needs to ensure that appropriate procedures and forms are available to cover the anticipated requests. Avoiding a bureaucratic approach to documenting a minor change removes some of the cultural barriers to adopting the change management process.

There are three different types of service change:

- **Standard change** A pre-authorized change that is low risk, relatively common and follows a procedure or work instruction.
- **Emergency change** A change that must be implemented as soon as possible, for example to resolve a major incident or implement a security patch.
- **Normal change** Any service change that is not a standard change or an emergency change (see Figure 5.3).

5.3.2.3 Change advisory board

A change advisory board (CAB) is a body that exists to support the authorization of changes and to assist change management in the assessment, prioritization and scheduling of changes. A CAB is often the change authority for one or more change categories, but in some organizations the CAB just plays an advisory role. In a large organization there may be many different CABs with a global CAB that is responsible for the most significant changes and other CABs supporting different business units, geographies or technologies. It is important that each CAB has full visibility of all changes that could have an impact on the services and configuration items within its control. For each CAB meeting, members should be chosen who are capable of ensuring that all changes within the scope of the

CAB are adequately assessed from both a business and a technical viewpoint.

5.3.3 Service asset and configuration management

Within the human body lie a number of intricate systems. The respiratory, nervous and circulatory systems have distinct functions, but they also have a critical dependency on one another. If one system fails, the others will eventually succumb, unless provided with additional life-supporting intervention. Services are systems with similar levels of interdependency. These are service assets which have configurations specific to the functions they perform and, ultimately, the service they collectively deliver.

No organization can be fully efficient or effective unless it manages its assets well, particularly those assets that are vital to the running of the customer's or organization's business. This process manages the service assets in order to support the other service management processes.

Optimizing the performance of service assets and configurations improves the overall service performance and optimizes the costs and risks caused by poorly managed assets, e.g. service outages, fines, incorrect licence fees and failed audits.

Service asset and configuration management (SACM) provides visibility of accurate representations of a service, release or environment that enables:

- IT staff to understand the configuration and relationships of services and the configuration items that provide them
- Better forecasting and planning of changes

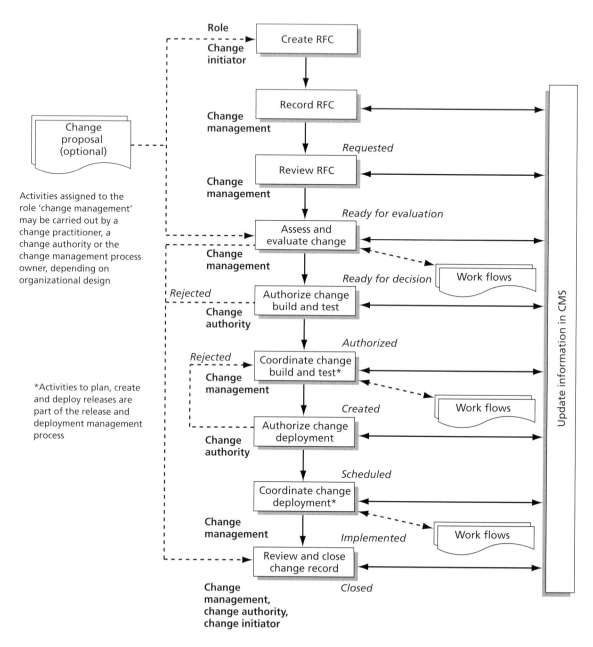

Figure 5.3 Example of a process flow for a normal change

- Successful assessment, planning and delivery of changes and releases
- Resolution of incidents and problems within the service level targets
- Delivery of service levels and warranties
- Better adherence to standards, legal and regulatory obligations (fewer non-conformances)
- More business opportunities as the service provider is able to demonstrate control of assets and services
- Traceability of changes from requirements
- The ability to identify the costs of a service
- Reduced cost and time to discover configuration information when it is needed
- Proper stewardship of fixed assets that are under the control of the service provider.

The purpose of the SACM process is to ensure that the assets required to deliver services are properly controlled, and that accurate and reliable information about those assets is available when and where it is needed. This information includes details of how the assets have been configured and the relationships between assets. The objectives of SACM are to:

- Ensure that assets under the control of the IT organization are identified, controlled and properly cared for throughout their lifecycle.
- Identify, control, record, report, audit and verify services and other configuration items (CIs), including versions, baselines, constituent components, their attributes and relationships.
- Account for, manage and protect the integrity of CIs through the service lifecycle by working with change management to ensure that only authorized components are used and only authorized changes are made.

- Ensure the integrity of CIs and configurations required to control the services by establishing and maintaining an accurate and complete CMS.
- Maintain accurate configuration information on the historical, planned and current state of services and other CIs.
- Support efficient and effective service management processes by providing accurate configuration information to enable people to make decisions at the right time – for example, to authorize changes and releases, or to resolve incidents and problems.

5.3.3.1 Configuration management system

To manage large and complex IT services and infrastructures, SACM requires the use of a supporting system known as the configuration management system (CMS).

It is important to distinguish between service assets, configuration items and configuration records, as these concepts are often confused:

- A **service asset** is any resource or capability that could contribute to the delivery of a service. Examples of service assets include a virtual server, a physical server, a software licence, a piece of information stored in a service management system, or some knowledge in the head of a senior manager.
- A **configuration item** is a service asset that needs to be managed in order to deliver an IT service. All CIs are service assets, but many service assets are not configuration items. Examples of configuration items are a server or a software licence. Every CI must be under the control of change management.
- A **configuration record** is a set of attributes and relationships about a CI. Configuration records

are stored in a configuration management database (CMDB) and managed with a CMS. It is important to note that CIs are not stored in a CMDB; configuration records that describe CIs are stored in the CMDB.

The CMS is also used for a wide range of purposes: for example, asset data held in the CMS may be made available to external fixed asset management systems to perform financial reporting outside service asset and configuration management.

The CMS maintains the relationships between all service components and may also include records for related incidents, problems, known errors, changes and releases. The CMS may also link to corporate data about employees, suppliers, locations and business units, customers and users; alternatively, the CMS may hold copies of this information, depending on the capabilities of the tools in use.

5.3.3.2 Asset management

Fixed assets of an organization are assets which have a financial value, can be used by the organization to help create products or services and have a long-term useful life. For an IT service provider these may include data centres, power distribution and air-handling components, servers, software licences, network components, PCs, data, information etc. Most organizations have a process that manages these assets. This process is usually called fixed asset management or financial asset management. It carries out activities such as:

- Identifying each asset, including unique naming and labels
- Identifying and recording asset owners
- Maintaining an asset register that includes details of all fixed assets

- Understanding the purchase cost, depreciation and net book value of each asset
- Helping to protect the assets from damage, theft etc.
- Carrying out regular audits to ensure the integrity of fixed assets.

Many configuration items that are managed by the service provider are fixed assets of the organization (or of its customer), and the service provider is responsible for protecting these assets in line with overall organizational policies. The service provider may carry out some or all of the following activities, depending on organizational policy and what has been agreed:

- Tracking and reporting CI lifecycle changes, for example when a CI has been received from a supplier or when it has been decommissioned. The service provider should also use this tracking as an opportunity to review maintenance contracts, to ensure that these are aligned with the assets that are in use.
- Providing unique names for assets and applying suitable labels to enable identification and audit.
- Protecting assets to ensure their integrity. For example by providing physical and logical security controls.
- Carrying out regular audits of the fixed assets under their control.

5.3.4 Release and deployment management

Effective release and deployment management enables the service provider to add value to the business by:

- Delivering change, faster and at optimum cost and minimized risk

■ Assuring that customers and users can use the new or changed service in a way that supports the business goals

■ Improving consistency in the implementation approach across the business change, service teams, suppliers and customers

■ Contributing to meeting auditable requirements for traceability through service transition.

Well-planned and implemented release and deployment management will make a significant difference to an organization's service costs. A poorly designed release or deployment will, at best, force IT personnel to spend significant amounts of time troubleshooting problems and managing complexity. At worst, it can cripple the environment and degrade live services.

The purpose of the release and deployment management process is to plan, schedule and control the build, test and deployment of releases, and to deliver new functionality required by the business while protecting the integrity of existing services.

The objectives of release and deployment management are to:

■ Define and agree release and deployment management plans with customers and stakeholders

■ Create and test release packages that consist of related configuration items that are compatible with each other

■ Ensure that the integrity of a release package and its constituent components is maintained throughout the transition activities, and that all release packages are stored in a definitive media library (DML) and recorded accurately in the CMS

■ Deploy release packages from the definative media library (DML) to the live environment following an agreed plan and schedule

■ Ensure that all release packages can be tracked, installed, tested, verified and/or uninstalled or backed out if appropriate

■ Ensure that organization and stakeholder change is managed during release and deployment activities

■ Ensure that a new or changed service and its enabling systems, technology and organization are capable of delivering the agreed utility and warranty

■ Record and manage deviations, risks and issues related to the new or changed service and take necessary corrective action

■ Ensure that there is knowledge transfer to enable the customers and users to optimize their use of the service to support their business activities

■ Ensure that skills and knowledge are transferred to service operation functions to enable them to effectively and efficiently deliver, support and maintain the service according to required warranties and service levels.

Figure 5.4 provides an example of how the architectural elements of a service may be changed from the current baseline to the new baseline with releases at each level. The architecture will be different in some organizations but is provided in this section to give a context for release activities. The release teams need to understand the relevant architecture in order to be able to plan, package, build and test a release to support the new or changed service. This helps to prioritize the release activities and manage dependencies: e.g. the technology infrastructure needs to be ready – with

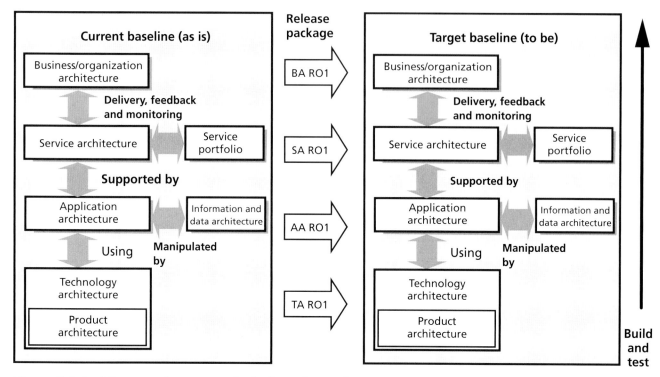

Figure 5.4 Architecture elements to be built and tested

service operation functions prepared to support it with new or changed procedures – before an application is installed.

The general aim is to decide the most appropriate release-unit level for each service asset or component. An organization may, for example, decide that the release unit for business-critical applications is the complete application in order to ensure that testing is comprehensive. The same organization may decide that a more appropriate release unit for a website is at the page level.

A 'release package' is a set of configuration items that will be built, tested and deployed together as a single release. Each release will take the documented release units into account when designing the contents of the release package. It may sometimes be necessary to create a release package that contains only part of one or more release units, but this would only happen in exceptional circumstances.

5.3.5 Service validation and testing

Service failures can harm the service provider's business and the customer's assets and result in outcomes such as loss of reputation, loss of money, loss of time, injury and death. Key values to the business and customers from service testing and validation are, firstly, confidence that a new or changed service will deliver the value and outcomes required of it and, secondly, an understanding of the risks.

Successful testing depends on all parties understanding that it cannot give, indeed should not give, any guarantees but provides a measured degree of confidence. The required degree of confidence varies depending on the customer's business requirements and pressures of an organization.

An IT service is, on most occasions, built from a number of technology resources or management assets. In the build phase, these different blocks, often from different suppliers, are installed and configured together to create the solution as designed. Standardization facilitates the integration of the different building blocks to provide a working solution and service.

Automating the installation of systems and application software onto servers and workstations reduces dependency on people and streamlines the procedures. Depending on the release and deployment plans, the installation may be performed in advance (for example, if equipment is being replaced) or it may have to take place in the live environment.

The physical infrastructure elements, together with the environment in which they will operate, need to be tested appropriately. This may include testing the replication of the infrastructure solution from one environment to another. This gives a better guarantee that the deployment to the live environment will be successful.

Test environments must be actively maintained and protected using service management best practices. For any significant change to a service, the following question should be asked (as it is for the continued relevance of continuity and capacity plans): 'If this change goes ahead, will there need to be a consequential change to the test data?'

During the build and test activities, operations and support teams need to be kept fully informed and involved as the solution is built to facilitate a structured transfer from the project to the operations team.

The purpose of the service validation and testing process is to ensure that a new or changed IT service matches its design specification and will meet the needs of the business.

The objectives of service validation and testing are to:

- Provide confidence that a release will create a new or changed service that delivers the expected outcomes and value for the customers within the projected costs, capacity and constraints
- Quality assure a release, its constituent service components, the resultant service and service capability delivered by a release
- Validate that a service is 'fit for purpose' – it will deliver the required utility
- Provide assurance that a service is 'fit for use' – it will deliver the agreed warranty
- Confirm that the customer and stakeholder requirements for the new or changed service are correctly defined and remedy any errors or variances early in the service lifecycle as this is considerably cheaper than fixing errors in the live environment
- Plan and implement a structured validation and testing process that provides objective evidence that the new or changed service will support the customer's business and stakeholder requirements, including the agreed service levels
- Identify, assess and address issues, errors and risks throughout service transition.

5.3.6 Change evaluation

Change evaluation is, by its very nature, concerned with value. Specifically, effective change evaluation will establish the use made of resources in terms of delivered benefit, and this information will allow a more accurate focus on value in future service development and change management. There is a great deal of intelligence that continual service improvement can take from change evaluation to inform future improvements to the process of change and the predictions and measurement of service change performance.

The purpose of the change evaluation process is to provide a consistent and standardized means of determining the performance of a service change in the context of likely impacts on business outcomes, and on existing and proposed services and IT infrastructure. The actual performance of a change is assessed against its predicted performance. Risks and issues related to the change are identified and managed.

The objectives of change evaluation are to:

- Set stakeholder expectations correctly and provide effective and accurate information to change management to make sure that changes which adversely affect service capability and introduce risk are not transitioned unchecked
- Evaluate the intended effects of a service change and as much of the unintended effects as is reasonably practical given capacity, resource and organizational constraints
- Provide good-quality outputs so that change management can expedite an effective decision about whether or not a service change is to be authorized.

Figure 5.5 shows the change evaluation process with key inputs and outputs.

5.3.7 Knowledge management

Knowledge management adds value to all stages of the service lifecycle by providing secure and controlled access to the knowledge, information and data that is needed to manage and deliver services.

Knowledge management is especially significant within service transition since relevant and appropriate knowledge is one of the key service elements being transitioned. Examples where successful transition rests on appropriate knowledge management include:

- User, service desk, support staff and supplier understanding of the new or changed service, including knowledge of errors signed off before deployment, to facilitate the roles within that service
- Awareness of the use of the service, and the discontinuation of previous versions
- Establishment of the acceptable risk and confidence levels associated with the transition, e.g. measuring, understanding and acting correctly on results of testing and other assurance results.

Effective knowledge management is a powerful asset for people in all roles across all stages of the service lifecycle. It is an excellent method for individuals and teams to share data, information and knowledge about all facets of an IT service. The creation of a single system for knowledge management is recommended.

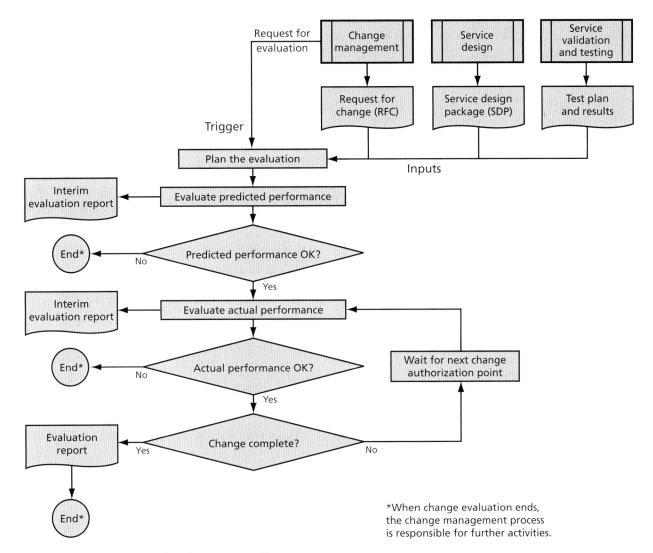

Figure 5.5 Change evaluation process flow

Specific application to the service transition domain can be illustrated through considering the following examples:

- Blurring of the concept of intellectual property and information when engaged in sourcing and partnering, therefore new approaches to controlling 'knowledge' must be addressed and managed during service transition

- Knowledge transfer often being a crucial factor in facilitating effective transition of new or changed services and essential to operational readiness
- Training of users, support staff, suppliers and other stakeholders in new or changed services
- Recording of errors, faults, workarounds etc. detected and documented during the service transition stage of the service lifecycle
- Capturing of implementation and testing information
- Re-using previously developed and quality-assured testing, training and documentation
- Compliance with legislative requirements, e.g. Sarbanes-Oxley, and conformance to standards such as ISO 9000 and ISO/IEC 20000
- Assisting decisions on whether to accept or proceed with items and services by delivering all available relevant information (and omitting unnecessary and confusing information) to key decision makers.

The objectives of knowledge management are to:

- Improve the quality of management decision-making by ensuring that reliable and secure knowledge, information and data is available throughout the service lifecycle
- Enable the service provider to be more efficient and improve quality of service, increase satisfaction and reduce the cost of service by reducing the need to rediscover knowledge
- Ensure that staff have a clear and common understanding of the value that their services provide to customers and the ways in which benefits are realized from the use of those services
- Maintain a service knowledge management system (SKMS) that provides controlled access

to knowledge, information and data that is appropriate for each audience
- Gather, analyse, store, share, use and maintain knowledge, information and data throughout the service provider organization.

5.3.7.1 Data-to-Information-to-Knowledge-to-Wisdom structure

Knowledge management is typically displayed within the Data-to-Information-to-Knowledge-to-Wisdom (DIKW) structure, as shown in Figure 5.6. The use of these terms is set out below.

Data is a set of discrete facts. Most organizations capture significant amounts of data in highly structured databases such as service management and service asset and configuration management tools/systems and databases.

The key knowledge management activities around data are the ability to:

- Capture accurate data
- Analyse, synthesize and then transform the data into information
- Identify relevant data and concentrate resources on its capture
- Maintain integrity of the data
- Archive and purge data to ensure optimal balance between availability of data and use of resources.

An example of data is the date and time at which an incident was logged.

Information comes from providing context to data. Information is typically stored in semi-structured content such as documents, email and multimedia.

The key knowledge management activity around information is managing the content in a way that makes it easy to capture, query, find, re-use and learn from experiences so that mistakes are not repeated and work is not duplicated.

An example of information is the average time to close priority 2 incidents. This information is created by combining data from the start time, end time and priority of many incidents.

Knowledge is composed of the tacit experiences, ideas, insights, values and judgements of individuals. People gain knowledge both from their own and from their peers' expertise, as well as from the analysis of information (and data). Through the synthesis of these elements, new knowledge is created.

Knowledge is dynamic and context-based. Knowledge puts information into an 'ease of use' form, which can facilitate decision-making. In service transition this knowledge is not solely based on the transition in progress, but is gathered from experience of previous transitions, awareness of recent and anticipated changes and other areas, which experienced staff will have been unconsciously collecting for some time.

An example of knowledge is that the average time to close priority 2 incidents has increased by about 10% since a new version of the service was released.

Wisdom makes use of knowledge to create value through correct and well-informed decisions. Wisdom involves having the application and contextual awareness to provide strong common-sense judgement.

5.3.7.2 The service knowledge management system

Specifically within IT service management, knowledge management will be focused within

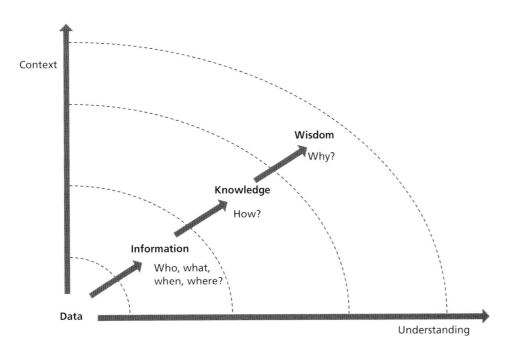

Figure 5.6 The flow from data to wisdom

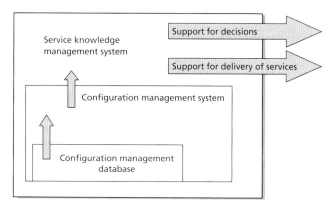

Figure 5.7 Relationship of the CMDB, the CMS and the SKMS

the service knowledge management system (SKMS), which is concerned, as its name implies, with knowledge. Underpinning this knowledge will be a considerable quantity of data, which will also be held in the SKMS. One very important part of the SKMS is the configuration management system (CMS). The CMS describes the attributes and relationships of configuration items, many of which are themselves knowledge, information or data assets stored in the SKMS.

Figure 5.7 is a very simplified illustration of the relationship of the three levels, with configuration data being recorded within the CMDB, and feeding through the CMS into the SKMS. The SKMS supports delivery of the services and informed decision-making.

The SKMS will contain many different types of data, information and knowledge. Examples of items that should be stored in an SKMS include:

- The service portfolio
- The configuration management system
- The definitive media library (DML)
- Service level agreements (SLAs), contracts and operation level agreements (OLAs)

- The information security policy
- The supplier and contract management information system (SCMIS), including suppliers' and partners' requirements, abilities and expectations
- Budgets
- Cost models
- Business plans
- CSI register
- Service improvement plans
- The capacity plan and capacity management information system (CMIS)
- The availability plan and availability management information system (AMIS)
- Service continuity invocation procedure
- Service reports
- A discussion forum where practitioners can ask questions, answer each other's questions, and search for previous questions and answers
- An indexed and searchable repository of project plans from previous projects
- A known error database provided by a vendor which lists common issues in their product and how to resolve them
- Skills register, and typical and anticipated user skill levels
- Diagnostic scripts
- A managed set of web-based training courses
- Weather reports, needed to support business and IT decision-making (for example, an organization may need to know whether rain is likely at the time of an outdoor event)
- Customer/user personal information, for example to support a blind user who needs to have specific support from the service desk.

Many of these knowledge and information assets are configuration items. Changes to CIs must be under the control of the change management process, and details of their attributes and relationships will be documented in the CMS.

5.4 SERVICE TRANSITION INPUTS AND OUTPUTS

The main input to service transition is a service design package, which includes all of the information needed to manage the entire lifecycle of a new or changed service. The main output is the deployment into live use of a new or changed service, with all the supporting knowledge and information, tools and processes required to support the service. Table 5.1 shows the major service transition inputs and outputs, by lifecycle stage. Appendix A provides a summary of the major inputs and outputs between each stage of the service lifecycle.

Table 5.1 Service transition inputs and outputs by lifecycle stage

Lifecycle stage	Service transition inputs (from the lifecycle stages in the first column)	Service transition outputs (to the lifecycle stages in the first column)
Service strategy	Vision and mission	Transitioned services
	Service portfolio	Information and feedback for business cases and service portfolio
	Policies	Response to change proposals
	Strategies and strategic plans	Service portfolio updates
	Priorities	Change schedule
	Change proposals, including utility and warranty requirements and expected timescales	Feedback on strategies and policies
	Financial information and budgets	Financial information for input to budgets
	Input to change evaluation and change advisory board (CAB) meetings	Financial reports
		Knowledge and information in the SKMS

Table continues

Table 5.1 – *continued*

Lifecycle stage	Service transition inputs (from the lifecycle stages in the first column)	Service transition outputs (to the lifecycle stages in the first column)
Service design	Service catalogue	Service catalogue updates
	Service design packages, including:	Feedback on all aspects of service design and service design packages
	■ Details of utility and warranty	Input and feedback on transition plans
	■ Acceptance criteria	Response to RFCs
	■ Service models	Knowledge and information in the SKMS (including the CMS)
	■ Designs and interface specifications	
	■ Transition plans	Design errors identified in transition for re-design
	■ Operational plans and procedures	Evaluation reports
	RFCs to transition or deploy new or changed services	
	Input to change evaluation and CAB meetings	
	Designs for service transition processes and procedures	
	Service level agreements, operational level agreements and underpinning contracts	
Service operation	RFCs to resolve operational issues	New or changed services
	Feedback on quality of transition activities	Known errors
	Input to operational testing	Standard changes for use in request fulfilment
	Actual performance information	Knowledge and information in the SKMS (including the CMS)
	Input to change evaluation and CAB meetings	
		Change schedule
Continual service improvement	Results of customer and user satisfaction surveys	Test reports
	Input to testing requirements	Change evaluation reports
	Data required for metrics, KPIs and CSFs	Knowledge and information in the SKMS
	Input to change evaluation and CAB meetings	Achievements against metrics, KPIs and CSFs
	Service reports	Improvement opportunities logged in the continual service improvement register
	RFCs for implementing improvements	

Service operation

6 Service operation

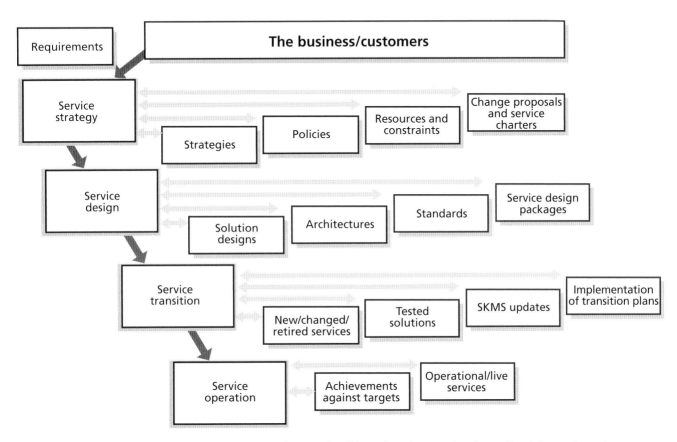

Figure 6.1 Service operation is the stage in the service lifecycle where value is realized from the other stages

So far, we have learned some of the key concepts of ITIL service management – service strategy, service design and service transition. Each of these has demonstrated how it contributes to service quality, but it is in service operation that the business customer sees the quality of the strategy, the design and the transition come to life in everyday use of the services (see Figure 6.1).

Service operation is the phase in the ITIL service management lifecycle that is responsible for business-as-usual activities. It can be viewed as the 'factory' of IT. This implies a closer focus on the day-to-day activities and infrastructure that are used to deliver services. The overriding purpose of service operation is to deliver and support services. Management of the infrastructure and the operational activities must always support this purpose.

6.1 SERVICE OPERATION OVERVIEW

6.1.1 Purpose and objectives of service operation

The purpose of the service operation stage of the service lifecycle is to coordinate and carry out the activities and processes required to deliver and manage services at agreed levels to business users and customers. Service operation is also responsible for the ongoing management of the technology that is used to deliver and support services.

Service operation is a critical stage of the service lifecycle. Well-planned and well-implemented processes will be to no avail if the day-to-day operation of those processes is not properly conducted, controlled and managed. Nor will service improvements be possible if day-to-day activities to monitor performance, assess metrics and gather operational data are not systematically conducted during service operation.

Staff involved in the service operation stage of the service lifecycle should have processes and support tools in place that allow them to have an overall view of service operation and delivery (rather than just the separate components, such as hardware, software applications and networks, that make up the end-to-end service from a business perspective). These processes and tools should also detect any threats or failures to service quality.

As services may be provided, in whole or in part, by one or more partner/supplier organizations, the service operation view of the end-to-end service should be extended to encompass external aspects of service provision. When necessary, shared or

interfacing processes and tools should be deployed to manage cross-organizational workflows.

The objectives of service operation are to:

■ Maintain business satisfaction and confidence in IT through effective and efficient delivery and support of agreed IT services
■ Minimize the impact of service outages on day-to-day business activities
■ Ensure that access to agreed IT services is only provided to those authorized to receive those services.

6.1.2 Scope

ITIL Service Operation describes the processes, functions, organization and tools used to underpin the ongoing activities required to deliver and support services. The guidance includes:

■ **The services themselves** Activities that form part of a service are included in service operation, whether it is performed by the service provider, an external supplier or the user or customer of that service.
■ **Service management processes** The ongoing management and execution of the many service management processes that are performed in service operation. Even though a number of ITIL processes (such as change and capacity management) originate at the service design or service transition stage of the service lifecycle, they are in use continually in service operation. Some processes are not included specifically in service operation, such as strategy management for IT services and the actual design process itself. These processes focus more on longer-term planning and improvement activities, which are outside the direct scope of service operation; however, service operation provides

input and influences these processes regularly as part of the lifecycle of service management.

- **Technology**   All services require some form of technology to deliver them. Managing this technology is not a separate issue, but an integral part of the management of the services themselves. Therefore a large part of *ITIL Service Operation* is concerned with the management of the infrastructure used to deliver services.

- **People**   Regardless of what services, processes and technology are managed, they are all about people. It is people who drive the demand for the organization's services and products and it is people who decide how this will be done. Ultimately, it is people who manage the technology, processes and services. Failure to recognize this will result (and has resulted) in the failure of service management activities.

6.1.3 Usage

ITIL Service Operation provides access to proven best practice based on the skill and knowledge of experienced industry practitioners in adopting a standardized and controlled approach to service management. Although this publication can be used and applied in isolation, it is recommended that it is used in conjunction with the other core ITIL publications. All of the core publications need to be read to fully appreciate and understand the overall lifecycle of services and IT service management.

6.1.4 Value to business

Selecting and adopting the best practice as recommended in *ITIL Service Operation* will assist organizations in delivering significant benefits.

Adopting and implementing standard and consistent approaches for service operation will:

- Reduce unplanned labour and costs for both the business and IT through optimized handling of service outages and identification of their root causes.

- Reduce the duration and frequency of service outages, which will allow the business to take full advantage of the value created by the services it is receiving.

- Provide operational results and data that can be used by other ITIL processes to improve services continually and provide justification for investing in ongoing service improvement activities and supporting technologies.

- Meet the goals and objectives of the organization's security policy by ensuring that IT services will be accessed only by those authorized to use them.

- Provide quick and effective access to standard services which business staff can use to improve their productivity or the quality of business services and products.

- Provide a basis for automated operations, thus increasing efficiencies and allowing expensive human resources to be used for more innovative work, such as designing new or improved functionality or defining new ways in which the business can exploit technology for increased competitive advantage.

6.2   SERVICE OPERATION PRINCIPLES

6.2.1 Realizing value in service operation

Each stage in the service lifecycle provides value to business. For example, service value is modelled in service strategy; the cost of the service is designed, predicted and validated in service design and service transition; and measures for optimization are identified in continual service improvement (CSI). The operation of service is where these plans, designs and optimizations are executed and measured. From a customer viewpoint, service operation is where actual value is seen.

To achieve business value, service operation cannot focus solely on the day-to-day operation and delivery of services.

6.2.2 Operational health

Many organizations find it helpful to compare the monitoring and control of service operation to health monitoring and control.

In this sense, the IT infrastructure is like an organism with vital life signs that can be monitored to check whether it is functioning normally. This means that it is not necessary to monitor continuously every component of every IT system to ensure that it is functioning.

Operational health can be determined by isolating a few important 'vital signs' on devices or services that are defined as critical for the successful execution of a vital business function. This could be the bandwidth utilization on a network segment, or memory utilization on a major server. If these signs are within normal ranges, the system is healthy and does not require additional attention. This reduction in the need for extensive monitoring will result in cost reduction and operational teams and departments that are focused on the appropriate areas for service success.

However, as with organisms, it is important to check systems more thoroughly from time to time, to look for problems that do not immediately affect vital signs. For example a disk may be

functioning perfectly, but it could be nearing its mean time between failures (MTBF) threshold. In this case the system should be taken out of service and given a thorough examination or 'health check'. At the same time, it should be stressed that the end result should be the healthy functioning of the service as a whole. This means that health checks on components should be balanced against checks of the 'end-to-end' service. The definition of what needs to be monitored and what is healthy versus unhealthy is defined during service design, especially availability management and SLM.

Operational health is dependent on the ability to prevent incidents and problems by investing in reliable and maintainable infrastructure. This is achieved through good availability design and proactive problem management. At the same time, operational health is also dependent on the ability to identify faults and localize them effectively so that they have minimal impact on the service. This requires strong (preferably automated) incident and problem management.

6.2.3 Service operation and project management

Because service operation is generally viewed as 'business as usual' and often focused on executing defined procedures in a standard way, there is a tendency not to use project management processes when they would in fact be appropriate. For example, major infrastructure upgrades, or the deployment of new or changed procedures, are significant tasks where formal project management can be used to improve control and manage costs/ resources.

Using project management to manage these types of activity has the following benefits:

- The project benefits are clearly stated and agreed
- There is more visibility of what is being done and how it is being managed, which makes it easier for other IT groups and the business to quantify the contributions made by operational teams
- This in turn makes it easier to obtain funding for projects that have traditionally been difficult to cost justify
- Greater consistency and improved quality
- Achievement of objectives results in higher credibility for operational groups.

6.2.4 Assessing and managing risk in service operation

There will be a number of occasions where it is imperative that risk assessment to service operation is quickly undertaken and acted upon.

The most obvious area is in assessing the risk of potential changes or known errors (already covered elsewhere) but in addition service operation staff may need to be involved in assessing the risk and impact of:

- Failures, or potential failures – either reported by event management or incident/problem management, or warnings raised by manufacturers, suppliers or contractors
- New projects that will ultimately result in delivery into the live environment
- Environmental risk (encompassing IT service continuity-type risks to the physical environment and locale as well as political, commercial or industrial relations-related risks)
- Suppliers, particularly where new suppliers are involved or where key service components are under the control of third parties

- Security risks – both theoretical or actual arising from security-related incidents or events
- New customers/services to be supported.

6.2.5 Operation staff involvement in other service lifecycle stages

It is extremely important that service operation staff are involved in activities taking place in other service lifecycle stages where appropriate. Resources must be made available for these activities and the time required should be taken into account, as appropriate.

6.2.6 Communication

Good communication is needed with other IT teams and departments, with users and internal customers, and between the service operation teams and departments themselves. Issues can often be prevented or mitigated with appropriate communication.

An important principle is that all communication must have an intended purpose or a resultant action. Information should not be communicated unless there is a clear audience. In addition, that audience should have been actively involved in determining the need for that communication and what they will do with the information. Further, there should be review of ongoing communications on a periodic basis to validate that they are still required by the audience.

6.2.7 Monitoring and control

The measurement and control of services is based on a continual cycle of monitoring, reporting and subsequent action. This cycle is discussed in detail in this section because it is fundamental to the delivery, support and improvement of services.

It is also important to note that, although this cycle takes place during service operation, it provides a basis for setting strategy, designing and testing services and achieving meaningful improvement. It is also the basis for SLM measurement. Therefore, although monitoring is performed by service operation functions, it should not be seen as a purely operational matter. All stages of the service lifecycle should ensure that measures and controls are clearly defined, executed and acted upon.

6.2.7.1 Monitor control loops

The most common model for defining control is the monitor control loop. Although it is a simple model, it has many complex applications within ITSM. This section will define the basic concepts of the monitor control loop model and subsequent sections will show how important these concepts are for the service lifecycle.

Figure 6.2 outlines the basic principles of control. A single activity and its output are measured using a predefined norm, or standard, to determine whether it is within an acceptable range of performance or quality. If not, action is taken to rectify the situation or to restore normal performance.

Typically there are two types of monitor control loops:

■ Open loop systems are designed to perform a specific activity regardless of environmental conditions. For example, a backup can be initiated at a given time and frequency – and will run regardless of other conditions.
■ Closed loop systems monitor an environment and respond to changes in that environment. For example, in network load balancing a monitor will evaluate the traffic on a circuit. If network traffic exceeds a certain range, the control system will begin to route traffic across a backup circuit. The monitor will continue to provide feedback to the control system, which will continue to regulate the flow of network traffic between the two circuits.

To help clarify the difference, solving capacity management through over-provisioning is open loop; a load-balancer that detects congestion/failure and redirects capacity is closed loop.

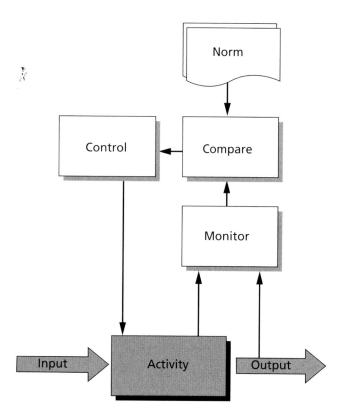

Figure 6.2 The monitor control loop

6.3   SERVICE OPERATION PROCESSES

6.3.1 Event management

The purpose of event management is to manage events throughout their lifecycle. This lifecycle of activities to detect events, make sense of them and determine the appropriate control action is coordinated by the event management process.

Event management is therefore the basis for operational monitoring and control. If events are programmed to communicate operational information as well as warnings and exceptions, they can be used as a basis for automating many routine operations management activities, for example executing scripts on remote devices, or submitting jobs for processing, or even dynamically balancing the demand for a service across multiple devices to enhance performance.

Event management's value to the business is generally indirect; however, it is possible to determine the basis for its value as follows:

- Event management provides mechanisms for early detection of incidents.
- Event management makes it possible for some types of automated activity to be monitored by exception – thus removing the need for expensive and resource-intensive real-time monitoring, while reducing downtime.
- When integrated into other service management processes (such as, for example, availability or capacity management), event management can signal status changes or exceptions that allow the appropriate person or team to perform early response, thus improving the performance of the process.
- Event management provides a basis for automated operations, thus increasing

efficiencies and allowing expensive human resources to be used for more innovative work, such as designing new or improved functionality or defining new ways in which the business can exploit technology for increased competitive advantage.

- Event management can have a direct bearing on service delivery and customer satisfaction.

The objectives of the event management process are to:

- Detect all changes of state that have significance for the management of a configuration item (CI) or IT service
- Determine the appropriate control action for events and ensure these are communicated to the appropriate functions
- Provide the trigger, or entry point, for the execution of many service operation processes and operations management activities
- Provide the means to compare actual operating performance and behaviour against design standards and SLAs
- Provide a basis for service assurance and reporting, and service improvement.

Effective service operation is dependent on knowing the status of the infrastructure and detecting any deviation from normal or expected operation. This is provided by good monitoring and control systems, which are based on two types of tools:

- Active monitoring tools that poll key CIs to determine their status and availability. Any exceptions will generate an alert that needs to be communicated to the appropriate tool or team for action.

■ Passive monitoring tools that detect and correlate operational alerts or communications generated by CIs.

Event management can be applied to any aspect of service management that needs to be controlled and which can be automated. This includes:

■ Configuration items
■ Environmental conditions (e.g. fire and smoke detection)
■ Software licence monitoring for usage to ensure optimum/legal licence utilization and allocation
■ Security (e.g. intrusion detection)
■ Normal activity (e.g. tracking the use of an application or the performance of a server).

Figure 6.3 is a high-level and generic representation of event management.

6.3.2 Incident management

Incident management includes any event which disrupts, or which could disrupt, a service. This includes events that are communicated directly by users, either through the service desk or through an interface from event management to incident management tools.

Incidents can also be reported and/or logged by technical staff (if, for example, they notice something untoward with a hardware or network component they may report or log an incident and refer it to the service desk). This does not mean, however, that all events are incidents. Many classes of events are not related to disruptions at all, but are indicators of normal operation or are simply informational.

The purpose of incident management is to restore normal service operation as quickly as possible

and minimize the adverse impact on business operations, thus ensuring that agreed levels of service quality are maintained. 'Normal service operation' is defined as an operational state where services and CIs are performing within their agreed service and operational levels.

Incident management is highly visible to the business, and it is therefore easier to demonstrate its value than most areas in service operation. For this reason, incident management is often one of the first processes to be implemented in service management projects. The added benefit of doing this is that incident management can be used to highlight other areas that need attention – thereby providing a justification for expenditure on implementing other processes.

The value of incident management includes:

■ The ability to reduce unplanned labour and costs for both the business and IT support staff caused by incidents.
■ The ability to detect and resolve incidents, which results in lower downtime to the business, which in turn means higher availability of the service. This means that the business is able to exploit the functionality of the service as designed.
■ The ability to align IT activity to real-time business priorities. This is because incident management includes the capability to identify business priorities and dynamically allocate resources as necessary.
■ The ability to identify potential improvements to services. This happens as a result of understanding what constitutes an incident and also from being in contact with the activities of business operational staff.

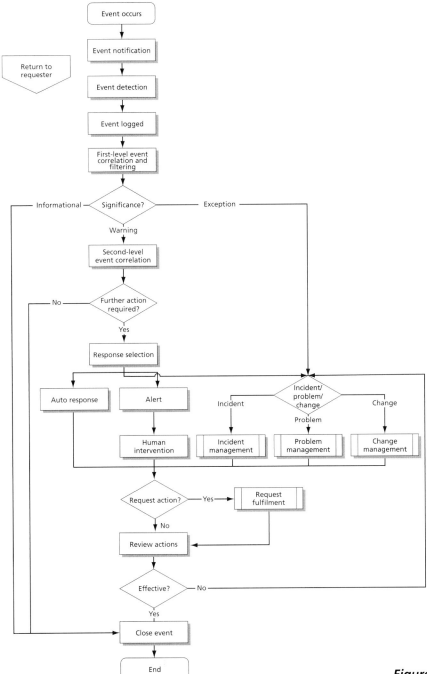

Figure 6.3 The event management process

■ The service desk can, during its handling of incidents, identify additional service or training requirements found in IT or the business.

6.3.2.1 Incident models

Many incidents are not new – they involve dealing with something that has happened before and may well happen again. For this reason, many organizations will find it helpful to predefine 'standard' incident models and apply them to appropriate incidents when they occur.

An incident model is a way of predefining the steps that should be taken to handle a process (in this case a process for dealing with a particular type of incident) in an agreed way. Support tools can then be used to manage the required process. This will ensure that 'standard' incidents are handled in a predefined path and within predefined timescales.

The incident model should include:

■ The steps that should be taken to handle the incident
■ The chronological order these steps should be taken in, with any dependencies or co-processing defined
■ Responsibilities: who should do what
■ Precautions to be taken before resolving the incident such as backing up data, configuration files, or steps to comply with health and safety-related guidelines
■ Timescales and thresholds for completion of the actions
■ Escalation procedures: who should be contacted and when
■ Any necessary evidence-preservation activities (particularly relevant for security- and capacity-related incidents).

The models should be input to the incident-handling support tools in use and the tools should then automate the handling, management and escalation of the process. Incident models should be stored in the SKMS.

6.3.2.2 Incident management process activities

The process activities to be followed during the management of an incident are shown in Figure 6.4, and include the following steps.

Incident identification

While work cannot begin on dealing with an incident until it is known that an incident has occurred, it is usually unacceptable, from a business perspective, to wait until a user is impacted and contacts the service desk. As far as possible, all key components should be monitored so that failures or potential failures are detected early. This means that the incident management process can be started quickly. Ideally, incidents should be resolved before they have an impact on users!

Incident logging

All incidents must be fully logged and date/time stamped, regardless of whether they are raised through a service desk telephone call, automatically detected via an event alert, or from any other source.

Incident categorization

Part of the initial logging must be to allocate suitable incident categorization coding so that the exact type of incident is recorded. This will be important later when looking at incident types/frequencies to establish trends for use in problem management, supplier management and other ITSM activities.

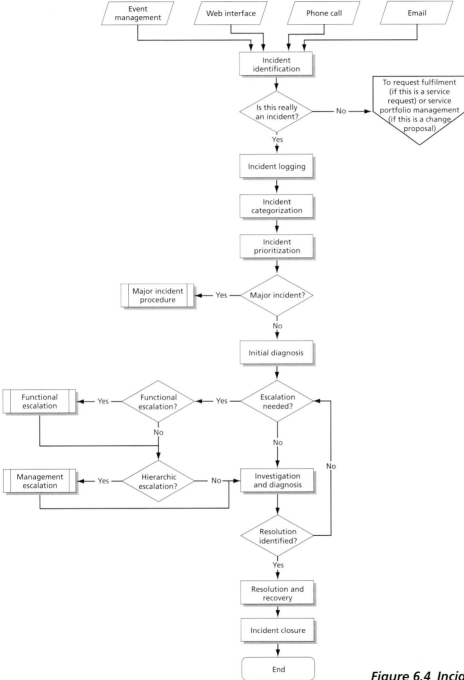

Figure 6.4 Incident management process flow

Incident prioritization

Prioritization can normally be determined by taking into account both the urgency of the incident (how quickly the business needs a resolution) and the level of business impact it is causing. An indication of impact is often (but not always) the number of users being affected. In some cases, and very importantly, the loss of service to a single user can have a major business impact – it all depends upon who is trying to do what – so numbers alone are not enough to evaluate overall priority.

Initial diagnosis

If the incident has been routed via the service desk, the service desk analyst must carry out initial diagnosis, typically while the user is still on the telephone – if the call is raised in this way – to try to discover the full symptoms of the incident and to determine exactly what has gone wrong and how to correct it. It is at this stage that diagnostic scripts and known error information can be most valuable in allowing earlier and accurate diagnosis.

Incident escalation

Incident escalation can take two forms:

- **Functional escalation** As soon as it becomes clear that the service desk is unable to resolve the incident itself (or when target times for first-point resolution have been exceeded – whichever comes first), the incident must be immediately escalated for further support.
- **Hierarchic escalation** If incidents are of a serious nature (for example, high-priority incidents), the appropriate IT managers must be notified, for informational purposes at least. Hierarchic escalation is also used if the 'investigation and diagnosis' and 'resolution and recovery' steps are taking too long or

proving too difficult. Hierarchic escalation should continue up the management chain so that senior managers are aware and can be prepared and take any necessary action, such as allocating additional resources or involving suppliers/maintainers. Hierarchic escalation is also used when there is contention about who the incident is allocated to.

Investigation and diagnosis

This investigation is likely to include such actions as:

- Establishing exactly what has gone wrong or is being sought by the user
- Understanding the chronological order of events
- Confirming the full impact of the incident, including the number and range of users affected
- Identifying any events that could have triggered the incident (e.g. a recent change, some user action?)
- Detailed knowledge searches looking for previous occurrences by searching incident/problem records and/or known error databases (KEDBs) or manufacturers'/suppliers' error logs or knowledge databases. These matches may not have been obvious during initial diagnosis.

Resolution and recovery

When a potential resolution has been identified, this should be applied and tested. The specific actions to be undertaken and the people who will be involved in taking the recovery actions may vary, depending upon the nature of the fault, but could involve:

- Asking the user to undertake directed activities on their own desktop or remote equipment

- The service desk implementing the resolution either centrally (say, rebooting a server) or remotely using software to take control of the user's desktop to diagnose and implement a resolution
- Specialist support groups being asked to implement specific recovery actions (e.g. network support reconfiguring a router)
- A third-party supplier or maintainer being asked to resolve the fault.

Incident closure

The service desk should check that the incident is fully resolved and that the users are satisfied and willing to agree the incident can be closed. The service desk should also check the following:

- **Closure categorization**   Check and confirm that the initial incident categorization was correct or, where the categorization subsequently turned out to be incorrect, update the record so that a correct closure categorization is recorded for the incident – seeking advice or guidance from the resolving group(s) as necessary.
- **User satisfaction survey**   Carry out a user satisfaction call-back or email survey for the agreed percentage of incidents.
- **Incident documentation**   Chase any outstanding details and ensure that the incident record is fully documented so that a full historic record at a sufficient level of detail is complete.
- **Ongoing or recurring problem?**   Determine (in conjunction with resolver groups) whether the incident was resolved without the root cause being identified. In this situation, it is likely that the incident could recur and require further preventive action to avoid this. In all such cases, determine if a problem record related

to the incident has already been raised. If not, raise a new problem record in conjunction with the problem management process so that preventive action is initiated.
- **Formal closure**   Formally close the incident record.

6.3.3 Request fulfilment

Request fulfilment is the process responsible for managing the lifecycle of all service requests from the users.

The term 'service request' is used as a generic description for many different types of demands that are placed upon the IT organization by the users. Many of these are typically requests for small changes that are low risk, frequently performed, low cost etc. (e.g. a request to change a password, a request to install an additional software application onto a particular workstation, a request to relocate some items of desktop equipment) or may be just a request for information.

Their scale and frequent, low-risk nature means that they are better handled by a separate process, rather than being allowed to congest and obstruct the normal incident and change management processes. Effective request fulfilment has a very important role in maintaining end user satisfaction with the services they are receiving and can directly impact how well IT is perceived throughout the business.

The value of the request fulfilment process includes:

- The ability to provide quick and effective access to standard services that business staff can use to improve their productivity or the quality of business services and products.

- The ability to effectively reduce the bureaucracy involved in requesting and receiving access to existing or new services, thus also reducing the cost of providing these services.
- The ability to increase the level of control over requested services through a centralized fulfilment function. This in turn can help reduce costs through centralized negotiation with suppliers, and can also help to reduce the cost of support.

The objectives of the request fulfilment process are to:

- Maintain user and customer satisfaction through efficient and professional handling of all service requests
- Provide a channel for users to request and receive standard services for which a predefined authorization and qualification process exists
- Provide information to users and customers about the availability of services and the procedure for obtaining them
- Source and deliver the components of requested standard services (e.g. licences and software media)
- Assist with general information, complaints or comments.

The process needed to fulfil a request will vary depending upon exactly what is being requested, but can usually be broken down into a set of activities that have to be performed. For each request, these activities should be documented into a request model and stored in the SKMS.

Some organizations will be comfortable letting the service requests be handled through their incident management process (and tools) – with service requests being handled as a particular type of 'incident' (using a high-level categorization system to identify those 'incidents' that are in fact service requests). Note, however, that there is a significant difference here – an incident is usually an unplanned event, whereas a service request is usually something that can and should be planned!

Therefore, in an organization where large numbers of service requests have to be handled, and where the actions to be taken to fulfil those requests are very varied or specialized, it may be appropriate to handle service requests as a completely separate work stream – and to record and manage them as a separate record type. This is essential if reporting is desired that more accurately separates incidents from requests.

Request models

Some service requests will occur frequently and will require handling consistently in order to meet agreed service levels. To assist this, many organizations will wish to create predefined request models (which typically include one or more standard changes in order to complete fulfilment activities). This is similar in concept to the idea of incident models already described in incident management, but applied to service requests.

Most requests will be triggered through either a user calling the service desk or a user completing some form of self-help web-based input screen to make their request. The latter will often involve selection from a portfolio of available request types.

6.3.4 Problem management

The purpose of problem management is to manage the lifecycle of all problems from first identification through further investigation, documentation and eventual removal. Problem management seeks to minimize the adverse impact of incidents and problems on the business that are caused by underlying errors within the IT infrastructure, and to proactively prevent recurrence of incidents related to these errors. In order to achieve this, problem management seeks to get to the root cause of incidents, document and communicate known errors, and initiate actions to improve or correct the situation.

Problem management includes the activities required to diagnose the root cause of incidents and to determine the resolution to those problems. It is also responsible for ensuring that the resolution is implemented through the appropriate control procedures, especially change management and release and deployment management.

Problem management will also maintain information about problems and the appropriate workarounds and resolutions, so that the organization is able to reduce the number and impact of incidents over time. In this respect, problem management has a strong interface with knowledge management, and tools such as the KEDB will be used for both.

Although incident and problem management are separate processes, they are closely related and will typically use the same tools, and may use similar categorization, impact and priority coding systems. This will ensure effective communication when dealing with related incidents and problems.

The value of problem management includes:

■ Higher availability of IT services by reducing the number and duration of incidents that those services may incur. Problem management works together with incident management and change management to ensure that IT service availability and quality are increased.

When incidents are resolved, information about the resolution is recorded. Over time, this information is used to speed up the resolution time and identify permanent solutions, reducing the number and resolution time of incidents.

■ Higher productivity of IT staff by reducing unplanned labour caused by incidents and creating the ability to resolve incidents more quickly through recorded known errors and workarounds.

■ Reduced expenditure on workarounds or fixes that do not work.

■ Reduction in cost of effort in fire-fighting or resolving repeat incidents.

6.3.4.1 Reactive and proactive problem management activities

Both reactive and proactive problem management activities seek to raise problems, manage them through the problem management process, find the underlying causes of the incidents they are associated with and prevent future recurrences of those incidents. The difference between reactive and proactive problem management lies in how the problem management process is triggered:

■ With reactive problem management, process activities will typically be triggered in reaction to an incident that has taken place. Reactive problem management complements incident management activities by focusing on the underlying cause of an incident to prevent its recurrence and identifying workarounds when necessary.

■ With proactive problem management, process activities are triggered by activities seeking to improve services. One example might be trend analysis activities to find common underlying causes of historical incidents that took place to prevent their recurrence. Proactive problem management complements CSI activities by helping to identify workarounds and improvement actions that can improve the quality of a service.

6.3.4.2 Problem models

The problem management process flow for handling a recognized problem is shown in Figure 6.5. This is a simplified chart to show the normal process flow, but in reality some of the states may be iterative or variations may have to be made in order to handle particular situations. For example, proactive problem management activities may raise new problem records, which in turn can become input to this process flow.

Problem detection

It is likely that multiple ways of detecting problems will exist in all organizations. These can include triggers for reactive and proactive problem management.

Reactive problem management triggers:

- Suspicion or detection of a cause of one or more incidents by the service desk, resulting in a problem record being raised – the desk may have resolved the incident but has not determined a definitive cause and suspects that it is likely to recur, so will raise a problem record to allow the underlying cause to be resolved. Alternatively, it may be immediately obvious from the outset that an incident, or incidents, has been caused by a major problem, so a problem record will be raised without delay.
- Analysis of an incident by a technical support group which reveals that an underlying problem exists, or is likely to exist.

- Automated detection of an infrastructure or application fault, using event/alert tools automatically to raise an incident which may reveal the need for a problem record.
- A notification from a supplier or contractor that a problem exists that has to be resolved.

Proactive problem management triggers:

- Analysis of incidents that result in the need to raise a problem record so that the underlying fault can be investigated further.
- Trending of historical incident records to identify one or more underlying causes so that removal of these causes can prevent their recurrence. In this case, a problem record is raised once the underlying trend or cause is discovered.
- Activities taken to improve the quality of a service that result in the need to raise a problem record to identify further improvement actions that should be taken.

Problem logging

A cross-reference must be made to the incident(s) which initiated the problem record – and all relevant details must be copied from the incident record(s) to the problem record. It is difficult to be exact, as cases may vary, but typically this will include details such as:

- User details
- Service details
- Equipment details
- Date/time initially logged
- Priority and categorization details
- Incident description
- Incident record numbers or other cross-references
- Details of all diagnostic or attempted recovery actions taken.

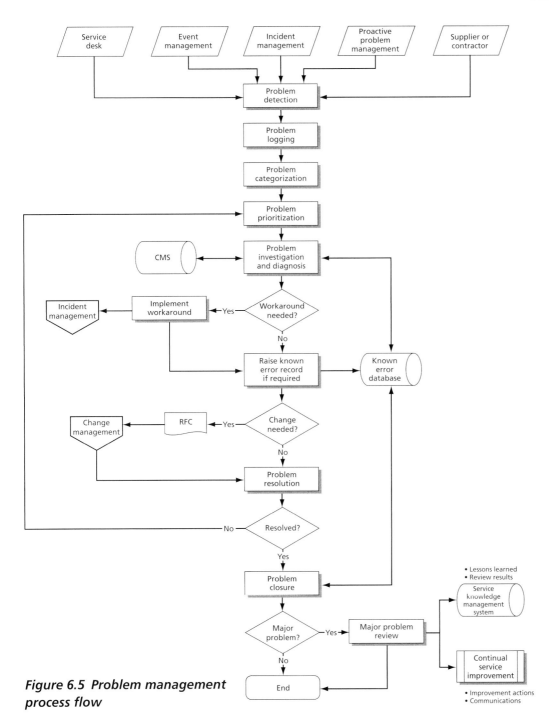

*Figure 6.5 Problem management
process flow*

Problem categorization

Problems should be categorized in the same way as incidents (and it is advisable to use the same coding system) so that the true nature of the problem can be easily traced in the future and meaningful management information can be obtained. This also allows for incidents and problems to be more readily matched.

Problem prioritization

Problems should be prioritized the same way using the same reasons as incidents. The frequency and impact of related incidents must also be taken into account, along with the severity of the problem. Severity in this context refers to how serious the problem is from a service or customer perspective as well as an infrastructure perspective, for example:

■ Can the system be recovered, or does it need to be replaced?

■ How much will it cost?

■ How many people, with what skills, will be needed to fix the problem?

■ How long will it take to fix the problem?

■ How extensive is the problem (e.g. how many CIs are affected)?

Problem investigation and diagnosis

At this stage, an investigation should be conducted to try to diagnose the root cause of the problem – the speed and nature of this investigation will vary depending upon the impact, severity and urgency of the problem – but the appropriate level of resources and expertise should be applied to finding a resolution commensurate with the priority code allocated and the service target in place for that priority level.

Workarounds

In some cases it may be possible to find a workaround for the incidents caused by the problem – a temporary way of overcoming the difficulties. For example, a manual amendment may be made to an input file to allow a program to complete its run successfully and allow a billing process to complete satisfactorily, but it is important that work on a permanent resolution continues where this is justified – in this example the reason for the file becoming corrupted in the first place must be found and corrected to prevent this happening again.

Raising a known error record

As soon as the diagnosis is complete, and particularly where a workaround has been found (even though it may not yet be a permanent resolution), a known error record must be raised and placed in the KEDB so that if further incidents or problems arise, they can be identified and the service restored more quickly. In some cases it may be advantageous to raise a known error record even earlier in the overall process, even though the diagnosis may not be complete or a workaround found. This might be used for information purposes or to identify a root cause or workaround that appears to address the problem but hasn't been fully confirmed. Therefore, it is inadvisable to set a concrete procedural point for exactly when a known error record must be raised. It should be done as soon as it becomes useful to do so!

Problem resolution

Once a root cause has been found and a solution to remove it has been developed, it should be applied to resolve the problem. In reality, safeguards may be needed to ensure that the resolution does not cause further difficulties. If any change in functionality is required, an RFC should be raised and authorized before the resolution can be applied. If the problem is very serious and an urgent fix is needed for business reasons, then an emergency RFC should be raised. The resolution should be applied only when the change has been authorized and scheduled for release. In the meantime, the KEDB should be used to help quickly resolve any further occurrences of the incidents/problems that occur.

Problem closure

When a final resolution has been applied, the problem record should be formally closed – as should any related incident records that are still open. A check should be performed at this time to ensure that the record contains a full historical description of all events – and if not, the record should be updated. The status of any related known error record should also be updated to show that the resolution has been applied.

Major problem review

After every major problem (as determined by the organization's priority system), and while memories are still fresh, a review should be conducted to learn any lessons for the future. Specifically, the review should examine:

■ Those things that were done correctly
■ Those things that were done wrong
■ What could be done better in the future
■ How to prevent recurrence
■ Whether there has been any third-party responsibility and whether follow-up actions are needed.

Such reviews can be used as part of training and awareness activities for support staff – and any lessons learned should be documented

in appropriate procedures, work instructions, diagnostic scripts or known error records. The problem manager facilitates the session and documents any agreed actions.

6.3.5 Access management

Access management is the process of granting authorized users the right to use a service, while preventing access to non-authorized users. It has also been referred to as rights management or identity management in different organizations.

Access management is effectively the execution of the policies in information security management, in that it enables the organization to manage the confidentiality, availability and integrity of the organization's data and intellectual property.

Access management ensures that users are given the right to use a service, but it does not ensure that this access is available at all agreed times – this is provided by availability management.

Access management is a process that is executed by all technical and application management functions and is usually not a separate function. However, there is likely to be a single control point of coordination, usually in IT operations management or on the service desk.

Access management can be initiated by a service request.

The value of access management includes:

■ Ensuring that controlled access to services will allow the organization to maintain effective confidentiality of its information
■ Ensuring that employees have the right level of access to execute their jobs effectively

- Reducing errors made in data entry or in the use of a critical service by an unskilled user (e.g. production control systems)
- Providing capabilities to audit use of services and to trace the abuse of services
- Providing capabilities to revoke access rights when needed on a timely basis – an important security consideration
- Providing and demonstrating compliance with regulatory requirements (e.g. SOX, HIPAA and COBIT).

While each user has an individual identity, and each IT service can be seen as an entity in its own right, it is often helpful to group them together so that they can be managed more easily. Sometimes the terms 'user profile', 'user template' or 'user role' are used to describe this type of grouping.

Most organizations have a standard set of services for all individual users, regardless of their position or job (excluding customers, who do not have any visibility to internal services and processes). These will include services such as messaging, office automation, desktop support, telephony etc. New users are automatically provided with rights to use these services. However, most users also have some specialized role that they perform. For example, in addition to the standard services, the user also performs a marketing management role, which requires that they have access to some specialized marketing and financial modelling tools and data.

Some groups may have unique requirements, such as field or home workers who may have to dial in or use virtual private network connections, with security implications that may have to be more tightly managed.

To make it easier for access management to provide the appropriate rights, it uses a catalogue

of all the roles in the organization and which services support each role. This catalogue of roles should be compiled and maintained by access management in conjunction with human resources and will often be automated in the directory services tools.

In addition to playing different roles, users may also belong to different groups. For example, all contractors are required to log their time sheets in a dedicated time card system, which is not used by employees. Access management will assess all the roles that a user plays as well as the groups that they belong to and ensure that they provide rights to use all associated services.

Role-based access control techniques may also be used by access management to authenticate and authorize users for specific operations. With these techniques, access is assigned to specific roles versus directly to users. Through this approach, users are indirectly authenticated and authorized through the roles they are assigned to.

Note that all data held on users will be subject to data protection legislation (this exists in most geographic locations in some form or other) so should be handled and protected as part of the organization's security procedures.

6.3.5.1 Access management process activities

The process to be followed during the management of an access request is shown in Figure 6.6. The process includes the following steps.

Request access

Access (or restriction) can be requested using one of any number of mechanisms, including:

- A service request generated by the human resource system. This is generally done

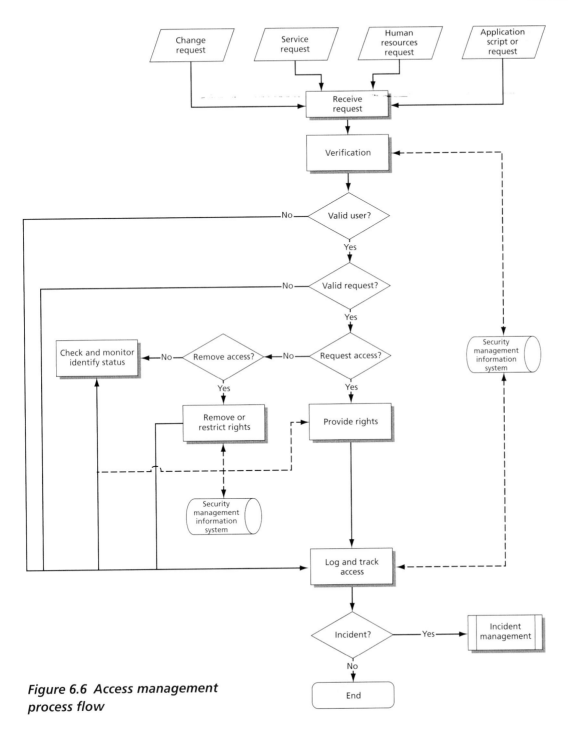

*Figure 6.6 Access management
process flow*

whenever a person is hired, promoted, transferred or when they leave the company

- An RFC
- A service request submitted via the request fulfilment system
- By executing a pre-authorized script or option (e.g. downloading an application from a staging server as and when it is needed).

Rules for requesting access are normally documented as part of the request fulfilment model associated with requests for access and may also be described in the service catalogue.

Verification

Access management needs to verify every request for access to an IT service from two perspectives:

- That the user requesting access is who they say they are
- That they have a legitimate requirement for that service.

Provide rights

As users work in the organization, their roles change and so also do their needs to access services. Examples of changes include:

- **Job changes** In this case the user will possibly need access to different or additional services.
- **Promotions or demotions** The user will probably use the same set of services, but will need access to different levels of functionality or data.
- **Transfers** In this situation, the user may need access to exactly the same set of services, but in a different region with different working practices and different sets of data.

- **Resignation or death** Access needs to be completely removed to prevent the user name being used as a security loophole.
- **Retirement** In many organizations, an employee who retires may still have access to a limited set of services, including benefits systems or systems that allow them to purchase company products at a reduced rate.
- **Disciplinary action** In some cases the organization will require a temporary restriction to prevent the user from accessing some or all of the services that they would normally have access to. There should be a feature in the process and tools to do this, rather than having to delete and reinstate the user's access rights.
- **Dismissals** Where an employee or contractor is dismissed, or where legal action is taken against a customer (for example for defaulting on payment for products purchased on the internet), access should be revoked immediately. In addition, access management, working together with information security management, should take active measures to prevent and detect malicious action against the organization from that user.

Access management should understand and document the typical lifecycle for each type of user and use it to automate the process. Access management tools should provide features that enable a user to be moved from one state to another, or from one group to another, easily and with an audit trail.

Log and track access

Access management should not only respond to requests. It is also responsible for ensuring that the rights it has provided are being properly used.

Remove or restrict rights

Just as access management provides rights to use a service, it is also responsible for revoking those rights. Again, this is not a decision that it makes on its own. Rather, it will execute the decisions and policies made during service strategy and design and also decisions made by managers in the organization.

6.4 SERVICE OPERATION FUNCTIONS

This section describes the main functions on which service operation depends: service desk, technical management, application management and IT operations management. Technical management and application management provide the technical resources and expertise to manage the whole service lifecycle, and practitioner roles within service operation may be performed by members of these functions.

6.4.1 Service desk function

A service desk is a functional unit made up of a dedicated number of staff responsible for dealing with a variety of service activities, usually made via telephone calls, a web interface or automatically reported infrastructure events.

The service desk is a vitally important part of an IT organization and should be the single point of contact for IT users on a day-by-day basis. It not only handles incidents, escalates incidents to problem management staff, manages service requests and answers questions, it may also provide an interface for other activities such as customer change requests, maintenance contracts, software licences, SLM, service asset and configuration management, availability management, financial management for IT services, and IT service continuity management.

The value of an effective service desk should not be underestimated – a good service desk can often compensate for deficiencies elsewhere in the IT organization, but a poor service desk (or the lack of a service desk) can give a poor impression of an otherwise very effective IT organization! It is therefore very important that the correct calibre of staff be used on the service desk and that IT managers do their best to make the desk an attractive place to work to improve staff retention.

The exact nature, type, size and location of a service desk will vary, depending upon the type of business, number of users, geography, complexity of calls, scope of services and many other factors. In alignment with customer and business requirements, the IT organization's senior managers should decide the exact nature of its required service desk (and whether it should be internal or outsourced to a third party) as part of its overall ITSM strategy (see *ITIL Service Strategy*). Subsequent planning must then be done to prepare for and then implement the appropriate service desk function (either when implementing a new function, or more likely these days when making necessary amendments to an existing function – see *ITIL Service Design* and *ITIL Service Transition*).

6.4.1.1 Service desk staffing

The issues involved in, and criteria for, establishing the appropriate staffing model and levels are discussed in more detail in *ITIL Service Operation*, along with typical service desk roles and responsibilities. These include the service desk manager, supervisor and analysts. In some organizations, these roles are complemented by business users ('super users') who provide first-line support.

An organization must ensure that the correct number of staff are available at any given time to match the demand being placed upon the desk by the business. Call rates can be very volatile, and often in the same day the arrival rate may go from very high to very low and back again. An organization planning a new desk should attempt to predict the call arrival rate and profile, and to staff accordingly. Statistical analysis of call arrival rates under current support arrangements must be undertaken and then closely monitored and adjusted as necessary.

6.4.1.2 Service desk performance

Metrics should be established so that performance of the service desk can be evaluated at regular intervals. This is important to assess the health, maturity, efficiency, effectiveness and any opportunities to improve service desk operations.

Metrics for service desk performance must be realistic and carefully chosen. It is common to select those metrics that are easily available and that may seem to be a possible indication of performance; however, this can be misleading. For example, the total number of calls received by the service desk is not in itself an indication of either good or bad performance and may in fact be caused by events completely outside the control of the service desk, for example a particularly busy period for the organization, or the release of a new version of a major corporate system.

6.4.2 Technical management function

Technical management refers to the groups, departments or teams that provide technical

expertise and overall management of the IT infrastructure. It plays a dual role:

- It is the custodian of technical knowledge and expertise related to managing the IT infrastructure. In this role, technical management ensures that the knowledge required to design, test, manage and improve IT services is identified, developed and refined.
- It provides the actual resources to support the service lifecycle. In this role, technical management ensures that resources are effectively trained and deployed to design, build, transition, operate and improve the technology required to deliver and support IT services.

By performing these two roles, technical management is able to ensure that the organization has access to the right type and level of human resources to manage technology and thus to meet business objectives. Defining the requirements for these roles starts in service strategy and is expanded in service design, validated in service transition and refined in CSI.

6.4.2.1 Technical management organization

Technical management is not normally provided by a single department or group. One or more technical support teams or departments will be needed to provide technical management and support for the IT infrastructure. In all but the smallest organizations, where a single combined team or department may suffice, separate teams or departments will be needed for each type of infrastructure being used.

Technical management consists of a number of technological areas. Each of these requires a specific set of skills to manage and operate it.

Some skillsets are related and can be performed by generalists, whereas others are specific to a component, system or platform. The primary criterion of a technical management organizational structure is that of specialization or division of labour. The principle is that people are grouped according to their technical skillsets, and that these skillsets are determined by the technology that needs to be managed.

ITIL Service Operation covers the organizational aspects of technical management in more detail, but this list provides some examples of typical technical management teams or departments:

■ Mainframe team or department – if one or more mainframe types are still being used by the organization

■ Server team or department – often split again by technology types (e.g. Unix server, Wintel server)

■ Storage team or department, responsible for the management of all data storage devices, storage area networks (SANs) and media

■ Network support team or department, looking after the organization's internal WANs/LANs and managing any external network suppliers

■ Virtualization team or department, responsible for designing, implementing, tuning and administering virtualized processing environments

■ Desktop team or department, responsible for all installed desktop equipment

■ Database team or department, responsible for the creation, maintenance and support of the organization's databases

■ Middleware team or department, responsible for the integration, testing and maintenance of all middleware in use in the organization

■ Directory services team or department, responsible for maintaining access and rights to service elements in the infrastructure

■ Internet or web team or department, responsible for managing the availability and security of access to servers and content by external customers, users and partners

■ Messaging team or department, responsible for email services

■ IP-based telephony team or department.

6.4.3 Application management function

Application management is responsible for managing applications throughout their lifecycle. This differs from application development as application management covers the entire ongoing lifecycle of an application, including requirements, design, build, deploy, operate and optimize. Application development is mainly concerned with the one-time activities for requirements, design and build of applications.

6.4.3.1 Application management roles

Application management is to applications what technical management is to the IT infrastructure. Application management activities are performed in all applications, whether purchased or developed in-house. One of the key decisions that they contribute to is the decision of whether to buy an application or build it (this is discussed in detail in *ITIL Service Design*). Once that decision is made, application management will have several roles:

■ It is the custodian of technical knowledge and expertise related to managing applications. In this role, application management, working together with technical management, ensures that the knowledge required to design, test, manage and improve IT services is identified, developed and refined.

■ It provides the actual resources to support the service lifecycle. In this role, application management ensures that resources are effectively trained and deployed to design, build, transition, operate and improve the technology required to deliver and support IT services.

By performing these roles, application management is able to ensure that the organization has access to the right type and level of human resources to manage applications and thus to meet business objectives. This starts in service strategy and is expanded in service design, tested in service transition and refined in CSI. A key objective is to ensure a balance between the skill level and the cost of these resources.

Application management also performs other specific roles:

■ Providing guidance to IT operations about how best to carry out the ongoing operational management of applications. This role is partly carried out during the service design process, but it is also a part of everyday communication with IT operations management as they seek to achieve stability and optimum performance.

■ The integration of the application management lifecycle into the service lifecycle.

6.4.3.2 Application management generic activities

While most application management teams or departments are dedicated to specific applications or sets of applications, there are a number of activities which they have in common. These include:

■ Identifying the knowledge and expertise required to manage and operate applications in the delivery of IT services. This process starts during the service strategy stage, is expanded in detail in service design, transitioned to the live environment in service transition and is executed in service operation. Ongoing assessment and updating of these skills are done during CSI.

■ Initiating training programmes to develop and refine the skills in the appropriate application management resources and maintaining training records for these resources.

■ Insourcing for specific activities where the required skills are not available internally or in the open market, or where it is more cost-efficient to do so.

■ Participating in the design and building of new services. All application management teams or departments will contribute to the design of the technical architecture and performance standards for IT services. They will also be responsible for specifying the operational activities required to manage applications on an ongoing basis.

■ Assistance in assessing risk, identifying critical service and system dependencies and defining and implementing countermeasures.

■ Managing suppliers. Many application management departments or groups are the only ones who know exactly what is required of a supplier and how to measure and manage them. For this reason, many organizations rely on application management to manage contracts with suppliers of specific applications. If this is the case it is important to ensure that these relationships are managed as part of the SLM and supplier management processes.

- Supporting change management with technical application knowledge and expertise to evaluate changes. Many changes may be built by application management teams.
- Defining, managing and maintaining attributes and relationships of application CIs in the CMS.
- Identifying opportunities for improvement and assisting in the evaluation of alternative solutions.
- Assisting financial management for IT services to identify the cost of the ongoing management of applications.

6.4.4 IT operations management function

In business, the term 'operations management' is used to mean the department, group or team of people responsible for performing the organization's day-to-day operational activities – such as running the production line in a manufacturing environment or managing the distribution centres and fleet movements within a logistics organization.

Operations management generally has the following characteristics:

- There is work to ensure that a device, system or process is actually running or working (as opposed to strategy or planning)
- This is where plans are turned into actions
- The focus is on daily or shorter-term activities, although it should be noted that these activities will generally be performed and repeated over a relatively long period (as opposed to one-off project-type activities)
- These activities are executed by specialized technical staff, who often have to undergo technical training to learn how to perform each activity

- There is a focus on building repeatable, consistent actions that – if repeated frequently enough at the right level of quality – will ensure the success of the operation
- This is where the actual value of the organization is delivered and measured
- There is a dependency on investment in equipment or human resources or both
- The value generated must exceed the cost of the investment and all other organizational overheads (such as management and marketing costs) if the business is to succeed.

In a similar way, IT operations management can be defined as the function responsible for the ongoing management and maintenance of an organization's IT infrastructure to ensure delivery of the agreed level of IT services to the business.

IT operations can be defined as the set of activities involved in the day-to-day running of the IT infrastructure for the purpose of delivering IT services at agreed levels to meet stated business objectives.

6.4.4.1 IT operations management role

The role of IT operations management is to execute the ongoing activities and procedures required to manage and maintain the IT infrastructure so as to deliver and support IT services at the agreed levels. These activities are summarized here for completeness.

IT operations control

IT operations control oversees the execution and monitoring of the operational activities and events in the IT infrastructure. This can be done with the help of an operations bridge or network operations centre. In addition to executing routine tasks from all technical areas, IT operations control also performs the following specific tasks:

- Console management/operations bridge, which refers to defining central observation and monitoring capability and then using those consoles to exercise event management, monitoring and control activities
- Job scheduling, or the management of routine batch jobs or scripts
- Backup and restore on behalf of all technical and application management teams and departments and often on behalf of users
- Print and output management for the collation and distribution of all centralized printing or electronic output
- Performance of maintenance activities on behalf of technical or application management teams or departments.

Facilities management

Facilities management refers to the management of the physical IT environment, typically a data centre or computer rooms and recovery sites together with all the power and cooling equipment. Facilities management also includes the coordination of large-scale consolidation projects, e.g. data centre consolidation or server consolidation projects. In some cases the management of a data centre is outsourced, in which case facilities management refers to the management of the outsourcing contract.

6.5 SERVICE OPERATION INPUTS AND OUTPUTS

Service operation does not operate independently, but interacts with all the other service lifecycle stages. Table 6.1 shows the major service operation inputs and outputs, by lifecycle stage. Appendix A provides a summary of the major inputs and outputs between each stage of the service lifecycle.

Table 6.1 Service operation inputs and outputs by lifecycle stage

Lifecycle stage	Service operation inputs (from the lifecycle stages in the first column)	Service operation outputs (to the lifecycle stages in the first column)
Service strategy	Vision and mission	Operating risks
	Service portfolio	Operating cost information for total cost of ownership (TCO) calculations
	Policies	Actual performance data
	Strategies and strategic plans	
	Priorities	
	Financial information and budgets	
	Demand forecasts and strategies	
	Strategic risks	

Table 6.1 – *continued*

Lifecycle stage	Service operation inputs (from the lifecycle stages in the first column)	Service operation outputs (to the lifecycle stages in the first column)
Service design	Service catalogue	Operational requirements
	Service design packages, including:	Actual performance data
	■ Details of utility and warranty	RFCs to resolve operational issues
	■ Operational plans and procedures	Historical incident and problem records
	■ Recovery procedures	
	Knowledge and information in the SKMS	
	Vital business functions	
	Hardware and software maintenance requirements	
	Designs for service operation processes and procedures	
	SLAs, OLAs and underpinning contracts	
	Security policies	
Service transition	New or changed services	RFCs to resolve operational issues
	Known errors	Feedback on quality of transition activities
	Standard changes for use in request fulfilment	Input to operational testing
	Knowledge and information in the SKMS (including the configuration management system)	Actual performance information
		Input to change evaluation and change advisory board meetings
	Change schedule	
Continual service improvement	Results of customer and user satisfaction surveys	Operational performance data and service records
	Service reports and dashboards	Proposed problem resolutions and proactive measures
	Data required for metrics, KPIs and CSFs	Knowledge and information in the SKMS
	RFCs for implementing improvements	Achievements against metrics, KPIs and CSFs
		Improvement opportunities logged in the continual service improvement register

Continual service
improvement

7 Continual service improvement

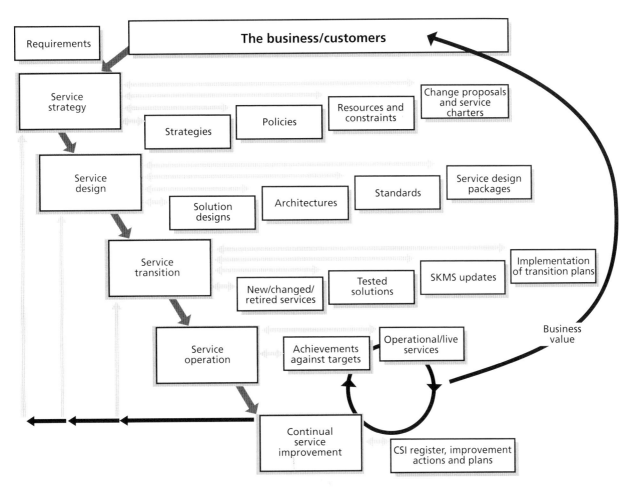

Figure 7.1 Continual service improvement acts in tandem with all the other stages in the service lifecycle

Continual service improvement (CSI) focuses on increasing the efficiency, maximizing the effectiveness and optimizing the cost of IT services and the underlying processes. These objectives are achieved by identifying improvement opportunities throughout the service lifecycle (see Figure 7.1).

7.1 CSI OVERVIEW

7.1.1 Purpose and objectives of CSI

The purpose of the CSI stage of the lifecycle is to align IT services with changing business needs by identifying and implementing improvements to IT services that support business processes. These improvement activities support the lifecycle approach through service strategy, service design, service transition and service operation. CSI is always seeking ways to improve service effectiveness, process effectiveness and cost effectiveness.

In order to identify improvement opportunities, the measurement of current performance is an important factor. Consider the following sayings about measurements and management:

> You cannot manage what you cannot control.
> You cannot control what you cannot measure.
> You cannot measure what you cannot define.

If services and processes are not implemented, managed and supported using clearly defined goals, objectives and relevant measurements that lead to actionable improvements, the business will suffer. Depending upon the criticality of a specific IT service to the business, the organization could lose productive hours, experience higher costs, suffer loss of reputation or, perhaps, even risk business failure. Ultimately it could also lead to loss of customer business. That is why it is critically important to understand what to measure, why it is being measured and what the successful outcome should be.

The objectives of CSI are to:

- Review, analyse, prioritize and make recommendations on improvement opportunities in each lifecycle stage: service strategy, service design, service transition, service operation and CSI itself
- Review and analyse service level achievement
- Identify and implement specific activities to improve IT service quality and improve the efficiency and effectiveness of the enabling processes
- Improve cost effectiveness of delivering IT services without sacrificing customer satisfaction
- Ensure that applicable quality management methods are used to support continual improvement activities
- Ensure that processes have clearly defined objectives and measurements that lead to actionable improvements
- Understand what to measure, why it is being measured and what the successful outcome should be.

7.1.2 Scope

ITIL Continual Service Improvement provides guidance in four main areas:

- The overall health of ITSM as a discipline
- The continual alignment of the service portfolio with the current and future business needs
- The maturity and capability of the organization, management, processes and people utilized by the services
- Continual improvement of all aspects of the IT service and the service assets that support them.

To implement CSI successfully it is important to understand the different activities that need to be applied. The following activities support CSI:

- Reviewing management information and trends to ensure that services are meeting agreed service levels
- Reviewing management information and trends to ensure that the output of the enabling processes are achieving the desired results
- Periodically conducting maturity assessments against the process activities and associated

roles to demonstrate areas of improvement or, conversely, areas of concern

- Periodically conducting internal audits verifying employee and process compliance
- Reviewing existing deliverables for appropriateness
- Periodically proposing recommendations for improvement opportunities
- Periodically conducting customer satisfaction surveys
- Reviewing business trends and changed priorities, and keeping abreast of business projections
- Conducting external and internal service reviews to identify CSI opportunities
- Measuring and identifying the value created by CSI improvements.

These activities do not happen automatically. They must be owned by individuals within the service provider organization who are empowered to make things happen. They must also be planned and scheduled on an ongoing basis. By default, 'improvement' becomes a process within ITSM with defined activities, inputs, outputs, roles and reporting levels. CSI must ensure that ITSM processes are developed and deployed in support of an end-to-end service management approach to business customers. It is essential to develop an ongoing continual improvement strategy for each of the processes as well as for the services that they support.

The deliverables of CSI must be reviewed on an ongoing basis to verify completeness, functionality and feasibility, and to ensure that they remain relevant and do not become stale and unusable. It is also important to ensure that monitoring of quality indicators and metrics will identify areas for process improvement.

Since any improvement initiative will more than likely necessitate changes, specific improvements will need to follow the defined change management process.

7.1.3 Usage

ITIL Continual Service Improvement provides access to proven best practice based on the skill and knowledge of experienced industry practitioners in adopting a standardized and controlled approach to service management. Although this publication can be used and applied in isolation, it is recommended that it is read in conjunction with the other core ITIL publications. All of the core publications need to be read to fully appreciate and understand the overall lifecycle of services and IT service management.

7.1.4 Value to business

Selecting and adopting the best practice as recommended in this publication will assist organizations in delivering significant benefits. It will help readers to set up CSI and the process that supports it, and to make effective use of the process to facilitate the effective improvement of service quality.

Adopting and implementing standard and consistent approaches for CSI will:

- Lead to a gradual and continual improvement in service quality, where justified
- Ensure that IT services remain continuously aligned to business requirements
- Result in gradual improvements in cost effectiveness through a reduction in costs and/ or the capability to handle more work at the same cost

■ Use monitoring and reporting to identify opportunities for improvement in all lifecycle stages and in all processes

■ Identify opportunities for improvements in organizational structures, resourcing capabilities, partners, technology, staff skills and training, and communications.

7.2 CSI PRINCIPLES

7.2.1 CSI approach

Figure 7.2 shows an overall approach to CSI and illustrates a continual cycle of improvement. This approach to improvement can be summarized as follows:

■ Embrace the vision by understanding the high-level business objectives. The vision should align the business and IT strategies.

■ Assess the current situation to obtain an accurate, unbiased snapshot of where the organization is right now. This baseline assessment is an analysis of the current position in terms of the business, organization, people, process and technology.

■ Understand and agree on the priorities for improvement based on a deeper development

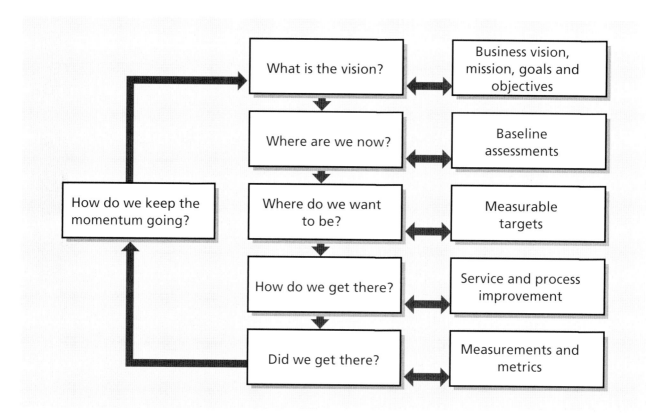

Figure 7.2 Continual service improvement approach

of the principles defined in the vision. The full vision may be years away but this step provides specific goals and a manageable timeframe.

- Detail the CSI plan to achieve higher-quality service provision by implementing or improving ITSM processes.
- Verify that measurements and metrics are in place and that the milestones were achieved, process compliance is high, and business objectives and priorities were met by the level of service.
- Finally, the approach should ensure that the momentum for quality improvement is maintained by assuring that changes become embedded in the organization.

7.2.2 CSI register

It is likely that several initiatives or possibilities for improvement are identified. It is recommended that a CSI register is kept to record all the improvement opportunities and that each one should be categorized into small, medium or large undertakings. Additionally they should be categorized into initiatives that can be achieved quickly, or in the medium term or longer term. Each improvement initiative should also show the benefits that will be achieved by its implementation. With this information a clear prioritized list can be produced. One failing that has been observed is that when something has been identified as a lower priority, it never makes its way higher up the list for further consideration; so automated raising of priorities over time may be a useful addition to the register.

The CSI register contains important information for the overall service provider and should be held and regarded as part of the service knowledge management system (SKMS).

The CSI register will introduce a structure and visibility to CSI ensuring that all initiatives are captured and recorded, and benefits realized. Additionally the benefits will be measured to show that they have given the desired results. In forecasting the benefits of each proposed improvement we should also try to quantify the benefit in terms of aspirational key performance indicator (KPI) metrics. This will assist in prioritizing those changes that deliver the most significant incremental benefit to the business.

The CSI register provides a coordinated, consistent view of the potentially numerous improvement activities. It is important to define the interface from the CSI register of initiatives with strategic initiatives and with processes such as problem management, capacity management and change management. In particular the service review meeting is likely to result in a number of requirements for improvement.

The CSI manager should have accountability and responsibility for the production and maintenance of the CSI register.

7.2.3 Service measurement and metrics

For services there are three basic measurements that most organizations utilize, which *ITIL Service Design* covers in more detail. They are:

- Availability of the service
- Reliability of the service
- Performance of the service.

In many cases, when an organization is monitoring, measuring and reporting on component levels it is doing so to protect itself and possibly to point the blame elsewhere – 'My server or my application was up 100% of the time.' Service measurement is not about placing blame or protecting oneself but instead provides a meaningful view of the IT service as the customer experiences it. The server may be up, but because the network is down, the customer is not able to connect to the server. Therefore the IT service was not available even though one or more of the components used to provide the service was available the whole time. Being able to measure against a service is directly linked to the components, systems and applications that are being monitored and reported on.

Measuring at the component level is necessary and valuable, but service measurement must go further than the component level. Service measurement will require someone to take the individual measurements and combine them to provide a view of the true customer experience. Too often we provide a report against a component, system or application but don't provide the true service level as experienced by the customer. Figure 5.3 in *ITIL Continual Service Improvement* shows how it is possible to measure and report against different levels of systems and components to provide a true service measurement. Even though the figure references availability measuring and reporting, the same can apply for performance measuring and reporting.

7.2.3.1 Metrics

It is important to remember that there are three types of metrics that an organization will need to collect to support CSI activities as well as other process activities:

- **Technology metrics** These metrics are often associated with component and application-based metrics such as performance, availability etc.
- **Process metrics** These metrics are captured in the form of critical success factors (CSFs), KPIs

and activity metrics for the service management processes. They can help determine the overall health of a process. KPIs can help to answer four key questions on quality, performance, value and compliance of following the process. CSI would use these metrics as input in identifying improvement opportunities for each process.

- **Service metrics** These metrics are a measure of the end-to-end service performance. Individual technology and process metrics are used when calculating the end-to-end service metrics.

Metrics can be classified into three categories: financial metrics, learning and growth metrics, and organizational or process effectiveness metrics. An example of financial metrics is the expenses and total percentage of hours spent on projects or maintenance, while an example of learning and growth is the percentage of education pursued in a target skill area, certification in a professional area, and contribution to knowledge management.

Some examples of service quality metrics are shown in Table 7.1. Process quality metrics are the quality metrics related to efficient and effective process management.

7.2.3.2 Interpreting metrics

When beginning to interpret the results it is important to know the data elements that make up the results, the purpose of producing the results and the expected normal ranges of the results.

Simply looking at some results and declaring a trend is dangerous. Figure 7.3 shows a trend that the service desk is opening fewer incidents over the last few months. One could believe that this is because there are fewer incidents or perhaps it is because the customers are not happy with the

Table 7.1 Examples of service quality metrics

Measure	Metric	Quality goal	Lower limit	Upper limit
Schedule	Variation against revised plan (%)	Within 7.5% of estimate	Not to be less than 7.5% of estimate	Not to exceed 7.5% of estimate
Effort	Variation against revised plan (%)	Within 10% of estimate	Not to be less than 10% of estimate	Not to exceed 10% of estimate
Cost	Variation against revised plan (%)	Within 10% of estimate	Not to be less than 10% of estimate	Not to exceed 10% of estimate
Defects	Variation against planned defect (%)	Within 10% of estimate	Not to be less than 10% of estimate	Not to exceed 10% of estimate
Productivity	Variation against productivity goal	Within 10% of estimate	Not to be less than 10% of estimate	Not to exceed 10% of estimate
Customer satisfaction	Customer satisfaction survey result	Greater than 8.9 on a range of 1 to 10	Not to be less than 8.9 on a range of 1 to 10	

Note: The figures in Table 7.1 are for illustrative purposes only and are not intended as generic targets. Organizations should consider and set their own targets.

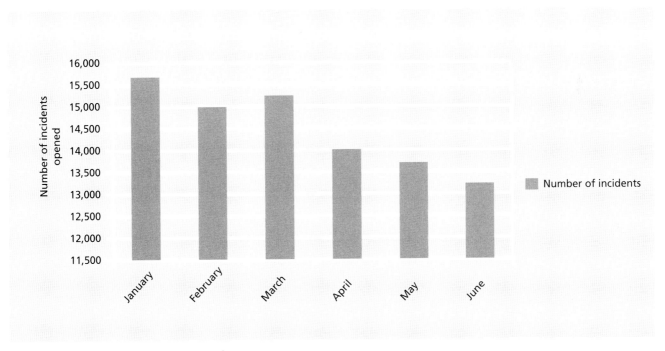

Figure 7.3 Number of incidents opened by service desk over time

service that is being provided, so they go elsewhere for their support needs. Perhaps the organization has implemented a self-help knowledge base and some customers are now using this service instead of contacting the service desk. Some investigation is required to understand what is driving these metrics.

7.2.3.3 Baselines

An important beginning point for highlighting improvement is to establish baselines as markers or starting points for later comparison. Baselines are also used to establish an initial data point to determine if a service or process needs to be improved. As a result, it is important that baselines are documented, recognized and accepted throughout the organization. Baselines must be established at each level: strategic goals and objectives, tactical process maturity, and operational metrics and KPIs.

If a baseline is not initially established the first measurement efforts will become the baseline. That is why it is essential to collect data at the outset, even if the integrity of the data is in question. It is better to have data to question than to have no data at all.

7.2.3.4 Why do we measure?

There are four reasons to monitor and measure:

- **To validate** Monitoring and measuring to validate previous decisions
- **To direct** Monitoring and measuring to set the direction for activities in order to meet set targets; this is the most prevalent reason for monitoring and measuring
- **To justify** Monitoring and measuring to justify, with factual evidence or proof, that a course of action is required

- **To intervene** Monitoring and measuring to identify a point of intervention including subsequent changes and corrective actions.

The four basic reasons to monitor and measure lead to three key questions: 'Why are we monitoring and measuring?', 'When do we stop?' and 'Is anyone using the data?' To answer these questions, it is important to identify which of the above reasons is driving the measurement effort. Too often, we continue to measure long after the need has passed. Every time you produce a report you should ask: 'Do we still need this?'

7.2.3.5 Service reporting

A significant amount of data is collated and monitored by IT in the daily delivery of quality service to the business; however, only a small subset is of real interest and importance to the business. Most data and its meaning are more suited to the internal management needs of IT.

The business likes to see a historical representation of the past period's performance that portrays its experience; however, it is more concerned with those historical events that continue to be a threat going forward, and how IT intends to militate against such threats.

Cross-referenced data must still be presented that align precisely to any contracted, chargeable elements of the delivery, which may or may not be technical depending on the business focus and language used within contracts and SLAs.

It is not satisfactory simply to present reports that depict adherence (or otherwise) to SLAs, which in themselves are prone to statistical ambiguity. IT needs to build an actionable approach to reporting: this is what happened, this is what we did, this is how we will ensure it doesn't impact you again, and this is how we are working to improve the delivery of IT services generally.

7.3 CSI PROCESS

7.3.1 Seven-step improvement process

CSI uses the seven-step improvement process shown in Figure 7.4, with each of the steps falling into one of the phases of the Plan-Do-Check-Act (PDCA) cycle. The PDCA cycle provides steady, ongoing improvement, which is a fundamental tenet of CSI.

Figure 7.4 also shows how the cycle fits into the Data-to-Information-to-Knowledge-to-Wisdom (DIKW) structure of knowledge management. The integration of the PDCA cycle and the seven-step improvement process is as follows:

■ Plan
  1. Identify the strategy for improvement
  2. Define what you will measure

■ Do
  3. Gather the data
  4. Process the data

■ Check
  5. Analyse the information and data
  6. Present and use the information

■ Act
  7. Implement improvement.

7.3.1.1 Step 1 – Identify the strategy for improvement

Before any further activity can be started it is imperative that the overall vision is identified. What are we trying to achieve for the business as a whole? The questions we need to ask are: What initiatives does the business have that could be undermined by poor IT service provision? Or, more positively: How can improvements in IT enable the business vision to be achieved? The answers to these questions will come from stepping through the seven-step improvement process.

What are the business and IT strategy and plans for the coming months and years? Why do we want to measure for improvement? The overall strategy should be assessed and analysed to see where we need to focus our measurements, for example. The technical and operational goals as well as the strategic goals need to be identified and assessed. The vision should not be to have state-of-the-art servers and desk-top computers, but to have state-of-the-art services that ensure and enable the overall business to perform as well as possible so it is not in any way constrained by the quality or cost of the IT services.

Like all the steps in the process, this should be revisited to reassess the potentially changing vision and goals. When revisiting this process we would apply any wisdom gained from previous iterations.

7.3.1.2 Step 2 – Define what you will measure

This step is directly related to the strategic, tactical and operational goals that have been defined for measuring services and service management processes as well as the existing technology and capability to support measuring and CSI activities. In this step you need to define what you should measure; define what you can actually measure; carry out a gap analysis; and then finalize the actual measurement plan.

As stated previously, measurement will take place at service, process and technology levels.

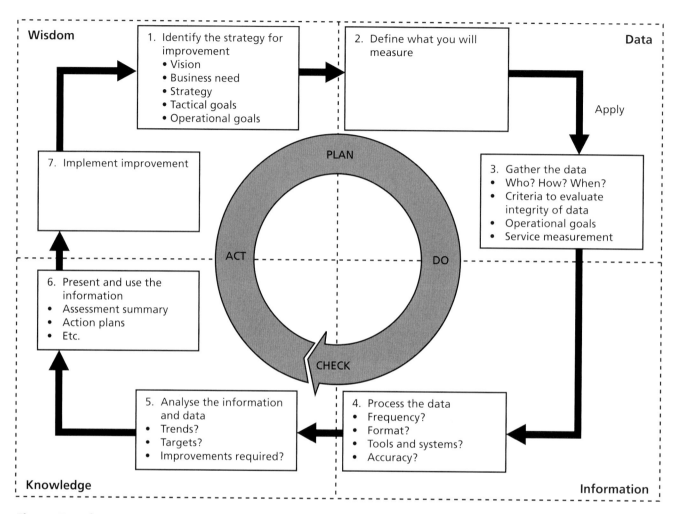

Figure 7.4 The seven-step improvement process

Step 2 is iterative during the rest of the activities. Depending on the goals and objectives to support service improvement activities, an organization may have to purchase and install new technology to support the gathering and processing of the data and/or hire staff with the required skills sets.

Effective service measures concentrate on a few vital, meaningful indicators that are economical, quantitative and usable for the desired results. If there are too many measures, organizations may become too intent on measurement and lose focus on improving results. A guiding principle is to measure that which matters most. IT has never lacked in the measuring area. In fact, many IT organizations measure far too many things that have little or no value. There is often no thought or effort given to aligning measures to the business and IT goals and objectives.

As part of the measuring process it is important to confirm regularly that the data being collected and collated is still required and that measurements are being adjusted where necessary. This responsibility falls on the owner of each report or dashboard. They are the individuals designated to keep the reports useful and to make sure that effective use is being made of the results.

7.3.1.3 Step 3 – Gather the data

Gathering data requires having monitoring in place. Monitoring could be executed using technology such as application, system and component monitoring tools as used in the event management process (documented in service operation) or it could even be a manual process for certain tasks. The accuracy and integrity of the data should always be maintained.

Quality is the key objective of monitoring for CSI. Monitoring will therefore focus on the effectiveness and efficiency of a service, process, tool, organization or configuration item (CI). The emphasis is not on assuring real-time service performance; rather it is on identifying where improvements can be made to the existing level of service, or IT performance. Monitoring for CSI will therefore tend to focus on detecting exceptions and resolutions. For example, CSI is not as interested in whether an incident was resolved, but whether it was resolved within the agreed time, and whether future incidents can be prevented.

CSI is not only interested in exceptions, though. If an SLA is consistently met over time, CSI will also be interested in determining whether that level of performance can be sustained at a lower cost or whether it needs to be upgraded to an even better level of performance because of changing business requirements. CSI may therefore also need access to regular performance reports.

However, since CSI is unlikely to need, or be able to cope with, the vast quantities of data that are produced by all monitoring activity, it will most likely focus on a specific subset of monitoring at any given time. This could be determined by input from the business or improvements to technology.

7.3.1.4 Step 4 – Process the data

This step is to convert the data into the required format and for the required audience. Follow the trail from metric to KPI to CSF, all the way back to the vision if necessary (see Figure 7.5).

Report-generating technologies are typically used at this stage as various amounts of data are condensed into information for use in the analysis activity. The data is also typically put into a format that provides an end-to-end perspective on the overall performance of a service. This activity begins the transformation of raw data into packaged information. Use the information to develop insight into the performance of the service and/or processes. Process the data into information (by creating logical groupings), which provides a better means to analyse the information and data – the next step in CSI.

The output of logical groupings could be in spreadsheets, reports generated directly from the service management tool suite, system monitoring and reporting tools, or telephony tools such as an automatic call distribution tool.

Processing the data is an important CSI activity that is often overlooked. While monitoring and collecting data on a single infrastructure component is important, it is also important to

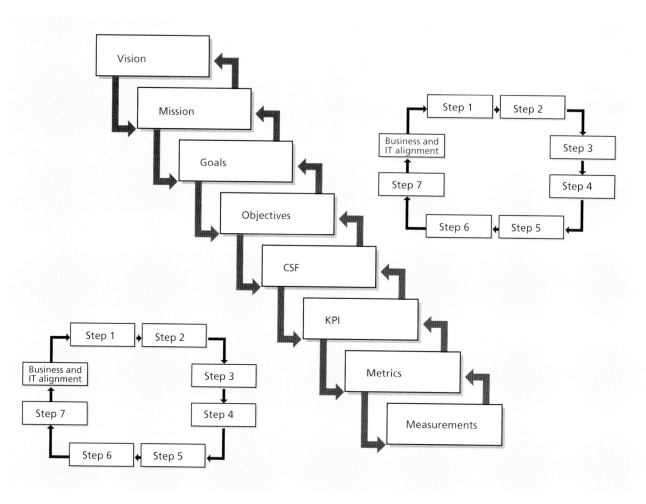

Figure 7.5 From vision to measurements

understand that component's impact on the larger infrastructure and IT service. Knowing that a server was up 99.99% of the time is one thing; knowing that no one could access the server is another. An example of processing the data is taking the data from monitoring of individual components, such as the mainframe, applications, WAN, LAN, servers etc., and processing it into a structure of an end-to-end service from the customer's perspective.

7.3.1.5 Step 5 – Analyse the data

Your organization's service desk has a trend of reduced call volumes consistently over the last four months. Even though this is a trend, you need to ask yourself the question: 'Is this a good trend or a bad trend?' You don't know if the call reduction is because you have reduced the number of recurring errors in the infrastructure by good problem management activities or if the customers feel that the service desk doesn't provide any value and have started bypassing the service desk and going directly to second-level support groups.

Data analysis transforms the information into knowledge of the events that are affecting the organization. More skill and experience is required to perform data analysis than data gathering and processing. Verification against goals and objectives is expected during this activity. This verification validates that objectives are being supported and value is being added. It is not sufficient to simply produce graphs of various types but to document the observations and conclusions.

Question: What do you actually analyse?

Answer: Once the data is processed into information, you can then analyse the results, looking for answers to questions such as:

■ Are there any clear trends?
■ Are they positive or negative trends?
■ Are changes required?
■ Are we operating according to plan?
■ Are we meeting targets?
■ Are improvements required?
■ Are there underlying structural problems?

In this step you apply knowledge to your information. Without this, you have nothing more than sets of numbers showing metrics that are meaningless. It is not enough to simply look at this month's figures and accept them without question, even if they meet SLA targets. You should analyse the figures to stay ahead of the game. Without analysis you merely have information. With analysis you have knowledge. If you find anomalies or poor results, then look for ways to improve.

7.3.1.6 Step 6 – Present and use the information

The sixth step is to take our knowledge, which is represented in the reports, monitors, action plans, reviews, evaluations and opportunities, and present it to the target audience in a clear, digestible and timely way. Consider the target audience; make sure that you identify exceptions to the service, benefits that have been revealed, or can be expected. Data gathering occurs at the operational level of an organization. Format this data into knowledge that all levels can appreciate and use to gain insight into their needs and expectations.

This stage involves presenting the information in a format that is understandable, at the right level, provides value, notes exceptions to service, identifies benefits that were revealed during the time period, and allows those receiving the information to make strategic, tactical and operational decisions. In other words, present the information in the manner that makes it most useful for the target audience.

Most organizations create reports and present information to some extent or another; however, it is often not done well. Many organizations simply take the gathered raw data (often straight from the tool) and report it to everyone, without necessarily processing or analysing the data. The report should emphasize and ideally highlight areas where the recipient needs to take action.

The other issue often associated with presenting and using information is that it is overdone. Managers at all levels are bombarded with too many emails, too many meetings, too many reports. The reality is that the managers often don't need this information or, at the very least, not in that format. It is often unclear what role the manager has in making decisions and providing guidance on improvement programmes.

As we have discussed, CSI is an ongoing activity of monitoring and gathering data, processing the data into logical groupings, and analysing it in order to meet targets and identify trends and improvement opportunities. There is no value in all the work done to this point if we don't do a good job of presenting our findings and then using them to make decisions that will lead to improvements.

'Begin with the end in mind' is habit number two in Stephen Covey's *The Seven Habits of Highly Effective People*.[5] Even though the book is about personal leadership, the habit holds true for presenting and using information. In addition to understanding the target audience, it is also important to understand the purpose of any information being presented. If the purpose and value cannot be articulated, then it is important to question if it is needed at all.

7.3.1.7 Step 7 – Implement improvement
Use the knowledge gained and combine it with previous experience to make informed decisions about optimizing, improving and correcting services. Managers need to identify issues and present solutions.

This stage may include any number of activities such as approval of improvement activities, prioritization and submitting a business case, integration with change management, integration with other lifecycle stages, and guidance on how to manage an ongoing improvement project successfully and on checking whether the improvement actually achieved its objective.

[5] Covey, S. (1989). *The Seven Habits of Highly Effective People*. Free Press, New York.

CSI identifies many opportunities for improvement, but organizations cannot afford to implement all of them. As discussed earlier, an organization needs to prioritize improvement activities for its goals, objectives, return on investment (ROI), types of service breaches etc., and document them in the CSI register. Improvement initiatives can also be externally driven by regulatory requirements, changes in competition, or even political decisions.

If organizations were implementing improvement according to CSI, there would be no need for this publication. Improvement often takes place in reaction to a single event that caused a (severe) outage to part or all of the organization. At other times, minor problems are noticed and specific improvements are implemented with no relation to the priorities of the organization, thus taking valuable resources away from real emergencies. This is common practice but obviously not best practice.

After a decision to improve a service and/or service management process is made, then the service lifecycle continues. A new service strategy may be defined, service design builds the changes, service transition implements the changes into production and then service operation manages the day-to-day operations of the service and/or service management processes. Keep in mind that CSI activities continue through each stage of the service lifecycle.

Each service lifecycle stage requires resources to build or modify the services and/or service management processes, potential new technology or modifications to existing technology, potential changes to KPIs and other metrics, and possibly even new or modified OLAs or underpinning contracts (UCs) to support SLAs. Communication, training and documentation are required to move a new or improved service, tool or service management process into production.

7.3.2 Interfaces

In order to support improvement activities it is important to have CSI practices integrated within each lifecycle stage and its associated processes and activities. Examples include monitoring the progress of strategies, standards, policies and architectural decisions that have been made and implemented. Service strategy will also analyse results associated with implemented strategies, policies and standards.

Within the service design stage, monitoring and gathering data are associated with creating and modifying services and service management processes. This part of the service lifecycle also measures against the effectiveness and ability to measure CSFs and KPIs that were defined through gathering business requirements. It is during service design that the definition of what should be measured is produced. Service design analyses current results of design and project activities. Trends are also noted with results compared against the design goals. Service design also identifies improvement opportunities and analyses the effectiveness and ability to measure CSFs and KPIs that were defined when gathering business requirements.

Service transition develops and tests the monitoring procedures and criteria to be used during and after implementation. Service transition monitors and gathers data on the actual release into production of services and service management processes. Service transition develops the monitoring procedures and criteria to be used during and after implementation.

It is during the service operation lifecycle stage that the actual monitoring of services in the live environment takes place. People working in the service operation functions will play a large part in the processing activity. Service operation staff provide input into what can be measured and processed into logical groupings, and then process the data. Service operation staff would also be responsible for taking the component data and processing it in a format which provides a better end-to-end perspective of the service achievements. Service operation staff analyse current results as well as trends over a period of time. Service operation staff also identify both incremental and large-scale improvement opportunities, providing input into what can be measured and processed into logical groupings. They also perform the actual data processing.

7.3.3 Role of other processes in gathering and processing the data

7.3.3.1 Service level management

SLM plays a key role in the data-gathering activity as SLM is responsible for defining not only business requirements but also IT's capabilities to achieve them:

- SLM needs to look at what is happening with the monitoring data to ensure that end-to-end service performance is being monitored and analysed.
- SLM should also identify who gets the data, whether any analysis takes place on the data before it is presented, and if any trend evaluation is undertaken to understand the performance over a period of time. This information will be helpful in following CSI activities.

7.3.3.2 Availability and capacity management

Availability management and capacity management support the data-processing activities of CSI by:

- Providing significant input into existing monitoring and data collection capabilities and tool requirements to meet new data collection requirements, and ensuring the availability and capacity plans are updated to reflect new or modified monitoring and data collection requirements
- Being accountable for the actual infrastructure monitoring and data collection activities that take place; therefore roles and responsibilities need to be defined and the roles filled with properly skilled and trained staff
- Being accountable for ensuring tools are in place to gather data
- Being accountable for ensuring that the actual monitoring and data collection activities are consistently performed
- Being responsible for processing the data at a component level and then working with SLM to provide service level data
- Processing data on KPIs such as availability or performance measures
- Utilizing the agreed reporting formats
- Analysing processed data for accuracy.

7.3.3.3 Event management, incident management and service desk

Event management, incident management and the service desk support the data-processing activities of CSI:

- Through incident management defining monitoring requirements to support event

and incident detection through automation; incident management also has the ability to automatically open incidents and/or auto-escalate incidents

- Through event management automatically monitoring events and producing alerts, some of which may require CSI activities to correct
- Through event and incident monitoring identifying abnormal situations and conditions, which helps with predicting and pre-empting situations and conditions, thereby avoiding possible service and component failures
- By monitoring the response times, repair times, resolution times and incident escalations
- By monitoring telephony items such as call volumes, average speed of answer, call abandonment rates etc. so that immediate action can be taken when there is an increase in contacts to the service desk; this is important for the service desk as a single point of contact; it also applies to those service desks that provide support via email and the web
- By processing data on incidents and service requests such as who is using the service desk and what is the nature of the incidents
- By collecting and processing data on KPIs such as MTRS and percentage of incidents resolved within service targets
- By processing data for telephony statistics at the service desk such as number of inbound/outbound calls, average talk time, average speed of answer, abandoned calls etc.
- By utilizing the agreed reporting format
- By analysing processed data for accuracy.

7.3.3.4 Information security management

Information security management contributes to monitoring and data collection by:

- Defining security monitoring and data collection requirements
- Monitoring, verifying and tracking the levels of security according to the organizational security policies and guidelines
- Assisting in determining the effects of security measures on the data monitoring and collection from the confidentiality (accessible only to those who should), integrity (data is accurate and not corrupted or not corruptible) and availability (data is available when needed) perspectives
- Processing response and resolution data on security incidents
- Creating trend analyses on security breaches
- Validating success of risk mitigation strategies
- Utilizing the agreed upon reporting format
- Analysing processed data for accuracy.

7.3.3.5 Financial management

Financial management for IT services is responsible for monitoring and collecting data associated with the actual expenditures versus budget and is able to provide input on questions such as whether costing or revenue targets are on track. Financial management for IT services should also monitor the ongoing cost per service etc.

In addition, financial management for IT services will provide the necessary templates to assist CSI to create the budget and expenditure reports for the various improvement initiatives as well as providing the means to compute the ROI of the improvements.

7.4 CSI INPUTS AND OUTPUTS

Table 7.2 shows the major CSI inputs and outputs, by lifecycle stage. Appendix A provides a summary of the major inputs and outputs between each stage of the service lifecycle.

Table 7.2 CSI inputs and outputs by lifecycle stage

Lifecycle stage	CSI inputs (from the lifecycle stages in the first column)	CSI outputs (to the lifecycle stages in the first column)
Service strategy	Vision and mission	Results of customer and user satisfaction surveys
	Service portfolio	Input to business cases and the service portfolio
	Policies	Feedback on strategies and policies
	Strategies and strategic plans	Financial information regarding improvement initiatives for input to budgets
	Priorities	
	Financial information and budgets	Data required for metrics, KPIs and CSFs
	Patterns of business activity	Service reports
	Achievements against metrics, KPIs and CSFs	Requests for change (RFCs) for implementing improvements
	Improvement opportunities logged in the CSI register	

Table continues

Table 7.2 – *continued*

Lifecycle stage	CSI inputs (from the lifecycle stages in the first column)	CSI outputs (to the lifecycle stages in the first column)
Service design	Service catalogue	Results of customer and user satisfaction surveys
	Service design packages including details of utility and warranty	Input to design requirements
		Data required for metrics, KPIs and CSFs
	Knowledge and information in the SKMS	Service reports
	Achievements against metrics, KPIs and CSFs	Feedback on service design packages
	Design of services, measurements, processes, infrastructure and systems	RFCs for implementing improvements
	Design for the seven-step improvement process and procedures	
	Improvement opportunities logged in the CSI register	
Service transition	Test reports	Results of customer and user satisfaction surveys
	Change evaluation reports	Input to testing requirements
	Knowledge and information in the SKMS	Data required for metrics, KPIs and CSFs
	Achievements against metrics, KPIs and CSFs	Input to change evaluation and change advisory board meetings
	Improvement opportunities logged in the CSI register	Service reports
		RFCs for implementing improvements
Service operation	Operational performance data and service records	Results of customer and user satisfaction surveys
	Proposed problem resolutions and proactive measures	Service reports and dashboards
		Data required for metrics, KPIs and CSFs
	Knowledge and information in the SKMS	RFCs for implementing improvements
	Achievements against metrics, KPIs and CSFs	
	Improvement opportunities logged in the CSI register	

ITIL qualifications
and credentials

8

8 ITIL qualifications and credentials

8.1 ITIL QUALIFICATION SCHEME

The Cabinet Office has established contractual arrangements with two organizations to provide support for their ITIL portfolio. As the official accreditor, the APM Group provides accreditation services related to training, registration and the examination scheme. The Stationery Office (TSO) is the official publisher of all official ITIL Best Management Practice framework publications, including this one.

The Cabinet Office retains the rights to all intellectual property, copyright and trademarks relating to ITIL. Its predominant role in the official scheme is one of stewardship of the ITIL Best Management Practice framework content and qualifications. The APM Group chairs the qualifications board (the steering committee made up of representatives from the community who make decisions about qualifications policy) and ensures that any decisions made are to the benefit of both the practice and users alike. Details can be found by visiting:

www.itil-officialsite.com/Qualifications/ITILQualificationScheme.aspx

Figure 8.1 shows the ITIL qualification scheme as administered by the APM Group.

8.2 *it*SMF

The IT Service Management Forum (*it*SMF) is the not-for-profit international community for IT service management professionals, with more

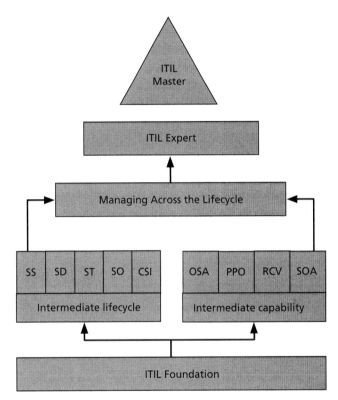

Figure 8.1 The ITIL qualification scheme

than 50 chapters worldwide and a coordinating organization – *it*SMF International. The chapters provide local support to those individuals and organizations using and implementing ITIL.

*it*SMF is recognized as an integral part of the ITIL community. It is a collaborative partner to the ITIL official scheme and participates on the qualifications board.

8.3 PROFESSIONAL RECOGNITION FOR INDIVIDUALS

Professional membership organizations promote professionalism in IT and IT service management. *it*SMF provides professional recognition to its members based on experience, professional contributions and qualifications under the priSM® scheme. priSM stands for Professional Recognition for IT Service Management, and is the credentialing scheme owned by *it*SMF International. It recognizes qualifications and roles across all of service management, including ITIL, COBIT, project/ programme management, competency schemes and ISO standards, amongst others.

Details can be found by visiting: www.theprisminstitute.org

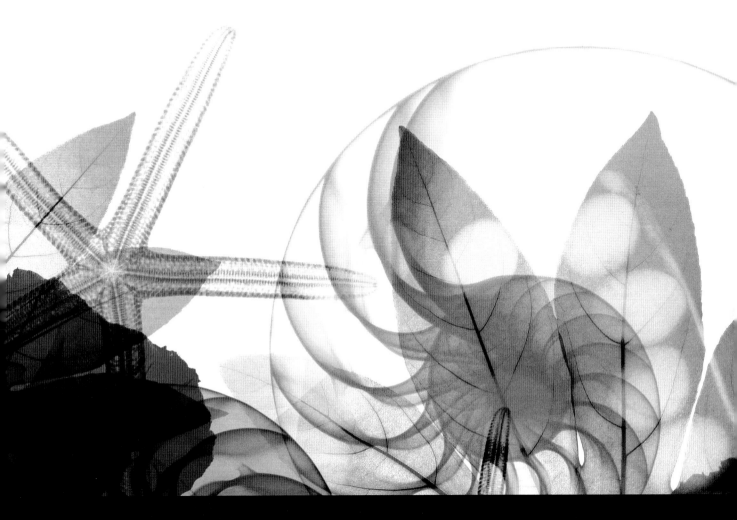

Appendix A:
Examples of inputs
and outputs across
the service lifecycle

Appendix A: Examples of inputs and outputs across the service lifecycle

This appendix identifies some of the major inputs and outputs between each stage of the service lifecycle. This is not an exhaustive list and is designed to help understand how the different lifecycle stages interact. See the tables at the end of each lifecycle chapter for more detail on the inputs and outputs of that stage of the service lifecycle.

Lifecycle stage	Examples of inputs from other service lifecycle stages	Examples of outputs to other service lifecycle stages
Service strategy	Information and feedback for business cases and service portfolio	Vision and mission
	Requirements for strategies and plans	Strategies, strategic plans and policies
	Inputs and feedback on strategies and policies	Financial information and budgets
	Financial reports, service reports, dashboards, and outputs of service review meetings	Service portfolio
	Response to change proposals	Change proposals
	Service portfolio updates including the service catalogue	Service charters including service packages, service models, and details of utility and warranty
	Change schedule	Patterns of business activity and demand forecasts
	Knowledge and information in the service knowledge management system (SKMS)	Updated knowledge and information in the SKMS
		Achievements against metrics, key performance indicators (KPIs) and critical success factors (CSFs)
		Feedback to other lifecycle stages
		Improvement opportunities logged in the CSI register

Lifecycle stage	Examples of inputs from other service lifecycle stages	Examples of outputs to other service lifecycle stages
Service design	Vision and mission	Service portfolio updates including the service catalogue
	Strategies, strategic plans and policies	Service design packages, including:
	Financial information and budgets	■ Details of utility and warranty
	Service portfolio	■ Acceptance criteria
	Service charters including service packages, service models, and details of utility and warranty	■ Updated service models
		■ Designs and interface specifications
	Feedback on all aspects of service design and service design packages	■ Transition plans
		■ Operational plans and procedures
	Requests for change (RFCs) for designing changes and improvements	Information security policies
	Input to design requirements from other lifecycle stages	Designs for new or changed services, management information systems and tools, technology architectures, processes, measurement methods and metrics
	Service reports, dashboards, and outputs of service review meetings	Service level agreements (SLAs), operational level agreements (OLAs) and underpinning contracts
	Knowledge and information in the SKMS	RFCs to transition or deploy new or changed services
		Financial reports
		Updated knowledge and information in the SKMS
		Achievements against metrics, KPIs and CSFs
		Feedback to other lifecycle stages
		Improvement opportunities logged in the CSI register

Lifecycle stage	Examples of inputs from other service lifecycle stages	Examples of outputs to other service lifecycle stages
Service transition	Vision and mission	New or changed services, management information systems and tools, technology architectures, processes, measurement methods and metrics
	Strategies, strategic plans and policies	
	Financial information and budgets	
	Service portfolio	Responses to change proposals and RFCs
	Change proposals, including utility and warranty requirements and expected timescales	Change schedule
		Known errors
	RFCs for implementing changes and improvements	Standard changes for use in request fulfilment
	Service design packages, including:	Knowledge and information in the SKMS (including the configuration management system)
	■ Details of utility and warranty	Financial reports
	■ Acceptance criteria	Updated knowledge and information in the SKMS
	■ Service models	
	■ Designs and interface specifications	Achievements against metrics, KPIs and CSFs
	■ Transition plans	Feedback to other lifecycle stages
	■ Operational plans and procedures	Improvement opportunities logged in the CSI register
	Input to change evaluation and change advisory board (CAB) meetings	
	Knowledge and information in the SKMS	

Lifecycle stage	Examples of inputs from other service lifecycle stages	Examples of outputs to other service lifecycle stages
Service operation	Vision and mission	Achievement of agreed service levels to deliver value to the business
	Strategies, strategic plans and policies	Operational requirements
	Financial information and budgets	Operational performance data and service records
	Service portfolio	
	Service reports, dashboards, and outputs of service review meetings	RFCs to resolve operational issues
	Service design packages, including:	Financial reports
	■ Details of utility and warranty	Updated knowledge and information in the SKMS
	■ Operational plans and procedures	Achievements against metrics, KPIs and CSFs
	■ Recovery procedures	Feedback to other lifecycle stages
	SLAs, OLAs and underpinning contracts	Improvement opportunities logged in the CSI register
	Known errors	
	Standard changes for use in request fulfilment	
	Information security policies	
	Change schedule	
	Patterns of business activity and demand forecasts	
	Knowledge and information in the SKMS	

Lifecycle stage	Examples of inputs from other service lifecycle stages	Examples of outputs to other service lifecycle stages
Continual service improvement	Vision and mission	RFCs for implementing improvements across all lifecycle stages
	Strategies, strategic plans and policies	Business cases for significant improvements
	Financial information and budgets	Updated CSI register
	Service portfolio	Service improvement plans
	Achievements against metrics, KPIs and CSFs from each lifecycle stage	Results of customer and user satisfaction surveys
	Operational performance data and service records	Service reports, dashboards, and outputs of service review meetings
	Improvement opportunities logged in the CSI register	Financial reports
	Knowledge and information in the SKMS	Updated knowledge and information in the SKMS
		Achievements against metrics, KPIs and CSFs
		Feedback to other lifecycle stages

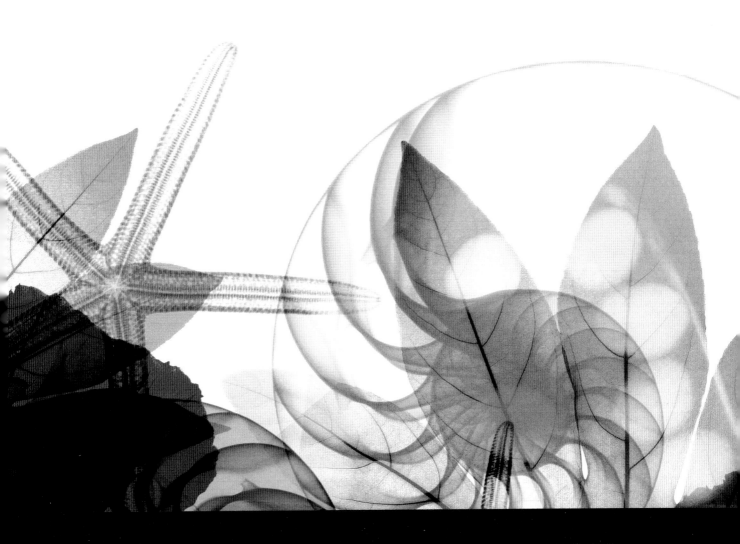

Appendix B:
Related guidance

Appendix B: Related guidance

This is a common appendix across the ITIL core publications. It includes frameworks, best practices, standards, models and quality systems that complement and have synergy with the ITIL service lifecycle.

Section 2.1.7 describes the role of best practices in the public domain and references some of the publications in this appendix. Each core publication references this appendix where relevant.

Related guidance may also be referenced within a single ITIL core publication where the topic is specific to that publication.

B.1 ITIL GUIDANCE AND WEB SERVICES

ITIL is part of the Best Management Practice (BMP) portfolio of best-practice guidance (see section 1.6). BMP products present flexible, practical and effective guidance, drawn from a range of the most successful global business experiences. Distilled to its essential elements, the guidance can then be applied to every type of business and organization.

The BMP website (www.best-management-practice. com) includes news, reviews, case studies and white papers on ITIL and all other BMP best-practice guidance.

The ITIL official website (www.itil-officialsite.com) contains reliable, up-to-date information on ITIL – including information on accreditation and the ITIL software scheme for the endorsement of ITIL-based tools.

Details of the core publications are as follows:

- Cabinet Office (2011). *ITIL Service Strategy.* TSO, London.
- Cabinet Office (2011). *ITIL Service Design.* TSO, London.
- Cabinet Office (2011). *ITIL Service Transition.* TSO, London.
- Cabinet Office (2011). *ITIL Service Operation.* TSO, London.
- Cabinet Office (2011). *ITIL Continual Service Improvement.* TSO, London.

The full ITIL glossary, in English and other languages, can be accessed through the ITIL official site at:

www.itil-officialsite.com/InternationalActivities/ ITILGlossaries.aspx

The range of translated glossaries is always growing, so check this website for the most up-to-date list.

Details of derived and complementary publications can be found in the publications library of the Best Management Practice website at:

www.best-management-practice.com/Publications-Library/IT-Service-Management-ITIL/

B.2 QUALITY MANAGEMENT SYSTEM

Quality management focuses on product/service quality as well as the quality assurance and control of processes to achieve consistent quality. Total quality management (TQM) is a methodology for managing continual improvement by using a quality management system. TQM establishes a culture involving all people in the organization in a process of continual monitoring and improvement.

ISO 9000:2005 describes the fundamentals of quality management systems that are applicable to all organizations which need to demonstrate their ability to consistently provide products that meet customer and applicable statutory and regulatory requirements. ISO 9001:2008 specifies generic requirements for a quality management system.

Many process-based quality management systems use the methodology known as 'Plan-Do-Check-Act' (PDCA), often referred to as the Deming Cycle, or Shewhart Cycle, that can be applied to all processes. PDCA can be summarized as:

■ **Plan** Establish the objectives and processes necessary to deliver results in accordance with customer requirements and the organization's policies.
■ **Do** Implement the processes.
■ **Check** Monitor and measure processes and product against policies, objectives and requirements for the product and report the results.
■ **Act** Take actions to continually improve process performance.

There are distinct advantages of tying an organization's ITSM processes, and service operation processes in particular, to its quality management system. If an organization has a formal quality management system that complies with ISO 9001, then this can be used to assess progress regularly and drive forward agreed service improvement initiatives through regular reviews and reporting.

Visit www.iso.org for information on ISO standards.

See www.deming.org for more information on the W. Edwards Deming Institute and the Deming Cycle for process improvement.

B.3 RISK MANAGEMENT

A number of different methodologies, standards and frameworks have been developed for the assessment and management of risk. Some focus more on generic techniques widely applicable to different levels and needs, while others are specifically concerned with risk management relating to important assets used by the organization in the pursuit of its objectives. Each organization should determine the approach to risk management that is best suited to its needs and circumstances. It is possible that the approach adopted will leverage the ideas reflected in more than one of the recognized standards and/or frameworks.

Each of the core publications has an appendix on risk management. See also:

■ Office of Government Commerce (2010). *Management of Risk: Guidance for Practitioners.* TSO, London.
■ ISO 31000:2009 Risk management – principles and guidelines.
■ ISO/IEC 27001: 2005 Information technology – security techniques – information security management systems – requirements.
■ ISACA (2009). *The Risk IT Framework* (based on COBIT, see section B.5).

B.4 GOVERNANCE OF IT

Corporate governance refers to the rules, policies, processes (and in some cases, laws) by which businesses are operated, regulated and controlled. These are often defined by the board or shareholders, or the constitution of the organization; but they can also be defined by legislation, regulation or consumer groups.

ISO 9004 (Managing for the sustained success of an organization – a quality management approach) provides guidance on governance for the board and executive of an organization.

The standard for corporate governance of IT is ISO/IEC 38500. The purpose of this standard is to promote effective, efficient and acceptable use of IT in all organizations by:

■ Assuring stakeholders (including consumers, shareholders and employees) that, if the standard is followed, they can have confidence in the organization's corporate governance of IT

■ Informing and guiding directors in governing the use of IT in their organization

■ Providing a basis for objective evaluation of the corporate governance of IT.

Typical examples of regulations that impact IT include: financial, safety, data protection, privacy, software asset management, environment management and carbon emission targets.

Further details are available at www.iso.org

Section 5.1.4 in *ITIL Service Strategy* references the concepts of ISO/IEC 38500 and how they can be applied.

B.5 COBIT

The Control OBjectives for Information and related Technology (COBIT) is a governance and control framework for IT management created by ISACA and the IT Governance Institute (ITGI).

COBIT is based on the analysis and harmonization of existing IT standards and good practices and conforms to generally accepted governance principles. It covers five key governance focus areas: strategic alignment, value delivery, resource management, risk management and performance management. COBIT is primarily aimed at internal and external stakeholders within an enterprise who wish to generate value from IT investments; those who provide IT services; and those who have a control/risk responsibility.

COBIT and ITIL are not 'competitive', nor are they mutually exclusive – on the contrary, they can be used in conjunction as part of an organization's overall governance and management framework. COBIT is positioned at a high level, is driven by business requirements, covers the full range of IT activities, and concentrates on what should be achieved rather than how to achieve effective governance, management and control. ITIL provides an organization with best-practice guidance on how to manage and improve its processes to deliver high-quality, cost-effective IT services. The following COBIT guidance supports strategy management and continual service improvement (CSI):

■ COBIT maturity models can be used to benchmark and drive improvement.

■ Goals and metrics can be aligned to the business goals for IT and used to create an IT management dashboard.

■ The COBIT 'monitor and evaluate' (ME) process domain defines the processes needed to assess current IT performance, IT controls and regulatory compliance.

Further details are available at www.isaca.org and www.itgi.org

B.6 ISO/IEC 20000 SERVICE MANAGEMENT SERIES

ISO/IEC 20000 is an internationally recognized standard for ITSM covering service providers who manage and deliver IT-enabled services to internal or external customers. ISO/IEC 20000-1 is aligned with other ISO management systems standards such as ISO 9001 and ISO/IEC 27001.

One of the most common routes for an organization to achieve the requirements of ISO/IEC 20000 is by adopting ITIL best practices. ISO/IEC 20000-1 is based on a service management system (SMS). The SMS is defined as a management system to direct and control the service management activities of the service provider. ISO/IEC 20000 includes:

■ ISO/IEC 20000-1:2005 – Information technology – Service management – Part 1: Specification

■ ISO/IEC 20000-1:2011 – Information technology – Service management – Part 1: Requirements for a service management system (the most recent edition of the ISO/IEC 20000 standard)

■ ISO/IEC 20000-2:2005 – Information technology – Service management – Part 2: Code of practice (being updated to include guidance on the application of service management systems and to support ISO/IEC 20000-1:2011)

■ ISO/IEC 20000-3:2005 – Information technology – Service management – Part 3: Scope and applicability

■ ISO/IEC TR 20000-4 – Information technology – Service management – Part 4: Process reference model

■ ISO/IEC TR 20000-5:2010 – Information technology – Service management – Part 5: Exemplar implementation plan for ISO/IEC 20000-1.

A closely related publication that is under development is ISO/IEC TR 15504-8 – Process assessment model for IT service management.

Further details can be found at www.iso.org or www.isoiec20000certification.com

Organizations using ISO/IEC 20000-1: 2005 for certification audits will transfer to the new edition, ISO/IEC 20000-1: 2011.

ITIL guidance supports organizations that are implementing service management practices to achieve the requirements of ISO/IEC 20000-1: 2005 and the new edition ISO/IEC 20000-1: 2011.

Other references include:

■ Dugmore, J. and Lacy, S. (2011). *Introduction to ISO/IEC 20000 Series: IT Service Management.* British Standards Institution, London.

■ Dugmore, J. and Lacy, S. (2011). *BIP 0005: A Manager's Guide to Service Management* (6th edition). British Standards Institution, London.

B.7 ENVIRONMENTAL MANAGEMENT AND GREEN/SUSTAINABLE IT

The transition to a low-carbon economy is a global challenge. Many governments have set targets to reduce carbon emissions or achieve carbon neutrality. IT is an enabler for environmental and cultural change that will help governments to achieve their targets – for example, through enabling tele- and video-conferencing, and remote and home working. However, IT is also a major user of energy and natural resources. Green IT refers to environmentally sustainable computing where the use and disposal of computers and printers are carried out in sustainable ways that do not have a negative impact on the environment.

Appendix E in *ITIL Service Design* includes further information on environmental architectures and standards. Appendix E in *ITIL Service Operation* also provides useful considerations for facilities management, including environmental aspects.

The ISO 14001 series of standards for an environment management system is designed to assure internal and external stakeholders that the organization is an environmentally responsible organization. It enables an organization of any size or type to:

■ Identify and control the environmental impact of its activities, products or services
■ Improve its environmental performance continually
■ Implement a systematic approach to setting and achieving environmental objectives and targets, and then demonstrating that they have been achieved.

Further details are available at www.iso.org

B.8 ISO STANDARDS AND PUBLICATIONS FOR IT

ISO 9241 is a series of standards and guidance on the ergonomics of human system interaction that cover people working with computers. It covers aspects that impact the utility of a service (whether it is fit for purpose) such as:

■ ISO 9241-11:1999 Guidance on usability
■ ISO 9241-210:2010 Human-centred design for interactive systems
■ ISO 9241-151:2008 Guidance on world wide web user interfaces.

ISO/IEC JTC1 is Joint Technical Committee 1 of ISO and the International Electrotechnical Commission

(IEC). It deals with information technology standards and other publications.

SC27 is a subcommittee under ISO/IEC JTC1 that develops ISO/IEC 27000, the information security management system (ISMS) family of standards. For further details, Appendix E in *ITIL Service Strategy* includes information on ISO/IEC 27001. SC7 is a subcommittee under ISO/IEC JTC1 that covers the standardization of processes, supporting tools and supporting technologies for the engineering of systems, services and software. SC7 publications include:

■ ISO/IEC 20000 Information technology – service management (see section B.6)
■ ISO/IEC 19770-1 Information technology – software asset management processes. ISO/IEC 19770-2:2009 establishes specifications for tagging software to optimize its identification and management
■ ISO/IEC 15288 Systems and software engineering – systems life cycle processes. The processes can be used as a basis for establishing business environments – e.g. methods, procedures, techniques, tools and trained personnel
■ ISO/IEC 12207 Systems and software engineering – software life cycle processes
■ ISO/IEC 15504 Process assessment series. Also known as SPICE (software process improvement and capability determination), it aims to ensure consistency and repeatability of the assessment ratings with evidence to substantiate the ratings. The series includes exemplar process assessment models (PAM), related to one or more conformant or compliant process reference model (PRM). ISO/IEC 15504-8 is an exemplar process assessment model for IT service management that is under development

- ISO/IEC 25000 series – provides guidance for the use of standards named Software product Quality Requirements and Evaluation (SQuaRE)
- ISO/IEC 42010 Systems and software engineering – recommended practice for architectural description of software-intensive systems.

SC7 is working on the harmonization of standards in the service management, software and IT systems domains. Further details are available at www.iso.org

B.9 ITIL AND THE OSI FRAMEWORK

At around the time that ITIL V1 was being written, the International Standards Organization launched an initiative that resulted in the Open Systems Interconnection (OSI) framework. Since this initiative covered many of the same areas as ITIL V1, it is not surprising that there was considerable overlap.

However, it is also not surprising that they classified their processes differently, used different terminology, or used the same terminology in different ways. To confuse matters even more, it is common for different groups in an organization to use terminology from both ITIL and the OSI framework.

The OSI framework made significant contributions to the definition and execution of ITSM programmes and projects around the world. It has also caused a great deal of debate between teams that do not realize the origins of the terminology that they are using. For example, some organizations have two change management departments – one following the ITIL change management process and the other using the OSI installation, moves, additions and changes

(IMAC) model. Each department is convinced that it is completely different from the other, and that it is performing a different role. Closer examination will reveal that there are several areas of commonality.

In service operation, the management of known errors may be mapped to fault management. There is also a section related to operational capacity management, which can be related to the OSI concept of performance management.

Information on the set of ISO standards for the OSI framework is available at: www.iso.org

B.10 PROGRAMME AND PROJECT MANAGEMENT

Large, complex deliveries are often broken down into manageable, interrelated projects. For those managing this overall delivery, the principles of programme management are key to delivering on time and within budget. Best management practice in this area is found in *Managing Successful Programmes* (MSP).

Guidance on effective portfolio, programme and project management is brought together in *Portfolio, Programme and Project Offices* (P3O), which is aimed at helping organizations to establish and maintain appropriate business support structures with proven roles and responsibilities.

Structured project management methods, such as PRINCE2 (PRojects IN Controlled Environments) or the Project Management Body of Knowledge (PMBOK) developed by the Project Management Institute (PMI), can be used when improving IT services. Not all improvements will require a structured project approach, but many will, due to the sheer scope and scale of the improvement. Project management is discussed in more detail in *ITIL Service Transition*.

Visit www.msp-officialsite.com for more information on MSP.

Visit www.p3o-officialsite.com for more information on P3O.

Visit www.prince-officialsite.com for more information on PRINCE2.

Visit www.pmi.org for more information on PMI and PMBOK.

See also the following publications:

■ Cleland, David I. and Ireland, Lewis R. (2006). *Project Management: Strategic Design and Implementation* (5th edition). McGraw-Hill Professional.
■ Haugan, Gregory T. (2006). *Project Management Fundamentals.* Management Concepts.
■ Office of Government Commerce (2009). *Managing Successful Projects with PRINCE2.* TSO, London.
■ Cabinet Office (2011). *Managing Successful Programmes.* TSO, London.
■ Office of Government Commerce (2008). Portfolio, *Programme and Project Offices.* TSO, London.
■ The Project Management Institute (2008). *A Guide to the Project Management Body of Knowledge* (PMBOK Guide) (4th edition). Project Management Institute.

B.11 ORGANIZATIONAL CHANGE

There is a wide range of publications that cover organizational change including the related

guidance for programme and project management referred to in the previous section.

Chapter 5 in *ITIL Service Transition* covers aspects of organizational change elements that are an essential part of, or a strong contributor towards, service transition. *ITIL Service Transition* and *ITIL Continual Service Improvement* refer to Kotter's 'eight steps for organizational change'.

Visit www.johnkotter.com for more information. See also the following publications:

■ Kotter, John P. (1996). *Leading Change.* Harvard Business School Press.
■ Kotter, John P. (1999). *What Leaders Really Do.* Harvard Business School Press.
■ Kotter, J. P. (2000). Leading change: why transformation efforts fail. *Harvard Business Review* January–February.
■ Kotter, John P. and Cohen, Dan S. (2002). *The Heart of Change: Real-Life Stories of How People Change their Organizations.* Harvard Business School Press.
■ Kotter, J. P. and Schlesinger, L. C. (1979). Choosing strategies for change. *Harvard Business Review* Vol. 57, No. 2, p.106.
■ Kotter, John P., Rathgeber, Holger, Mueller, Peter and Johnson, Spenser (2006). *Our Iceberg Is Melting: Changing and Succeeding Under Any Conditions.* St. Martin's Press.

B.12 SKILLS FRAMEWORK FOR THE INFORMATION AGE

The Skills Framework for the Information Age (SFIA) enables employers of IT professionals to carry out a range of human resource activities against a common framework including a skills audit, planning future skill requirements, development programmes, standardization of job titles and functions, and resource allocation.

SFIA provides a standardized view of the wide range of professional skills needed by people working in IT. SFIA is constructed as a simple two-dimensional matrix consisting of areas of work on one axis and levels of responsibility on the other. It uses a common language and a sensible, logical structure that can be adapted to the training and development needs of a very wide range of businesses.

Visit www.sfia.org.uk for further details.

B.13 CARNEGIE MELLON: CMMI AND eSCM FRAMEWORK

The Capability Maturity Model Integration (CMMI) is a process improvement approach developed by the Software Engineering Institute (SEI) of Carnegie Mellon University. CMMI provides organizations with the essential elements of effective processes. It can be used to guide process improvement across a project, a division or an entire organization. CMMI helps integrate traditionally separate organizational functions, sets process improvement goals and priorities, provides guidance for quality processes, and suggests a point of reference for appraising current processes. There are several CMMI models covering different domains of application.

The eSourcing Capability Model for Service Providers (eSCM-SP) is a framework developed by ITSqc at Carnegie Mellon to improve the relationship between IT service providers and their customers.

Organizations can be assessed against CMMI models using SCAMPI (Standard CMMI Appraisal Method for Process Improvement).

For more information, see www.sei.cmu.edu/cmmi/

B.14 BALANCED SCORECARD

A new approach to strategic management was developed in the early 1990s by Drs Robert Kaplan (Harvard Business School) and David Norton. They named this system the 'balanced scorecard'. Recognizing some of the weaknesses and vagueness of previous management approaches, the balanced scorecard approach provides a clear prescription as to what companies should measure in order to 'balance' the financial perspective. The balanced scorecard suggests that the organization be viewed from four perspectives, and it is valuable to develop metrics, collect data and analyse the organization relative to each of these perspectives:

- The learning and growth perspective
- The business process perspective
- The customer perspective
- The financial perspective.

Some organizations may choose to use the balanced scorecard method as a way of assessing and reporting their IT quality performance in general and their service operation performance in particular.

Further details are available through the balanced scorecard user community at www.scorecardsupport.com

B.15 SIX SIGMA

Six Sigma is a data-driven process improvement approach that supports continual improvement. It is business-output-driven in relation to customer specification. The objective is to implement a measurement-oriented strategy focused on process improvement and defects reduction. A Six Sigma defect is defined as anything outside customer specifications.

Six Sigma focuses on dramatically reducing process variation using statistical process control (SPC) measures. The fundamental objective is to reduce errors to fewer than 3.4 defects per million executions (regardless of the process). Service providers must determine whether it is reasonable to expect delivery at a Six Sigma level given the wide variation in IT deliverables, roles and tasks within IT operational environments.

There are two primary sub-methodologies within Six Sigma: DMAIC (Define, Measure, Analyse, Improve, Control) and DMADV (Define, Measure, Analyse, Design, Verify). DMAIC is an improvement method for existing processes for which performance does not meet expectations, or for which incremental improvements are desired. DMADV focuses on the creation of new processes. For more information, see:

- George, Michael L. (2003). *Lean Six Sigma for Service: How to Use Lean Speed and Six Sigma Quality to Improve Services and Transactions.* McGraw-Hill.
- Pande, Pete and Holpp, Larry (2001). *What Is Six Sigma?* McGraw-Hill.
- Pande, Peter S., Neuman, Robert P. and Cavanagh, Roland R. (2000). *The Six Sigma Way: How GE, Motorola, and Other Top Companies are Honing their Performance.* McGraw-Hill.

Abbreviations
and glossary

Abbreviations

ACD	automatic call distribution		DIKW	Data-to-Information-to-Knowledge-to-Wisdom
AM	availability management		DML	definitive media library
AMIS	availability management information system		ECAB	emergency change advisory board
ASP	application service provider		ELS	early life support
AST	agreed service time		eSCM-CL	eSourcing Capability Model for Client Organizations
BCM	business continuity management		eSCM-SP	eSourcing Capability Model for Service Providers
BCP	business continuity plan		FTA	fault tree analysis
BIA	business impact analysis		IRR	internal rate of return
BMP	Best Management Practice		ISG	IT steering group
BRM	business relationship manager		ISM	information security management
BSI	British Standards Institution		ISMS	information security management system
CAB	change advisory board		ISO	International Organization for Standardization
CAPEX	capital expenditure		ISP	internet service provider
CCM	component capacity management		IT	information technology
CFIA	component failure impact analysis		ITSCM	IT service continuity management
CI	configuration item		ITSM	IT service management
CMDB	configuration management database		itSMF	IT Service Management Forum
CMIS	capacity management information system		IVR	interactive voice response
CMM	capability maturity model		KEDB	known error database
CMMI	Capability Maturity Model Integration		KPI	key performance indicator
CMS	configuration management system		LOS	line of service
COBIT	Control OBjectives for Information and related Technology		MIS	management information system
COTS	commercial off the shelf		M_o_R	Management of Risk
CSF	critical success factor		MTBF	mean time between failures
CSI	continual service improvement			
CTI	computer telephony integration			

MTBSI	mean time between service incidents	SDP	service design package
MTRS	mean time to restore service	SFA	service failure analysis
MTTR	mean time to repair	SIP	service improvement plan
NPV	net present value	SKMS	service knowledge management system
OLA	operational level agreement	SLA	service level agreement
OPEX	operational expenditure	SLM	service level management
PBA	pattern of business activity	SLP	service level package
PDCA	Plan-Do-Check-Act	SLR	service level requirement
PFS	prerequisite for success	SMART	specific, measurable, achievable, relevant and time-bound
PIR	post-implementation review		
PMBOK	Project Management Body of Knowledge	SMIS	security management information system
PMI	Project Management Institute	SMO	service maintenance objective
PMO	project management office	SoC	separation of concerns
PRINCE2	PRojects IN Controlled Environments	SOP	standard operating procedure
PSO	projected service outage	SOR	statement of requirements
QA	quality assurance	SOX	Sarbanes-Oxley (US law)
QMS	quality management system	SPI	service provider interface
RACI	responsible, accountable, consulted and informed	SPM	service portfolio management
		SPOF	single point of failure
RCA	root cause analysis	TCO	total cost of ownership
RFC	request for change	TCU	total cost of utilization
ROA	return on assets	TO	technical observation
ROI	return on investment	TOR	terms of reference
RPO	recovery point objective	TQM	total quality management
RTO	recovery time objective	UC	underpinning contract
SAC	service acceptance criteria	UP	user profile
SACM	service asset and configuration management	VBF	vital business function
SAM	software asset management	VOI	value on investment
SCM	service capacity management	WIP	work in progress
SCMIS	supplier and contract management information system		

Glossary

The core ITIL publications (*ITIL Service Strategy*, *ITIL Service Design*, *ITIL Service Operation*, *ITIL Service Transition*, *ITIL Continual Service Improvement*) referred to in parentheses at the beginning of a definition indicate where a reader can find more information. Terms without such a reference may either be used generically across all five core publications, or simply may not be explained in any greater detail elsewhere in the ITIL series. In other words, readers are only directed to other sources where they can expect to expand on their knowledge or to see a greater context.

acceptance

Formal agreement that an IT service, process, plan or other deliverable is complete, accurate, reliable and meets its specified requirements. Acceptance is usually preceded by change evaluation or testing and is often required before proceeding to the next stage of a project or process. *See also* service acceptance criteria.

access management

(*ITIL Service Operation*) The process responsible for allowing users to make use of IT services, data or other assets. Access management helps to protect the confidentiality, integrity and availability of assets by ensuring that only authorized users are able to access or modify them. Access management implements the policies of information security management and is sometimes referred to as rights management or identity management.

account manager

(*ITIL Service Strategy*) A role that is very similar to that of the business relationship manager, but includes more commercial aspects. Most commonly used by Type III service providers when dealing with external customers.

accounting

(*ITIL Service Strategy*) The process responsible for identifying the actual costs of delivering IT services, comparing these with budgeted costs, and managing variance from the budget.

accounting period

(*ITIL Service Strategy*) A period of time (usually one year) for which budgets, charges, depreciation and other financial calculations are made. *See also* financial year.

accredited

Officially authorized to carry out a role. For example, an accredited body may be authorized to provide training or to conduct audits.

active monitoring

(*ITIL Service Operation*) Monitoring of a configuration item or an IT service that uses automated regular checks to discover the current status. *See also* passive monitoring.

activity

A set of actions designed to achieve a particular result. Activities are usually defined as part of processes or plans, and are documented in procedures.

agreed service time (AST)

(*ITIL Service Design*) A synonym for service hours, commonly used in formal calculations of availability. *See also* downtime.

agreement

A document that describes a formal understanding between two or more parties. An agreement is not legally binding, unless it forms part of a contract. *See also* operational level agreement; service level agreement.

alert

(ITIL Service Operation) A notification that a threshold has been reached, something has changed, or a failure has occurred. Alerts are often created and managed by system management tools and are managed by the event management process.

analytical modelling

(ITIL Continual Service Improvement) (ITIL Service Design) (ITIL Service Strategy) A technique that uses mathematical models to predict the behaviour of IT services or other configuration items. Analytical models are commonly used in capacity management and availability management. *See also* modelling; simulation modelling.

application

Software that provides functions which are required by an IT service. Each application may be part of more than one IT service. An application runs on one or more servers or clients. *See also* application management; application portfolio.

application management

(ITIL Service Operation) The function responsible for managing applications throughout their lifecycle.

application portfolio

(ITIL Service Design) A database or structured document used to manage applications throughout their lifecycle. The application portfolio contains key attributes of all applications. The application portfolio is sometimes implemented as part of the service portfolio, or as part of the configuration management system.

application service provider (ASP)

(ITIL Service Design) An external service provider that provides IT services using applications running at the service provider's premises. Users access the applications by network connections to the service provider.

application sizing

(ITIL Service Design) The activity responsible for understanding the resource requirements needed to support a new application, or a major change to an existing application. Application sizing helps to ensure that the IT service can meet its agreed service level targets for capacity and performance.

architecture

(ITIL Service Design) The structure of a system or IT service, including the relationships of components to each other and to the environment they are in. Architecture also includes the standards and guidelines that guide the design and evolution of the system.

assembly

(ITIL Service Transition) A configuration item that is made up of a number of other CIs. For example, a server CI may contain CIs for CPUs, disks, memory etc.; an IT service CI may contain many hardware, software and other CIs. *See also* build; component CI.

assessment

Inspection and analysis to check whether a standard or set of guidelines is being followed, that records are accurate, or that efficiency and effectiveness targets are being met. *See also* audit.

asset

(ITIL Service Strategy) Any resource or capability. The assets of a service provider include anything that could contribute to the delivery of a service. Assets can be one of the following types: management, organization, process, knowledge, people, information, applications,

infrastructure or financial capital. *See also* customer asset; service asset; strategic asset.

asset management

(ITIL Service Transition) A generic activity or process responsible for tracking and reporting the value and ownership of assets throughout their lifecycle. *See also* service asset and configuration management; fixed asset management; software asset management.

asset register

(ITIL Service Transition) A list of fixed assets that includes their ownership and value. *See also* fixed asset management.

asset specificity

(ITIL Service Strategy) One or more attributes of an asset that make it particularly useful for a given purpose. Asset specificity may limit the use of the asset for other purposes.

attribute

(ITIL Service Transition) A piece of information about a configuration item. Examples are name, location, version number and cost. Attributes of CIs are recorded in a configuration management database (CMDB) and maintained as part of a configuration management system (CMS). *See also* relationship; configuration management system.

audit

Formal inspection and verification to check whether a standard or set of guidelines is being followed, that records are accurate, or that efficiency and effectiveness targets are being met. An audit may be carried out by internal or external groups. *See also* assessment; certification.

authority matrix

See RACI.

automatic call distribution (ACD)

(ITIL Service Operation) Use of information technology to direct an incoming telephone call to the most appropriate person in the shortest possible time. ACD is sometimes called automated call distribution.

availability

(ITIL Service Design) Ability of an IT service or other configuration item to perform its agreed function when required. Availability is determined by reliability, maintainability, serviceability, performance and security. Availability is usually calculated as a percentage. This calculation is often based on agreed service time and downtime. It is best practice to calculate availability of an IT service using measurements of the business output.

availability management (AM)

(ITIL Service Design) The process responsible for ensuring that IT services meet the current and future availability needs of the business in a cost-effective and timely manner. Availability management defines, analyses, plans, measures and improves all aspects of the availability of IT services, and ensures that all IT infrastructures, processes, tools, roles etc. are appropriate for the agreed service level targets for availability. *See also* availability management information system.

availability management information system (AMIS)

(ITIL Service Design) A set of tools, data and information that is used to support availability management. *See also* service knowledge management system.

availability plan

(ITIL Service Design) A plan to ensure that existing and future availability requirements for IT services can be provided cost-effectively.

back-out

(ITIL Service Transition) An activity that restores a service or other configuration item to a previous baseline. Back-out is used as a form of remediation when a change or release is not successful.

backup

(ITIL Service Design) (ITIL Service Operation) Copying data to protect against loss of integrity or availability of the original.

balanced scorecard

(ITIL Continual Service Improvement) A management tool developed by Drs Robert Kaplan (Harvard Business School) and David Norton. A balanced scorecard enables a strategy to be broken down into key performance indicators. Performance against the KPIs is used to demonstrate how well the strategy is being achieved. A balanced scorecard has four major areas, each of which has a small number of KPIs. The same four areas are considered at different levels of detail throughout the organization.

baseline

(ITIL Continual Service Improvement) (ITIL Service Transition) A snapshot that is used as a reference point. Many snapshots may be taken and recorded over time but only some will be used as baselines. For example:

- An ITSM baseline can be used as a starting point to measure the effect of a service improvement plan
- A performance baseline can be used to measure changes in performance over the lifetime of an IT service
- A configuration baseline can be used as part of a back-out plan to enable the IT infrastructure to be restored to a known configuration if a change or release fails.

See also benchmark.

benchmark

(ITIL Continual Service Improvement) (ITIL Service Transition) A baseline that is used to compare related data sets as part of a benchmarking exercise. For example, a recent snapshot of a process can be compared to a previous baseline of that process, or a current baseline can be compared to industry data or best practice. *See also* benchmarking; baseline.

benchmarking

(ITIL Continual Service Improvement) The process responsible for comparing a benchmark with related data sets such as a more recent snapshot, industry data or best practice. The term is also used to mean creating a series of benchmarks over time, and comparing the results to measure progress or improvement. This process is not described in detail within the core ITIL publications.

Best Management Practice (BMP)

The Best Management Practice portfolio is owned by the Cabinet Office, part of HM Government. Formerly owned by CCTA and then OGC, the BMP functions moved to the Cabinet Office in June 2010. The BMP portfolio includes guidance on IT service management and project, programme, risk, portfolio and value management. There is also a management maturity model as well as related glossaries of terms.

best practice

Proven activities or processes that have been successfully used by multiple organizations. ITIL is an example of best practice.

billing

(ITIL Service Strategy) Part of the charging process. Billing is the activity responsible for producing an invoice or a bill and recovering the money from customers. *See also* pricing.

brainstorming

(ITIL Service Design) (ITIL Service Operation) A technique that helps a team to generate ideas. Ideas are not reviewed during the brainstorming session, but at a later stage. Brainstorming is often used by problem management to identify possible causes.

British Standards Institution (BSI)

The UK national standards body, responsible for creating and maintaining British standards. See www.bsi-global.com for more information. *See also* International Organization for Standardization.

budget

A list of all the money an organization or business unit plans to receive, and plans to pay out, over a specified period of time. *See also* budgeting; planning.

budgeting

The activity of predicting and controlling the spending of money. Budgeting consists of a periodic negotiation cycle to set future budgets (usually annual) and the day-to-day monitoring and adjusting of current budgets.

build

(ITIL Service Transition) The activity of assembling a number of configuration items to create part of an IT service. The term is also used to refer to a release that is authorized for distribution – for example, server build or laptop build. *See also* configuration baseline.

build environment

(ITIL Service Transition) A controlled environment where applications, IT services and other builds are assembled prior to being moved into a test or live environment.

business

(ITIL Service Strategy) An overall corporate entity or organization formed of a number of business units. In the context of ITSM, the term includes public sector and not-for-profit organizations, as well as companies. An IT service provider provides IT services to a customer within a business. The IT service provider may be part of the same business as its customer (internal service provider), or part of another business (external service provider).

business capacity management

(ITIL Continual Service Improvement) (ITIL Service Design) In the context of ITSM, business capacity management is the sub-process of capacity management responsible for understanding future business requirements for use in the capacity plan. *See also* service capacity management; component capacity management.

business case

(ITIL Service Strategy) Justification for a significant item of expenditure. The business case includes information about costs, benefits, options, issues, risks and possible problems. *See also* cost benefit analysis.

business continuity management (BCM)

(ITIL Service Design) The business process responsible for managing risks that could seriously affect the business. Business continuity management safeguards the interests of key stakeholders, reputation, brand and value-creating activities. The process involves reducing risks to an acceptable level and planning for the recovery of business processes should a disruption to the business occur. Business continuity management sets the objectives, scope and requirements for IT service continuity management.

business continuity plan (BCP)

(ITIL Service Design) A plan defining the steps required to restore business processes following a disruption. The plan also identifies the triggers for invocation, people to be involved, communications etc. IT service continuity plans form a significant part of business continuity plans.

business customer

(ITIL Service Strategy) A recipient of a product or a service from the business. For example, if the business is a car manufacturer, then the business customer is someone who buys a car.

business impact analysis (BIA)

(ITIL Service Strategy) Business impact analysis is the activity in business continuity management that identifies vital business functions and their dependencies. These dependencies may include suppliers, people, other business processes, IT services etc. Business impact analysis defines the recovery requirements for IT services. These requirements include recovery time objectives, recovery point objectives and minimum service level targets for each IT service.

business objective

(ITIL Service Strategy) The objective of a business process, or of the business as a whole. Business objectives support the business vision, provide guidance for the IT strategy, and are often supported by IT services.

business operations

(ITIL Service Strategy) The day-to-day execution, monitoring and management of business processes.

business perspective

(ITIL Continual Service Improvement) An understanding of the service provider and IT services from the point of view of the business, and an understanding of the business from the point of view of the service provider.

business process

A process that is owned and carried out by the business. A business process contributes to the delivery of a product or service to a business customer. For example, a retailer may have a purchasing process that helps to deliver services to its business customers. Many business processes rely on IT services.

business relationship management

(ITIL Service Strategy) The process responsible for maintaining a positive relationship with customers. Business relationship management identifies customer needs and ensures that the service provider is able to meet these needs with an appropriate catalogue of services. This process has strong links with service level management.

business relationship manager (BRM)

(ITIL Service Strategy) A role responsible for maintaining the relationship with one or more customers. This role is often combined with the service level manager role.

business service

A service that is delivered to business customers by business units. For example, delivery of financial services to customers of a bank, or goods to the customers of a retail store. Successful delivery of business services often depends on one or more IT services. A business service may consist almost entirely of an IT service – for example, an online banking service or an external website where product orders can be placed by business customers. *See also* customer-facing service.

business service management

The management of business services delivered to business customers. Business service management is performed by business units.

business unit

(ITIL Service Strategy) A segment of the business that has its own plans, metrics, income and costs. Each business unit owns assets and uses these to create value for customers in the form of goods and services.

call

(ITIL Service Operation) A telephone call to the service desk from a user. A call could result in an incident or a service request being logged.

call centre

(ITIL Service Operation) An organization or business unit that handles large numbers of incoming and outgoing telephone calls. *See also* service desk.

call type

(ITIL Service Operation) A category that is used to distinguish incoming requests to a service desk. Common call types are incident, service request and complaint.

capability

(ITIL Service Strategy) The ability of an organization, person, process, application, IT service or other configuration item to carry out an activity. Capabilities are intangible assets of an organization. *See also* resource.

Capability Maturity Model Integration (CMMI)

(ITIL Continual Service Improvement) A process improvement approach developed by the Software Engineering Institute (SEI) of Carnegie Mellon University, US. CMMI provides organizations with the essential elements of effective processes. It can be used to guide process improvement across a project, a division or an entire organization. CMMI helps integrate traditionally separate organizational functions, set process improvement goals and priorities, provide guidance for quality processes, and provide a point of reference for appraising current processes. See www.sei.cmu.edu/cmmi for more information. *See also* maturity.

capacity

(ITIL Service Design) The maximum throughput that a configuration item or IT service can deliver. For some types of CI, capacity may be the size or volume – for example, a disk drive.

capacity management

(ITIL Continual Service Improvement) (ITIL Service Design) The process responsible for ensuring that the capacity of IT services and the IT infrastructure is able to meet agreed capacity- and performance-related requirements in a cost-effective and timely manner. Capacity management considers all resources required to deliver an IT service, and is concerned with meeting both the current and future capacity and performance needs of the business. Capacity management includes three sub-processes: business capacity management, service capacity management, and component capacity management. *See also* capacity management information system.

capacity management information system (CMIS)

(ITIL Service Design) A set of tools, data and information that is used to support capacity management. *See also* service knowledge management system.

capacity plan

(ITIL Service Design) A plan used to manage the resources required to deliver IT services. The plan contains details of current and historic usage of IT services and components, and any issues that need to be addressed (including related improvement activities). The plan also contains scenarios for different predictions of business demand and costed options to deliver the agreed service level targets.

capacity planning

(ITIL Service Design) The activity within capacity management responsible for creating a capacity plan.

capital budgeting

(ITIL Service Strategy) The present commitment of funds in order to receive a return in the future in the form of additional cash inflows or reduced cash outflows.

capital cost

(ITIL Service Strategy) The cost of purchasing something that will become a financial asset – for example, computer equipment and buildings. The value of the asset depreciates over multiple accounting periods. *See also* operational cost.

capital expenditure (CAPEX)

See capital cost.

capitalization

(ITIL Service Strategy) Identifying major cost as capital, even though no asset is purchased. This is done to spread the impact of the cost over multiple accounting periods. The most common example of this is software development, or purchase of a software licence.

category

A named group of things that have something in common. Categories are used to group similar things together. For example, cost types are used to group similar types of cost. Incident categories are used to group similar types of incident, while CI types are used to group similar types of configuration item.

certification

Issuing a certificate to confirm compliance to a standard. Certification includes a formal audit by an independent and accredited body. The term is also used to mean awarding a certificate to provide evidence that a person has achieved a qualification.

change

(ITIL Service Transition) The addition, modification or removal of anything that could have an effect on IT services. The scope should include changes to all architectures, processes, tools, metrics and documentation, as well as changes to IT services and other configuration items.

change advisory board (CAB)

(ITIL Service Transition) A group of people that support the assessment, prioritization, authorization and scheduling of changes. A change advisory board is usually made up of representatives from: all areas within the IT service provider; the business; and third parties such as suppliers.

change evaluation

(ITIL Service Transition) The process responsible for formal assessment of a new or changed IT service to ensure that risks have been managed and to help determine whether to authorize the change.

change history

(ITIL Service Transition) Information about all changes made to a configuration item during its life. Change history consists of all those change records that apply to the CI.

change management

(ITIL Service Transition) The process responsible for controlling the lifecycle of all changes, enabling beneficial changes to be made with minimum disruption to IT services.

change model

(ITIL Service Transition) A repeatable way of dealing with a particular category of change. A change model defines specific agreed steps that will be followed for a change of this category. Change models may be very complex with many steps that require authorization (e.g.

major software release) or may be very simple with no requirement for authorization (e.g. password reset). *See also* change advisory board; standard change.

change proposal

(ITIL Service Strategy) (ITIL Service Transition) A document that includes a high level description of a potential service introduction or significant change, along with a corresponding business case and an expected implementation schedule. Change proposals are normally created by the service portfolio management process and are passed to change management for authorization. Change management will review the potential impact on other services, on shared resources, and on the overall change schedule. Once the change proposal has been authorized, service portfolio management will charter the service.

change record

(ITIL Service Transition) A record containing the details of a change. Each change record documents the lifecycle of a single change. A change record is created for every request for change that is received, even those that are subsequently rejected. Change records should reference the configuration items that are affected by the change. Change records may be stored in the configuration management system, or elsewhere in the service knowledge management system.

change request

See request for change.

change schedule

(ITIL Service Transition) A document that lists all authorized changes and their planned implementation dates, as well as the estimated dates of longer-term changes. A change schedule is sometimes called a forward schedule of change, even though it also contains information about changes that have already been implemented.

change window

(ITIL Service Transition) A regular, agreed time when changes or releases may be implemented with minimal impact on services. Change windows are usually documented in service level agreements.

chargeable item

(ITIL Service Strategy) A deliverable of an IT service that is used in calculating charges to customers (for example, number of transactions, number of desktop PCs).

charging

(ITIL Service Strategy) Requiring payment for IT services. Charging for IT services is optional, and many organizations choose to treat their IT service provider as a cost centre. *See also* charging process; charging policy.

charging policy

(ITIL Service Strategy) A policy specifying the objective of the charging process and the way in which charges will be calculated. *See also* cost.

charging process

(ITIL Service Strategy) The process responsible for deciding how much customers should pay (pricing) and recovering money from them (billing). This process is not described in detail within the core ITIL publications.

charter

(ITIL Service Strategy) A document that contains details of a new service, a significant change or other significant project. Charters are typically authorized by service portfolio management or by a project management office. The term charter is also used to describe the act of authorizing the work required to complete the service change or project. *See also* change proposal; service charter; project portfolio.

chronological analysis

(ITIL Service Operation) A technique used to help identify possible causes of problems. All available data about the problem is collected and sorted by date and time to provide a detailed timeline. This can make it possible to identify which events may have been triggered by others.

CI type

(ITIL Service Transition) A category that is used to classify configuration items. The CI type identifies the required attributes and relationships for a configuration record. Common CI types include hardware, document, user etc.

classification

The act of assigning a category to something. Classification is used to ensure consistent management and reporting. Configuration items, incidents, problems, changes etc. are usually classified.

client

A generic term that means a customer, the business or a business customer. For example, client manager may be used as a synonym for business relationship manager. The term is also used to mean:

- A computer that is used directly by a user – for example, a PC, a handheld computer or a work station
- The part of a client server application that the user directly interfaces with – for example, an email client.

closed

(ITIL Service Operation) The final status in the lifecycle of an incident, problem, change etc. When the status is closed, no further action is taken.

closure

(ITIL Service Operation) The act of changing the status of an incident, problem, change etc. to closed.

COBIT

(ITIL Continual Service Improvement) Control OBjectives for Information and related Technology (COBIT) provides guidance and best practice for the management of IT processes. COBIT is published by ISACA in conjunction with the IT Governance Institute (ITGI). See www.isaca.org for more information.

code of practice

A guideline published by a public body or a standards organization, such as ISO or BSI. Many standards consist of a code of practice and a specification. The code of practice describes recommended best practice.

cold standby

See gradual recovery.

commercial off the shelf (COTS)

(ITIL Service Design) Pre-existing application software or middleware that can be purchased from a third party.

compliance

Ensuring that a standard or set of guidelines is followed, or that proper, consistent accounting or other practices are being employed.

component

A general term that is used to mean one part of something more complex. For example, a computer system may be a component of an IT service; an application may be a component of a release unit. Components that need to be managed should be configuration items.

component capacity management (CCM)

(ITIL Continual Service Improvement) *(ITIL Service Design)* The sub-process of capacity management responsible for understanding the capacity, utilization and performance of configuration items. Data is collected, recorded and

analysed for use in the capacity plan. *See also* business capacity management; service capacity management.

component CI

(ITIL Service Transition) A configuration item that is part of an assembly. For example, a CPU or memory CI may be part of a server CI.

component failure impact analysis (CFIA)

(ITIL Service Design) A technique that helps to identify the impact of configuration item failure on IT services and the business. A matrix is created with IT services on one axis and CIs on the other. This enables the identification of critical CIs (that could cause the failure of multiple IT services) and fragile IT services (that have multiple single points of failure).

computer telephony integration (CTI)

(ITIL Service Operation) Computer telephony integration is a general term covering any kind of integration between computers and telephone systems. It is most commonly used to refer to systems where an application displays detailed screens relating to incoming or outgoing telephone calls. *See also* automatic call distribution; interactive voice response.

concurrency

A measure of the number of users engaged in the same operation at the same time.

confidentiality

(ITIL Service Design) A security principle that requires that data should only be accessed by authorized people.

configuration

(ITIL Service Transition) A generic term used to describe a group of configuration items that work together to deliver an IT service, or a recognizable part of an IT service. Configuration is also used to describe the parameter settings for one or more configuration items.

configuration baseline

(ITIL Service Transition) The baseline of a configuration that has been formally agreed and is managed through the change management process. A configuration baseline is used as a basis for future builds, releases and changes.

configuration control

(ITIL Service Transition) The activity responsible for ensuring that adding, modifying or removing a configuration item is properly managed – for example, by submitting a request for change or service request.

configuration identification

(ITIL Service Transition) The activity responsible for collecting information about configuration items and their relationships, and loading this information into the configuration management database. Configuration identification is also responsible for labelling the configuration items themselves, so that the corresponding configuration records can be found.

configuration item (CI)

(ITIL Service Transition) Any component or other service asset that needs to be managed in order to deliver an IT service. Information about each configuration item is recorded in a configuration record within the configuration management system and is maintained throughout its lifecycle by service asset and configuration management. Configuration items are under the control of change management. They typically include IT services, hardware, software, buildings, people and formal documentation such as process documentation and service level agreements.

configuration management

See service asset and configuration management.

configuration management database (CMDB)

(ITIL Service Transition) A database used to store configuration records throughout their lifecycle. The configuration management system maintains one or more configuration management databases, and each database stores attributes of configuration items, and relationships with other configuration items.

configuration management system (CMS)

(ITIL Service Transition) A set of tools, data and information that is used to support service asset and configuration management. The CMS is part of an overall service knowledge management system and includes tools for collecting, storing, managing, updating, analysing and presenting data about all configuration items and their relationships. The CMS may also include information about incidents, problems, known errors, changes and releases. The CMS is maintained by service asset and configuration management and is used by all IT service management processes. *See also* configuration management database.

configuration record

(ITIL Service Transition) A record containing the details of a configuration item. Each configuration record documents the lifecycle of a single configuration item. Configuration records are stored in a configuration management database and maintained as part of a configuration management system.

configuration structure

(ITIL Service Transition) The hierarchy and other relationships between all the configuration items that comprise a configuration.

continual service improvement (CSI)

(ITIL Continual Service Improvement) A stage in the lifecycle of a service. Continual service improvement ensures that services are aligned with changing business needs by identifying and implementing improvements to IT services that support business processes. The performance of the IT service provider is continually measured and improvements are made to processes, IT services and IT infrastructure in order to increase efficiency, effectiveness and cost effectiveness. Continual service improvement includes the seven-step improvement process. Although this process is associated with continual service improvement, most processes have activities that take place across multiple stages of the service lifecycle. *See also* Plan-Do-Check-Act.

continuous availability

(ITIL Service Design) An approach or design to achieve 100% availability. A continuously available IT service has no planned or unplanned downtime.

continuous operation

(ITIL Service Design) An approach or design to eliminate planned downtime of an IT service. Note that individual configuration items may be down even though the IT service is available.

contract

A legally binding agreement between two or more parties.

control

A means of managing a risk, ensuring that a business objective is achieved or that a process is followed. Examples of control include policies, procedures, roles, RAID, door locks etc. A control is sometimes called a countermeasure or safeguard. Control also means to manage the utilization or behaviour of a configuration item, system or IT service.

Control OBjectives for Information and related Technology

See COBIT.

control perspective

(ITIL Service Strategy) An approach to the management of IT services, processes, functions, assets etc. There can be several different control perspectives on the same IT service, process etc., allowing different individuals or teams to focus on what is important and relevant to their specific role. Examples of control perspective include reactive and proactive management within IT operations, or a lifecycle view for an application project team.

control processes

The ISO/IEC 20000 process group that includes change management and configuration management.

core service

(ITIL Service Strategy) A service that delivers the basic outcomes desired by one or more customers. A core service provides a specific level of utility and warranty. Customers may be offered a choice of utility and warranty through one or more service options. *See also* enabling service; enhancing service; IT service; service package.

cost

The amount of money spent on a specific activity, IT service or business unit. Costs consist of real cost (money), notional cost (such as people's time) and depreciation.

cost benefit analysis

An activity that analyses and compares the costs and the benefits involved in one or more alternative courses of action. *See also* business case; internal rate of return; net present value; return on investment; value on investment.

cost centre

(ITIL Service Strategy) A business unit or project to which costs are assigned. A cost centre does not charge for services provided. An IT service provider can be run as a cost centre or a profit centre.

cost effectiveness

A measure of the balance between the effectiveness and cost of a service, process or activity. A cost-effective process is one that achieves its objectives at minimum cost. *See also* key performance indicator; return on investment; value for money.

cost element

(ITIL Service Strategy) The middle level of category to which costs are assigned in budgeting and accounting. The highest-level category is cost type. For example, a cost type of 'people' could have cost elements of payroll, staff benefits, expenses, training, overtime etc. Cost elements can be further broken down to give cost units. For example, the cost element 'expenses' could include cost units of hotels, transport, meals etc.

cost management

(ITIL Service Strategy) A general term that is used to refer to budgeting and accounting, and is sometimes used as a synonym for financial management.

cost model

(ITIL Service Strategy) A framework used in budgeting and accounting in which all known costs can be recorded, categorized and allocated to specific customers, business units or projects. *See also* cost type; cost element; cost unit.

cost type

(ITIL Service Strategy) The highest level of category to which costs are assigned in budgeting and accounting – for example, hardware, software, people, accommodation, external and transfer. *See also* cost element; cost unit.

cost unit

(ITIL Service Strategy) The lowest level of category to which costs are assigned; cost units are usually things that can be easily counted (e.g. staff numbers, software licences) or things easily measured (e.g. CPU usage, electricity consumed). Cost units are included within cost elements. For example, a cost element of 'expenses' could include cost units of hotels, transport, meals etc. *See also* cost type.

countermeasure

Can be used to refer to any type of control. The term is most often used when referring to measures that increase resilience, fault tolerance or reliability of an IT service.

course corrections

Changes made to a plan or activity that has already started to ensure that it will meet its objectives. Course corrections are made as a result of monitoring progress.

crisis management

Crisis management is the process responsible for managing the wider implications of business continuity. A crisis management team is responsible for strategic issues such as managing media relations and shareholder confidence, and decides when to invoke business continuity plans.

critical success factor (CSF)

Something that must happen if an IT service, process, plan, project or other activity is to succeed. Key performance indicators are used to measure the achievement of each critical success factor. For example, a critical success factor of 'protect IT services when making changes' could be measured by key performance indicators such as 'percentage reduction of unsuccessful changes', 'percentage reduction in changes causing incidents' etc.

CSI register

(ITIL Continual Service Improvement) A database or structured document used to record and manage improvement opportunities throughout their lifecycle.

culture

A set of values that is shared by a group of people, including expectations about how people should behave, their ideas, beliefs and practices. *See also* vision.

customer

Someone who buys goods or services. The customer of an IT service provider is the person or group who defines and agrees the service level targets. The term is also sometimes used informally to mean user – for example, 'This is a customer-focused organization.'

customer agreement portfolio

(ITIL Service Strategy) A database or structured document used to manage service contracts or agreements between an IT service provider and its customers. Each IT service delivered to a customer should have a contract or other agreement that is listed in the customer agreement portfolio. *See also* customer-facing service; service catalogue; service portfolio.

customer asset

Any resource or capability of a customer. *See also* asset.

customer portfolio

(ITIL Service Strategy) A database or structured document used to record all customers of the IT service provider. The customer portfolio is the business relationship manager's view of the customers who receive services from the IT service provider. *See also* customer agreement portfolio; service catalogue; service portfolio.

customer-facing service

(ITIL Service Design) An IT service that is visible to the customer. These are normally services that support the customer's business processes and facilitate one or more outcomes desired by the customer. All live customer-facing services, including those available for deployment, are recorded in the service catalogue along with customer-visible information about deliverables, prices, contact points, ordering and request processes. Other information such as relationships to supporting services and other CIs will also be recorded for internal use by the IT service provider.

dashboard

(ITIL Service Operation) A graphical representation of overall IT service performance and availability. Dashboard images may be updated in real time, and can also be included in management reports and web pages. Dashboards can be used to support service level management, event management and incident diagnosis.

Data-to-Information-to-Knowledge-to-Wisdom (DIKW)

(ITIL Service Transition) A way of understanding the relationships between data, information, knowledge and wisdom. DIKW shows how each of these builds on the others.

definitive media library (DML)

(ITIL Service Transition) One or more locations in which the definitive and authorized versions of all software configuration items are securely stored. The definitive media library may also contain associated configuration items such as licences and documentation. It is a single logical storage area even if there are multiple locations. The definitive media library is controlled by service asset and configuration management and is recorded in the configuration management system.

deliverable

Something that must be provided to meet a commitment in a service level agreement or a contract. It is also used in a more informal way to mean a planned output of any process.

demand management

(ITIL Service Design) *(ITIL Service Strategy)* The process responsible for understanding, anticipating and influencing customer demand for services. Demand management works with capacity management to ensure that the service provider has sufficient capacity to meet the required demand. At a strategic level, demand management can involve analysis of patterns of business activity and user profiles, while at a tactical level, it can involve the use of differential charging to encourage customers to use IT services at less busy times, or require short-term activities to respond to unexpected demand or the failure of a configuration item.

Deming Cycle

See Plan-Do-Check-Act.

dependency

The direct or indirect reliance of one process or activity on another.

deployment

(ITIL Service Transition) The activity responsible for movement of new or changed hardware, software, documentation, process etc. to the live environment. Deployment is part of the release and deployment management process.

depreciation

(ITIL Service Strategy) A measure of the reduction in value of an asset over its life. This is based on wearing out, consumption or other reduction in the useful economic value.

design

(ITIL Service Design) An activity or process that identifies requirements and then defines a solution that is able to meet these requirements. *See also* service design.

design coordination

(ITIL Service Design) The process responsible for coordinating all service design activities, processes and resources. Design coordination ensures the consistent and effective design of new or changed IT services, service management information systems, architectures, technology, processes, information and metrics.

detection

(ITIL Service Operation) A stage in the expanded incident lifecycle. Detection results in the incident becoming known to the service provider. Detection can be automatic or the result of a user logging an incident.

development

(ITIL Service Design) The process responsible for creating or modifying an IT service or application ready for subsequent release and deployment. Development is also used to mean the role or function that carries out development work. This process is not described in detail within the core ITIL publications.

development environment

(ITIL Service Design) An environment used to create or modify IT services or applications. Development environments are not typically subjected to the same degree of control as test or live environments. *See also* development.

diagnosis

(ITIL Service Operation) A stage in the incident and problem lifecycles. The purpose of diagnosis is to identify a workaround for an incident or the root cause of a problem.

diagnostic script

(ITIL Service Operation) A structured set of questions used by service desk staff to ensure they ask the correct questions, and to help them classify, resolve and assign incidents. Diagnostic scripts may also be made available to users to help them diagnose and resolve their own incidents.

differential charging

A technique used to support demand management by charging different amounts for the same function of an IT service under different circumstances. For example, reduced charges outside peak times, or increased charges for users who exceed a bandwidth allocation.

direct cost

(ITIL Service Strategy) The cost of providing an IT service which can be allocated in full to a specific customer, cost centre, project etc. For example, the cost of providing non-shared servers or software licences. *See also* indirect cost.

directory service

(ITIL Service Operation) An application that manages information about IT infrastructure available on a network, and corresponding user access rights.

document

Information in readable form. A document may be paper or electronic – for example, a policy statement, service level agreement, incident record or diagram of a computer room layout. *See also* record.

downtime

(ITIL Service Design) (ITIL Service Operation) The time when an IT service or other configuration item is not available during its agreed service time. The availability of an IT service is often calculated from agreed service time and downtime.

driver

Something that influences strategy, objectives or requirements – for example, new legislation or the actions of competitors.

early life support (ELS)

(ITIL Service Transition) A stage in the service lifecycle that occurs at the end of deployment and before the service is fully accepted into operation. During early life support, the service provider reviews key performance indicators, service levels and monitoring thresholds and may implement improvements to ensure that service targets can be met. The service provider may also provide additional resources for incident and problem management during this time.

economies of scale

(ITIL Service Strategy) The reduction in average cost that is possible from increasing the usage of an IT service or asset. See also economies of scope.

economies of scope

(ITIL Service Strategy) The reduction in cost that is allocated to an IT service by using an existing asset for an additional purpose. For example, delivering a new IT service from an existing IT infrastructure. See also economies of scale.

effectiveness

(ITIL Continual Service Improvement) A measure of whether the objectives of a process, service or activity have been achieved. An effective process or activity is one that achieves its agreed objectives. See also key performance indicator.

efficiency

(ITIL Continual Service Improvement) A measure of whether the right amount of resource has been used to deliver a process, service or activity. An efficient process achieves its objectives with the minimum amount of

time, money, people or other resources. See also key performance indicator.

emergency change

(ITIL Service Transition) A change that must be introduced as soon as possible – for example, to resolve a major incident or implement a security patch. The change management process will normally have a specific procedure for handling emergency changes. See also emergency change advisory board.

emergency change advisory board (ECAB)

(ITIL Service Transition) A subgroup of the change advisory board that makes decisions about emergency changes. Membership may be decided at the time a meeting is called, and depends on the nature of the emergency change.

enabling service

(ITIL Service Strategy) A service that is needed in order to deliver a core service. Enabling services may or may not be visible to the customer, but they are not offered to customers in their own right. See also enhancing service.

enhancing service

(ITIL Service Strategy) A service that is added to a core service to make it more attractive to the customer. Enhancing services are not essential to the delivery of a core service but are used to encourage customers to use the core service or to differentiate the service provider from its competitors. See also enabling service; excitement factor.

enterprise financial management

(ITIL Service Strategy) The function and processes responsible for managing the overall organization's budgeting, accounting and charging requirements. Enterprise financial management is sometimes referred to as the 'corporate' financial department. See also financial management for IT services.

environment

(ITIL Service Transition) A subset of the IT infrastructure that is used for a particular purpose – for example, live environment, test environment, build environment. Also used in the term 'physical environment' to mean the accommodation, air conditioning, power system etc. Environment is used as a generic term to mean the external conditions that influence or affect something.

error

(ITIL Service Operation) A design flaw or malfunction that causes a failure of one or more IT services or other configuration items. A mistake made by a person or a faulty process that impacts a configuration item is also an error.

escalation

(ITIL Service Operation) An activity that obtains additional resources when these are needed to meet service level targets or customer expectations. Escalation may be needed within any IT service management process, but is most commonly associated with incident management, problem management and the management of customer complaints. There are two types of escalation: functional escalation and hierarchic escalation.

eSourcing Capability Model for Client Organizations (eSCM-CL)

(ITIL Service Strategy) A framework to help organizations in their analysis and decision-making on service-sourcing models and strategies. It was developed by Carnegie Mellon University in the US. *See also* eSourcing Capability Model for Service Providers.

eSourcing Capability Model for Service Providers (eSCM-SP)

(ITIL Service Strategy) A framework to help IT service providers develop their IT service management capabilities from a service sourcing perspective. It was developed by Carnegie Mellon University in the US. *See also* eSourcing Capability Model for Client Organizations.

estimation

The use of experience to provide an approximate value for a metric or cost. Estimation is also used in capacity and availability management as the cheapest and least accurate modelling method.

event

(ITIL Service Operation) A change of state that has significance for the management of an IT service or other configuration item. The term is also used to mean an alert or notification created by any IT service, configuration item or monitoring tool. Events typically require IT operations personnel to take actions, and often lead to incidents being logged.

event management

(ITIL Service Operation) The process responsible for managing events throughout their lifecycle. Event management is one of the main activities of IT operations.

exception report

A document containing details of one or more key performance indicators or other important targets that have exceeded defined thresholds. Examples include service level agreement targets being missed or about to be missed, and a performance metric indicating a potential capacity problem.

excitement attribute

See excitement factor.

excitement factor

(ITIL Service Strategy) An attribute added to something to make it more attractive or more exciting to the customer. For example, a restaurant may provide a free drink with every meal. *See also* enhancing service.

expanded incident lifecycle

(ITIL Continual Service Improvement) (ITIL Service Design) Detailed stages in the lifecycle of an incident. The stages are detection, diagnosis, repair, recovery and restoration. The expanded incident lifecycle is used to help understand all contributions to the impact of incidents and to plan for how these could be controlled or reduced.

external customer

A customer who works for a different business from the IT service provider. *See also* external service provider; internal customer.

external metric

A metric that is used to measure the delivery of IT service to a customer. External metrics are usually defined in service level agreements and reported to customers. *See also* internal metric.

external service provider

(ITIL Service Strategy) An IT service provider that is part of a different organization from its customer. An IT service provider may have both internal and external customers. *See also* outsourcing; Type III service provider.

facilities management

(ITIL Service Operation) The function responsible for managing the physical environment where the IT infrastructure is located. Facilities management includes all aspects of managing the physical environment – for example, power and cooling, building access management, and environmental monitoring.

failure

(ITIL Service Operation) Loss of ability to operate to specification, or to deliver the required output. The term may be used when referring to IT services, processes, activities, configuration items etc. A failure often causes an incident.

fast recovery

(ITIL Service Design) A recovery option that is also known as hot standby. Fast recovery normally uses a dedicated fixed facility with computer systems and software configured ready to run the IT services. Fast recovery typically takes up to 24 hours but may be quicker if there is no need to restore data from backups.

fault

See error.

fault tolerance

(ITIL Service Design) The ability of an IT service or other configuration item to continue to operate correctly after failure of a component part. *See also* countermeasure; resilience.

fault tree analysis (FTA)

(ITIL Continual Service Improvement) (ITIL Service Design) A technique that can be used to determine a chain of events that has caused an incident, or may cause an incident in the future. Fault tree analysis represents a chain of events using Boolean notation in a diagram.

financial management

(ITIL Service Strategy) A generic term used to describe the function and processes responsible for managing an organization's budgeting, accounting and charging requirements. Enterprise financial management is the specific term used to describe the function and processes from the perspective of the overall organization. Financial management for IT services is the specific term used to describe the function and processes from the perspective of the IT service provider.

financial management for IT services

(ITIL Service Strategy) The function and processes responsible for managing an IT service provider's budgeting, accounting and charging requirements. Financial management for IT services secures an

appropriate level of funding to design, develop and deliver services that meet the strategy of the organization in a cost-effective manner. *See also* enterprise financial management.

financial year

(ITIL Service Strategy) An accounting period covering 12 consecutive months. A financial year may start on any date (for example, 1 April to 31 March).

first-line support

(ITIL Service Operation) The first level in a hierarchy of support groups involved in the resolution of incidents. Each level contains more specialist skills, or has more time or other resources. *See also* escalation.

fishbone diagram

See Ishikawa diagram.

fit for purpose

(ITIL Service Strategy) The ability to meet an agreed level of utility. Fit for purpose is also used informally to describe a process, configuration item, IT service etc. that is capable of meeting its objectives or service levels. Being fit for purpose requires suitable design, implementation, control and maintenance.

fit for use

(ITIL Service Strategy) The ability to meet an agreed level of warranty. Being fit for use requires suitable design, implementation, control and maintenance.

fixed asset

(ITIL Service Transition) A tangible business asset that has a long-term useful life (for example, a building, a piece of land, a server or a software licence). *See also* service asset; configuration item.

fixed asset management

(ITIL Service Transition) The process responsible for tracking and reporting the value and ownership of fixed assets throughout their lifecycle. Fixed asset management maintains the asset register and is usually carried out by the overall business, rather than by the IT organization. Fixed asset management is sometimes called financial asset management and is not described in detail within the core ITIL publications.

fixed cost

(ITIL Service Strategy) A cost that does not vary with IT service usage – for example, the cost of server hardware. *See also* variable cost.

fixed facility

(ITIL Service Design) A permanent building, available for use when needed by an IT service continuity plan. *See also* portable facility; recovery option.

follow the sun

(ITIL Service Operation) A methodology for using service desks and support groups around the world to provide seamless 24/7 service. Calls, incidents, problems and service requests are passed between groups in different time zones.

fulfilment

Performing activities to meet a need or requirement – for example, by providing a new IT service, or meeting a service request.

function

A team or group of people and the tools or other resources that they use to carry out one or more processes or activities – for example, the service desk. The term also has two other meanings:

■ An intended purpose of a configuration item, person, team, process or IT service. For example, one function of an email service may be to store and forward outgoing messages, while the function of a business process may be to despatch goods to customers.

- To perform the intended purpose correctly, as in 'The computer is functioning.'

functional escalation

(ITIL Service Operation) Transferring an incident, problem or change to a technical team with a higher level of expertise to assist in an escalation.

gap analysis

(ITIL Continual Service Improvement) An activity that compares two sets of data and identifies the differences. Gap analysis is commonly used to compare a set of requirements with actual delivery. *See also* benchmarking.

governance

Ensures that policies and strategy are actually implemented, and that required processes are correctly followed. Governance includes defining roles and responsibilities, measuring and reporting, and taking actions to resolve any issues identified.

gradual recovery

(ITIL Service Design) A recovery option that is also known as cold standby. Gradual recovery typically uses a portable or fixed facility that has environmental support and network cabling, but no computer systems. The hardware and software are installed as part of the IT service continuity plan. Gradual recovery typically takes more than three days, and may take significantly longer.

guideline

A document describing best practice, which recommends what should be done. Compliance with a guideline is not normally enforced. *See also* standard.

hierarchic escalation

(ITIL Service Operation) Informing or involving more senior levels of management to assist in an escalation.

high availability

(ITIL Service Design) An approach or design that minimizes or hides the effects of configuration item failure from the users of an IT service. High availability solutions are designed to achieve an agreed level of availability and make use of techniques such as fault tolerance, resilience and fast recovery to reduce the number and impact of incidents.

hot standby

See fast recovery; immediate recovery.

identity

(ITIL Service Operation) A unique name that is used to identify a user, person or role. The identity is used to grant rights to that user, person or role. Examples of identities might be the username SmithJ or the role 'change manager'.

immediate recovery

(ITIL Service Design) A recovery option that is also known as hot standby. Provision is made to recover the IT service with no significant loss of service to the customer. Immediate recovery typically uses mirroring, load balancing and split-site technologies.

impact

(ITIL Service Operation) (ITIL Service Transition) A measure of the effect of an incident, problem or change on business processes. Impact is often based on how service levels will be affected. Impact and urgency are used to assign priority.

incident

(ITIL Service Operation) An unplanned interruption to an IT service or reduction in the quality of an IT service. Failure of a configuration item that has not yet affected service is also an incident – for example, failure of one disk from a mirror set.

incident management

(ITIL Service Operation) The process responsible for managing the lifecycle of all incidents. Incident management ensures that normal service operation is restored as quickly as possible and the business impact is minimized.

incident record

(ITIL Service Operation) A record containing the details of an incident. Each incident record documents the lifecycle of a single incident.

indirect cost

(ITIL Service Strategy) The cost of providing an IT service which cannot be allocated in full to a specific customer – for example, the cost of providing shared servers or software licences. Also known as overhead. *See also* direct cost.

information security management (ISM)

(ITIL Service Design) The process responsible for ensuring that the confidentiality, integrity and availability of an organization's assets, information, data and IT services match the agreed needs of the business. Information security management supports business security and has a wider scope than that of the IT service provider, and includes handling of paper, building access, phone calls etc. for the entire organization. *See also* security management information system.

information security management system (ISMS)

(ITIL Service Design) The framework of policy, processes, functions, standards, guidelines and tools that ensures an organization can achieve its information security management objectives. *See also* security management information system.

information security policy

(ITIL Service Design) The policy that governs the organization's approach to information security management.

information system

See management information system.

information technology (IT)

The use of technology for the storage, communication or processing of information. The technology typically includes computers, telecommunications, applications and other software. The information may include business data, voice, images, video etc. Information technology is often used to support business processes through IT services.

infrastructure service

A type of supporting service that provides hardware, network or other data centre components. The term is also used as a synonym for supporting service.

insourcing

(ITIL Service Strategy) Using an internal service provider to manage IT services. The term insourcing is also used to describe the act of transferring the provision of an IT service from an external service provider to an internal service provider. *See also* service sourcing.

integrity

(ITIL Service Design) A security principle which ensures that data and configuration items are modified only by authorized personnel and activities. Integrity considers all possible causes of modification, including software and hardware failure, environmental events, and human intervention.

interactive voice response (IVR)

(ITIL Service Operation) A form of automatic call distribution that accepts user input, such as key presses and spoken commands, to identify the correct destination for incoming calls.

intermediate recovery

(ITIL Service Design) A recovery option that is also known as warm standby. Intermediate recovery usually uses a shared portable or fixed facility that has computer systems and network components. The hardware and software will need to be configured, and data will need to be restored, as part of the IT service continuity plan. Typical recovery times for intermediate recovery are one to three days.

internal customer

A customer who works for the same business as the IT service provider. See also external customer; internal service provider.

internal metric

A metric that is used within the IT service provider to monitor the efficiency, effectiveness or cost effectiveness of the IT service provider's internal processes. Internal metrics are not normally reported to the customer of the IT service. *See also* external metric.

internal rate of return (IRR)

(ITIL Service Strategy) A technique used to help make decisions about capital expenditure. It calculates a figure that allows two or more alternative investments to be compared. A larger internal rate of return indicates a better investment. *See also* net present value; return on investment.

internal service provider

(ITIL Service Strategy) An IT service provider that is part of the same organization as its customer. An IT service provider may have both internal and external customers. *See also* insourcing; Type I service provider; Type II service provider.

International Organization for Standardization (ISO)

The International Organization for Standardization (ISO) is the world's largest developer of standards. ISO is a non-governmental organization that is a network of the national standards institutes of 156 countries. See www.iso.org for further information about ISO.

International Standards Organization

See International Organization for Standardization.

internet service provider (ISP)

An external service provider that provides access to the internet. Most ISPs also provide other IT services such as web hosting.

invocation

(ITIL Service Design) Initiation of the steps defined in a plan – for example, initiating the IT service continuity plan for one or more IT services.

Ishikawa diagram

(ITIL Continual Service Improvement) (ITIL Service Operation) A technique that helps a team to identify all the possible causes of a problem. Originally devised by Kaoru Ishikawa, the output of this technique is a diagram that looks like a fishbone.

ISO 9000

A generic term that refers to a number of international standards and guidelines for quality management systems. See www.iso.org for more information. *See also* International Organization for Standardization.

ISO 9001

An international standard for quality management systems. *See also* ISO 9000; standard.

ISO/IEC 20000

An international standard for IT service management.

ISO/IEC 27001

(ITIL Continual Service Improvement) (ITIL Service Design) An international specification for information security management. The corresponding code of practice is ISO/IEC 27002. *See also* standard.

ISO/IEC 27002

(ITIL Continual Service Improvement) An international code of practice for information security management. The corresponding specification is ISO/IEC 27001. *See also* standard.

IT accounting

See accounting.

IT infrastructure

All of the hardware, software, networks, facilities etc. that are required to develop, test, deliver, monitor, control or support applications and IT services. The term includes all of the information technology but not the associated people, processes and documentation.

IT operations

(ITIL Service Operation) Activities carried out by IT operations control, including console management/operations bridge, job scheduling, backup and restore, and print and output management. IT operations is also used as a synonym for service operation.

IT operations control

(ITIL Service Operation) The function responsible for monitoring and control of the IT services and IT infrastructure. *See also* operations bridge.

IT operations management

(ITIL Service Operation) The function within an IT service provider that performs the daily activities needed to manage IT services and the supporting IT infrastructure. IT operations management includes IT operations control and facilities management.

IT service

A service provided by an IT service provider. An IT service is made up of a combination of information technology, people and processes. A customer-facing IT service directly supports the business processes of one or more customers and its service level targets should be defined in a service level agreement. Other IT services, called supporting services, are not directly used by the business but are required by the service provider to deliver customer-facing services. *See also* core service; enabling service; enhancing service; service; service package.

IT service continuity management (ITSCM)

(ITIL Service Design) The process responsible for managing risks that could seriously affect IT services. IT service continuity management ensures that the IT service provider can always provide minimum agreed service levels, by reducing the risk to an acceptable level and planning for the recovery of IT services. IT service continuity management supports business continuity management.

IT service continuity plan

(ITIL Service Design) A plan defining the steps required to recover one or more IT services. The plan also identifies

the triggers for invocation, people to be involved, communications etc. The IT service continuity plan should be part of a business continuity plan.

IT service management (ITSM)

The implementation and management of quality IT services that meet the needs of the business. IT service management is performed by IT service providers through an appropriate mix of people, process and information technology. *See also* service management.

IT Service Management Forum (*it*SMF)

The IT Service Management Forum is an independent organization dedicated to promoting a professional approach to IT service management. The *it*SMF is a not-for-profit membership organization with representation in many countries around the world (*it*SMF chapters). The *it*SMF and its membership contribute to the development of ITIL and associated IT service management standards. See www.itsmf.com for more information.

IT service provider

(ITIL Service Strategy) A service provider that provides IT services to internal or external customers.

IT steering group (ISG)

(ITIL Service Design) (ITIL Service Strategy) A formal group that is responsible for ensuring that business and IT service provider strategies and plans are closely aligned. An IT steering group includes senior representatives from the business and the IT service provider. Also known as IT strategy group or IT steering committee.

ITIL

A set of best-practice publications for IT service management. Owned by the Cabinet Office (part of HM Government), ITIL gives guidance on the provision of quality IT services and the processes, functions and other capabilities needed to support them. The ITIL framework is based on a service lifecycle and consists of five lifecycle stages (service strategy, service design, service transition, service operation and continual service improvement), each of which has its own supporting publication. There is also a set of complementary ITIL publications providing guidance specific to industry sectors, organization types, operating models and technology architectures. See www.itil-officialsite.com for more information.

job description

A document that defines the roles, responsibilities, skills and knowledge required by a particular person. One job description can include multiple roles – for example, the roles of configuration manager and change manager may be carried out by one person.

job scheduling

(ITIL Service Operation) Planning and managing the execution of software tasks that are required as part of an IT service. Job scheduling is carried out by IT operations management, and is often automated using software tools that run batch or online tasks at specific times of the day, week, month or year.

Kano model

(ITIL Service Strategy) A model developed by Noriaki Kano that is used to help understand customer preferences. The Kano model considers attributes of an IT service grouped into areas such as basic factors, excitement factors, performance factors etc.

Kepner and Tregoe analysis

(ITIL Service Operation) A structured approach to problem solving. The problem is analysed in terms of what, where, when and extent. Possible causes are identified, the most probable cause is tested, and the true cause is verified.

key performance indicator (KPI)

(ITIL Continual Service Improvement) (ITIL Service Design) A metric that is used to help manage an IT service, process, plan, project or other activity. Key performance indicators are used to measure the achievement of critical success factors. Many metrics may be measured, but only the most important of these are defined as key performance indicators and used to actively manage and report on the process, IT service or activity. They should be selected to ensure that efficiency, effectiveness and cost effectiveness are all managed.

knowledge base

(ITIL Service Transition) A logical database containing data and information used by the service knowledge management system.

knowledge management

(ITIL Service Transition) The process responsible for sharing perspectives, ideas, experience and information, and for ensuring that these are available in the right place and at the right time. The knowledge management process enables informed decisions, and improves efficiency by reducing the need to rediscover knowledge. *See also* Data-to-Information-to-Knowledge-to-Wisdom; service knowledge management system.

known error

(ITIL Service Operation) A problem that has a documented root cause and a workaround. Known errors are created and managed throughout their lifecycle by problem management. Known errors may also be identified by development or suppliers.

known error database (KEDB)

(ITIL Service Operation) A database containing all known error records. This database is created by problem management and used by incident and problem management. The known error database may be part of the configuration management system, or may be stored elsewhere in the service knowledge management system.

known error record

(ITIL Service Operation) A record containing the details of a known error. Each known error record documents the lifecycle of a known error, including the status, root cause and workaround. In some implementations, a known error is documented using additional fields in a problem record.

lifecycle

The various stages in the life of an IT service, configuration item, incident, problem, change etc. The lifecycle defines the categories for status and the status transitions that are permitted. For example:

- The lifecycle of an application includes requirements, design, build, deploy, operate, optimize
- The expanded incident lifecycle includes detection, diagnosis, repair, recovery and restoration
- The lifecycle of a server may include: ordered, received, in test, live, disposed etc.

line of service (LOS)

(ITIL Service Strategy) A core service or service package that has multiple service options. A line of service is managed by a service owner and each service option is designed to support a particular market segment.

live

(ITIL Service Transition) Refers to an IT service or other configuration item that is being used to deliver service to a customer.

live environment

(ITIL Service Transition) A controlled environment containing live configuration items used to deliver IT services to customers.

maintainability

(ITIL Service Design) A measure of how quickly and effectively an IT service or other configuration item can be restored to normal working after a failure. Maintainability is often measured and reported as MTRS. Maintainability is also used in the context of software or IT service development to mean ability to be changed or repaired easily.

major incident

(ITIL Service Operation) The highest category of impact for an incident. A major incident results in significant disruption to the business.

manageability

An informal measure of how easily and effectively an IT service or other component can be managed.

management information

Information that is used to support decision-making by managers. Management information is often generated automatically by tools supporting the various IT service management processes. Management information often includes the values of key performance indicators, such as 'percentage of changes leading to incidents' or 'first-time fix rate'.

management information system (MIS)

(ITIL Service Design) A set of tools, data and information that is used to support a process or function. Examples include the availability management information system and the supplier and contract management information system. *See also* service knowledge management system.

Management of Risk (M_o_R)

M_o_R includes all the activities required to identify and control the exposure to risk, which may have an impact on the achievement of an organization's business objectives. See www.mor-officialsite.com for more details.

management system

The framework of policy, processes, functions, standards, guidelines and tools that ensures an organization or part of an organization can achieve its objectives. This term is also used with a smaller scope to support a specific process or activity – for example, an event management system or risk management system. *See also* system.

manual workaround

(ITIL Continual Service Improvement) A workaround that requires manual intervention. Manual workaround is also used as the name of a recovery option in which the business process operates without the use of IT services. This is a temporary measure and is usually combined with another recovery option.

marginal cost

(ITIL Service Strategy) The increase or decrease in the cost of producing one more, or one less, unit of output – for example, the cost of supporting an additional user.

market space

(ITIL Service Strategy) Opportunities that an IT service provider could exploit to meet the business needs of customers. Market spaces identify the possible IT services that an IT service provider may wish to consider delivering.

maturity

(ITIL Continual Service Improvement) A measure of the reliability, efficiency and effectiveness of a process, function, organization etc. The most mature processes and functions are formally aligned to business objectives and strategy, and are supported by a framework for continual improvement.

maturity level

A named level in a maturity model, such as the Carnegie Mellon Capability Maturity Model Integration.

mean time between failures (MTBF)

(ITIL Service Design) A metric for measuring and reporting reliability. MTBF is the average time that an IT service or other configuration item can perform its agreed function without interruption. This is measured from when the configuration item starts working, until it next fails.

mean time between service incidents (MTBSI)

(ITIL Service Design) A metric used for measuring and reporting reliability. It is the mean time from when a system or IT service fails, until it next fails. MTBSI is equal to MTBF plus MTRS.

mean time to repair (MTTR)

The average time taken to repair an IT service or other configuration item after a failure. MTTR is measured from when the configuration item fails until it is repaired. MTTR does not include the time required to recover or restore. It is sometimes incorrectly used instead of mean time to restore service.

mean time to restore service (MTRS)

The average time taken to restore an IT service or other configuration item after a failure. MTRS is measured from when the configuration item fails until it is fully restored and delivering its normal functionality. *See also* maintainability; mean time to repair.

metric

(ITIL Continual Service Improvement) Something that is measured and reported to help manage a process, IT service or activity. *See also* key performance indicator.

middleware

(ITIL Service Design) Software that connects two or more software components or applications. Middleware is usually purchased from a supplier, rather than developed within the IT service provider. *See also* commercial off the shelf.

mission

A short but complete description of the overall purpose and intentions of an organization. It states what is to be achieved, but not how this should be done. *See also* vision.

model

A representation of a system, process, IT service, configuration item etc. that is used to help understand or predict future behaviour.

modelling

A technique that is used to predict the future behaviour of a system, process, IT service, configuration item etc. Modelling is commonly used in financial management, capacity management and availability management.

monitor control loop

(ITIL Service Operation) Monitoring the output of a task, process, IT service or other configuration item; comparing this output to a predefined norm; and taking appropriate action based on this comparison.

monitoring

(ITIL Service Operation) Repeated observation of a configuration item, IT service or process to detect events and to ensure that the current status is known.

near-shore

(ITIL Service Strategy) Provision of services from a country near the country where the customer is based. This can be the provision of an IT service, or of supporting functions such as a service desk. *See also* offshore; onshore.

net present value (NPV)

(ITIL Service Strategy) A technique used to help make decisions about capital expenditure. It compares cash inflows with cash outflows. Positive net present value indicates that an investment is worthwhile. *See also* internal rate of return; return on investment.

normal change

(ITIL Service Transition) A change that is not an emergency change or a standard change. Normal changes follow the defined steps of the change management process.

normal service operation

(ITIL Service Operation) An operational state where services and configuration items are performing within their agreed service and operational levels.

notional charging

(ITIL Service Strategy) An approach to charging for IT services. Charges to customers are calculated and customers are informed of the charge, but no money is actually transferred. Notional charging is sometimes introduced to ensure that customers are aware of the costs they incur, or as a stage during the introduction of real charging.

objective

The outcomes required from a process, activity or organization in order to ensure that its purpose will be fulfilled. Objectives are usually expressed as measurable targets. The term is also informally used to mean a requirement.

off the shelf

See commercial off the shelf.

Office of Government Commerce (OGC)

OGC (former owner of Best Management Practice) and its functions have moved into the Cabinet Office as part of HM Government. See www.cabinetoffice.gov.uk

offshore

(ITIL Service Strategy) Provision of services from a location outside the country where the customer is based, often in a different continent. This can be the provision of an IT service, or of supporting functions such as a service desk. *See also* near-shore; onshore.

onshore

(ITIL Service Strategy) Provision of services from a location within the country where the customer is based. *See also* near-shore; offshore.

operate

To perform as expected. A process or configuration item is said to operate if it is delivering the required outputs. Operate also means to perform one or more operations. For example, to operate a computer is to do the day-to-day operations needed for it to perform as expected.

operation

(ITIL Service Operation) Day-to-day management of an IT service, system or other configuration item. Operation is also used to mean any predefined activity or transaction – for example, loading a magnetic tape, accepting money at a point of sale, or reading data from a disk drive.

operational

The lowest of three levels of planning and delivery (strategic, tactical, operational). Operational activities include the day-to-day or short-term planning or delivery of a business process or IT service management process. The term is also a synonym for live.

operational cost

The cost resulting from running the IT services, which often involves repeating payments – for example, staff costs, hardware maintenance and electricity (also known as current expenditure or revenue expenditure). *See also* capital expenditure.

operational expenditure (OPEX)

See operational cost.

operational level agreement (OLA)

(ITIL Continual Service Improvement) (ITIL Service Design) An agreement between an IT service provider and another part of the same organization. It supports the IT service provider's delivery of IT services to customers and defines the goods or services to be provided and the responsibilities of both parties. For example, there could be an operational level agreement:

- Between the IT service provider and a procurement department to obtain hardware in agreed times
- Between the service desk and a support group to provide incident resolution in agreed times.

See also service level agreement.

operations bridge

(ITIL Service Operation) A physical location where IT services and IT infrastructure are monitored and managed.

operations control

See IT operations control.

operations management

See IT operations management.

opportunity cost

(ITIL Service Strategy) A cost that is used in deciding between investment choices. Opportunity cost represents the revenue that would have been generated by using the resources in a different way. For example, the opportunity cost of purchasing a new server may include not carrying out a service improvement activity that the money could have been spent on. Opportunity cost analysis is used as part of a decision-making process, but opportunity cost is not treated as an actual cost in any financial statement.

optimize

Review, plan and request changes, in order to obtain the maximum efficiency and effectiveness from a process, configuration item, application etc.

organization

A company, legal entity or other institution. The term is sometimes used to refer to any entity that has people, resources and budgets – for example, a project or business unit.

outcome

The result of carrying out an activity, following a process, or delivering an IT service etc. The term is used to refer to intended results as well as to actual results. *See also* objective.

outsourcing

(ITIL Service Strategy) Using an external service provider to manage IT services. *See also* service sourcing.

overhead

See indirect cost.

pain value analysis

(ITIL Service Operation) A technique used to help identify the business impact of one or more problems. A formula is used to calculate pain value based on the number of users affected, the duration of the downtime, the impact on each user, and the cost to the business (if known).

Pareto principle

(ITIL Service Operation) A technique used to prioritize activities. The Pareto principle says that 80% of the value of any activity is created with 20% of the effort. Pareto analysis is also used in problem management to prioritize possible problem causes for investigation.

partnership

A relationship between two organizations that involves working closely together for common goals or mutual benefit. The IT service provider should have a partnership with the business and with third parties who are critical to the delivery of IT services. *See also* value network.

passive monitoring

(ITIL Service Operation) Monitoring of a configuration item, an IT service or a process that relies on an alert or notification to discover the current status. *See also* active monitoring.

pattern of business activity (PBA)

(ITIL Service Strategy) A workload profile of one or more business activities. Patterns of business activity are used to help the IT service provider understand and plan for different levels of business activity. *See also* user profile.

percentage utilization

(ITIL Service Design) The amount of time that a component is busy over a given period of time. For example, if a CPU is busy for 1,800 seconds in a one-hour period, its utilization is 50%.

performance

A measure of what is achieved or delivered by a system, person, team, process or IT service.

performance management

Activities to ensure that something achieves its expected outcomes in an efficient and consistent manner.

pilot

(ITIL Service Transition) A limited deployment of an IT service, a release or a process to the live environment. A pilot is used to reduce risk and to gain user feedback and acceptance. *See also* change evaluation; test.

plan

A detailed proposal that describes the activities and resources needed to achieve an objective – for example, a plan to implement a new IT service or process. ISO/IEC 20000 requires a plan for the management of each IT service management process.

Plan-Do-Check-Act (PDCA)

(ITIL Continual Service Improvement) A four-stage cycle for process management, attributed to W. Edwards Deming. Plan-Do-Check-Act is also called the Deming Cycle. **Plan** – design or revise processes that support the IT services; **Do** – implement the plan and manage the processes; **Check** – measure the processes and IT services, compare with objectives and produce reports; **Act** – plan and implement changes to improve the processes.

planned downtime

(ITIL Service Design) Agreed time when an IT service will not be available. Planned downtime is often used for maintenance, upgrades and testing. *See also* change window; downtime.

planning

An activity responsible for creating one or more plans – for example, capacity planning.

policy

Formally documented management expectations and intentions. Policies are used to direct decisions, and to ensure consistent and appropriate development and implementation of processes, standards, roles, activities, IT infrastructure etc.

portable facility

(ITIL Service Design) A prefabricated building, or a large vehicle, provided by a third party and moved to a site when needed according to an IT service continuity plan. *See also* fixed facility; recovery option.

post-implementation review (PIR)

A review that takes place after a change or a project has been implemented. It determines if the change or project was successful, and identifies opportunities for improvement.

practice

A way of working, or a way in which work must be done. Practices can include activities, processes, functions, standards and guidelines. *See also* best practice.

prerequisite for success (PFS)

An activity that needs to be completed, or a condition that needs to be met, to enable successful implementation of a plan or process. It is often an output from one process that is a required input to another process.

pricing

(ITIL Service Strategy) Pricing is the activity for establishing how much customers will be charged.

PRINCE2

See PRojects IN Controlled Environments.

priority

(ITIL Service Operation) (ITIL Service Transition) A category used to identify the relative importance of an incident, problem or change. Priority is based on impact and urgency, and is used to identify required times for actions to be taken. For example, the service level agreement may state that Priority 2 incidents must be resolved within 12 hours.

proactive monitoring

(ITIL Service Operation) Monitoring that looks for patterns of events to predict possible future failures. *See also* reactive monitoring.

proactive problem management

(ITIL Service Operation) Part of the problem management process. The objective of proactive problem management is to identify problems that might otherwise be missed. Proactive problem management analyses incident records, and uses data collected by other IT service management processes to identify trends or significant problems.

problem

(ITIL Service Operation) A cause of one or more incidents. The cause is not usually known at the time a problem record is created, and the problem management process is responsible for further investigation.

problem management

(ITIL Service Operation) The process responsible for managing the lifecycle of all problems. Problem management proactively prevents incidents from happening and minimizes the impact of incidents that cannot be prevented.

problem record

(ITIL Service Operation) A record containing the details of a problem. Each problem record documents the lifecycle of a single problem.

procedure

A document containing steps that specify how to achieve an activity. Procedures are defined as part of processes. *See also* work instruction.

process

A structured set of activities designed to accomplish a specific objective. A process takes one or more defined inputs and turns them into defined outputs. It may include any of the roles, responsibilities, tools and management controls required to reliably deliver the outputs. A process may define policies, standards, guidelines, activities and work instructions if they are needed.

process control

The activity of planning and regulating a process, with the objective of performing the process in an effective, efficient and consistent manner.

process manager

A role responsible for the operational management of a process. The process manager's responsibilities include planning and coordination of all activities required to carry out, monitor and report on the process. There may be several process managers for one process – for example, regional change managers or IT service continuity managers for each data centre. The process manager role is often assigned to the person who carries out the process owner role, but the two roles may be separate in larger organizations.

process owner

The person who is held accountable for ensuring that a process is fit for purpose. The process owner's responsibilities include sponsorship, design, change management and continual improvement of the process and its metrics. This role can be assigned to the same person who carries out the process manager role, but the two roles may be separate in larger organizations.

production environment

See live environment.

profit centre

(ITIL Service Strategy) A business unit that charges for services provided. A profit centre can be created with the objective of making a profit, recovering costs, or running at a loss. An IT service provider can be run as a cost centre or a profit centre.

pro-forma

A template or example document containing sample data that will be replaced with real values when these are available.

programme

A number of projects and activities that are planned and managed together to achieve an overall set of related objectives and other outcomes.

project

A temporary organization, with people and other assets, that is required to achieve an objective or other outcome. Each project has a lifecycle that typically includes initiation, planning, execution, and closure. Projects are usually managed using a formal methodology such as PRojects IN Controlled Environments (PRINCE2) or the Project Management Body of Knowledge (PMBOK). *See also* charter; project management office; project portfolio.

project charter

See charter.

Project Management Body of Knowledge (PMBOK)

A project management standard maintained and published by the Project Management Institute. See www.pmi.org for more information. *See also* PRojects IN Controlled Environments (PRINCE2).

Project Management Institute (PMI)

A membership association that advances the project management profession through globally recognized standards and certifications, collaborative communities, an extensive research programme, and professional development opportunities. PMI is a not-for-profit membership organization with representation in many countries around the world. PMI maintains and publishes the Project Management Body of Knowledge (PMBOK). See www.pmi.org for more information. *See also* PRojects IN Controlled Environments (PRINCE2).

project management office (PMO)

(ITIL Service Design) (ITIL Service Strategy) A function or group responsible for managing the lifecycle of projects. *See also* charter; project portfolio.

project portfolio

(ITIL Service Design) (ITIL Service Strategy) A database or structured document used to manage projects throughout their lifecycle. The project portfolio is used to coordinate projects and ensure that they meet their objectives in a cost-effective and timely manner. In larger organizations, the project portfolio is typically defined and maintained by a project management office. The project portfolio is important to service portfolio management as new services and significant changes are normally managed as projects. *See also* charter.

projected service outage (PSO)

(ITIL Service Transition) A document that identifies the effect of planned changes, maintenance activities and test plans on agreed service levels.

PRojects IN Controlled Environments (PRINCE2)

The standard UK government methodology for project management. See www.prince-officialsite.com for more information. *See also* Project Management Body of Knowledge (PMBOK).

qualification

(ITIL Service Transition) An activity that ensures that the IT infrastructure is appropriate and correctly configured to support an application or IT service. *See also* validation.

quality

The ability of a product, service or process to provide the intended value. For example, a hardware component can be considered to be of high quality if it performs as expected and delivers the required reliability. Process quality also requires an ability to monitor effectiveness and efficiency, and to improve them if necessary. *See also* quality management system.

quality assurance (QA)

(ITIL Service Transition) The process responsible for ensuring that the quality of a service, process or other service asset will provide its intended value. Quality assurance is also used to refer to a function or team that performs quality assurance. This process is not described in detail within the core ITIL publications. *See also* service validation and testing.

quality management system (QMS)

(ITIL Continual Service Improvement) The framework of policy, processes, functions, standards, guidelines and tools that ensures an organization is of a suitable quality to reliably meet business objectives or service levels. *See also* ISO 9000.

quick win

(ITIL Continual Service Improvement) An improvement activity that is expected to provide a return on investment in a short period of time with relatively small cost and effort. *See also* Pareto principle.

RACI

(ITIL Service Design) A model used to help define roles and responsibilities. RACI stands for responsible, accountable, consulted and informed.

reactive monitoring

(ITIL Service Operation) Monitoring that takes place in response to an event. For example, submitting a batch job when the previous job completes, or logging an incident when an error occurs. *See also* proactive monitoring.

real charging

(ITIL Service Strategy) A charging policy where actual money is transferred from the customer to the IT service provider in payment for the delivery of IT services. *See also* notional charging.

reciprocal arrangement

(ITIL Service Design) A recovery option. An agreement between two organizations to share resources in an emergency – for example, high-speed printing facilities or computer room space.

record

A document containing the results or other output from a process or activity. Records are evidence of the fact that an activity took place and may be paper or electronic – for example, an audit report, an incident record or the minutes of a meeting.

recovery

(ITIL Service Design) (ITIL Service Operation) Returning a configuration item or an IT service to a working state. Recovery of an IT service often includes recovering data to a known consistent state. After recovery, further steps may be needed before the IT service can be made available to the users (restoration).

recovery option

(ITIL Service Design) A strategy for responding to an interruption to service. Commonly used strategies are manual workaround, reciprocal arrangement, gradual recovery, intermediate recovery, fast recovery, and immediate recovery. Recovery options may make use of dedicated facilities or third-party facilities shared by multiple businesses.

recovery point objective (RPO)

(ITIL Service Design) (ITIL Service Operation) The maximum amount of data that may be lost when service is restored after an interruption. The recovery point objective is expressed as a length of time before the failure. For example, a recovery point objective of one day may be supported by daily backups, and up to 24 hours of data may be lost. Recovery point objectives for each IT service should be negotiated, agreed and documented, and used as requirements for service design and IT service continuity plans.

recovery time objective (RTO)

(ITIL Service Design) (ITIL Service Operation) The maximum time allowed for the recovery of an IT service following an interruption. The service level to be provided may be less than normal service level targets. Recovery time objectives for each IT service should be negotiated, agreed and documented. *See also* business impact analysis.

redundancy

(ITIL Service Design) Use of one or more additional configuration items to provide fault tolerance. The term also has a generic meaning of obsolescence, or no longer needed.

relationship

A connection or interaction between two people or things. In business relationship management, it is the interaction between the IT service provider and the business. In service asset and configuration management, it is a link between two configuration items that identifies a dependency or connection between them. For example, applications may be linked to the servers they run on, and IT services have many links to all the configuration items that contribute to that IT service.

relationship processes

The ISO/IEC 20000 process group that includes business relationship management and supplier management.

release

(ITIL Service Transition) One or more changes to an IT service that are built, tested and deployed together. A single release may include changes to hardware, software, documentation, processes and other components.

release and deployment management

(ITIL Service Transition) The process responsible for planning, scheduling and controlling the build, test and deployment of releases, and for delivering new functionality required by the business while protecting the integrity of existing services.

release identification

(ITIL Service Transition) A naming convention used to uniquely identify a release. The release identification typically includes a reference to the configuration item and a version number – for example, Microsoft Office 2010 SR2.

release management

See release and deployment management.

release package

(ITIL Service Transition) A set of configuration items that will be built, tested and deployed together as a single

release. Each release package will usually include one or more release units.

release record

(ITIL Service Transition) A record that defines the content of a release. A release record has relationships with all configuration items that are affected by the release. Release records may be in the configuration management system or elsewhere in the service knowledge management system.

release unit

(ITIL Service Transition) Components of an IT service that are normally released together. A release unit typically includes sufficient components to perform a useful function. For example, one release unit could be a desktop PC, including hardware, software, licences, documentation etc. A different release unit may be the complete payroll application, including IT operations procedures and user training.

release window

See change window.

reliability

(ITIL Continual Service Improvement) (ITIL Service Design) A measure of how long an IT service or other configuration item can perform its agreed function without interruption. Usually measured as MTBF or MTBSI. The term can also be used to state how likely it is that a process, function etc. will deliver its required outputs. *See also* availability.

remediation

(ITIL Service Transition) Actions taken to recover after a failed change or release. Remediation may include back-out, invocation of service continuity plans, or other actions designed to enable the business process to continue.

repair

(ITIL Service Operation) The replacement or correction of a failed configuration item.

request for change (RFC)

(ITIL Service Transition) A formal proposal for a change to be made. It includes details of the proposed change, and may be recorded on paper or electronically. The term is often misused to mean a change record, or the change itself.

request fulfilment

(ITIL Service Operation) The process responsible for managing the lifecycle of all service requests.

request model

(ITIL Service Operation) A repeatable way of dealing with a particular category of service request. A request model defines specific agreed steps that will be followed for a service request of this category. Request models may be very simple, with no requirement for authorization (e.g. password reset), or may be more complex with many steps that require authorization (e.g. provision of an existing IT service). *See also* request fulfilment.

requirement

(ITIL Service Design) A formal statement of what is needed – for example, a service level requirement, a project requirement or the required deliverables for a process. *See also* statement of requirements.

resilience

(ITIL Service Design) The ability of an IT service or other configuration item to resist failure or to recover in a timely manner following a failure. For example, an armoured cable will resist failure when put under stress. *See also* fault tolerance.

resolution

(ITIL Service Operation) Action taken to repair the root cause of an incident or problem, or to implement a workaround. In ISO/IEC 20000, resolution processes is the process group that includes incident and problem management.

resolution processes

The ISO/IEC 20000 process group that includes incident and problem management.

resource

(ITIL Service Strategy) A generic term that includes IT infrastructure, people, money or anything else that might help to deliver an IT service. Resources are considered to be assets of an organization. *See also* capability; service asset.

response time

A measure of the time taken to complete an operation or transaction. Used in capacity management as a measure of IT infrastructure performance, and in incident management as a measure of the time taken to answer the phone, or to start diagnosis.

responsiveness

A measurement of the time taken to respond to something. This could be response time of a transaction, or the speed with which an IT service provider responds to an incident or request for change etc.

restoration of service

See restore.

restore

(ITIL Service Operation) Taking action to return an IT service to the users after repair and recovery from an incident. This is the primary objective of incident management.

retire

(ITIL Service Transition) To permanently remove an IT service, or other configuration item, from the live environment. Being retired is a stage in the lifecycle of many configuration items.

return on assets (ROA)

(ITIL Service Strategy) A measurement of the profitability of a business unit or organization. Return on assets is calculated by dividing the annual net income by the total value of assets. *See also* return on investment.

return on investment (ROI)

(ITIL Continual Service Improvement) (ITIL Service Strategy) A measurement of the expected benefit of an investment. In the simplest sense, it is the net profit of an investment divided by the net worth of the assets invested. *See also* net present value; value on investment.

return to normal

(ITIL Service Design) The phase of an IT service continuity plan during which full normal operations are resumed. For example, if an alternative data centre has been in use, then this phase will bring the primary data centre back into operation, and restore the ability to invoke IT service continuity plans again.

review

An evaluation of a change, problem, process, project etc. Reviews are typically carried out at predefined points in the lifecycle, and especially after closure. The purpose of a review is to ensure that all deliverables have been provided, and to identify opportunities for improvement. *See also* change evaluation; post-implementation review.

rights

(ITIL Service Operation) Entitlements, or permissions, granted to a user or role – for example, the right to modify particular data, or to authorize a change.

risk

A possible event that could cause harm or loss, or affect the ability to achieve objectives. A risk is measured by the probability of a threat, the vulnerability of the asset to that threat, and the impact it would have if it occurred. Risk can also be defined as uncertainty of outcome, and can be used in the context of measuring the probability of positive outcomes as well as negative outcomes.

risk assessment

The initial steps of risk management: analysing the value of assets to the business, identifying threats to those assets, and evaluating how vulnerable each asset is to those threats. Risk assessment can be quantitative (based on numerical data) or qualitative.

risk management

The process responsible for identifying, assessing and controlling risks. Risk management is also sometimes used to refer to the second part of the overall process after risks have been identified and assessed, as in 'risk assessment and management'. This process is not described in detail within the core ITIL publications. *See also* risk assessment.

role

A set of responsibilities, activities and authorities assigned to a person or team. A role is defined in a process or function. One person or team may have multiple roles – for example, the roles of configuration manager and change manager may be carried out by a single person. Role is also used to describe the purpose of something or what it is used for.

root cause

(ITIL Service Operation) The underlying or original cause of an incident or problem.

root cause analysis (RCA)

(ITIL Service Operation) An activity that identifies the root cause of an incident or problem. Root cause analysis typically concentrates on IT infrastructure failures. *See also* service failure analysis.

running costs

See operational cost.

Sarbanes-Oxley (SOX)

US law that regulates financial practice and corporate governance.

scalability

The ability of an IT service, process, configuration item etc. to perform its agreed function when the workload or scope changes.

scope

The boundary or extent to which a process, procedure, certification, contract etc. applies. For example, the scope of change management may include all live IT services and related configuration items; the scope of an ISO/IEC 20000 certificate may include all IT services delivered out of a named data centre.

second-line support

(ITIL Service Operation) The second level in a hierarchy of support groups involved in the resolution of incidents and investigation of problems. Each level contains more specialist skills, or is allocated more time or other resources.

security

See information security management.

security management

See information security management.

security management information system (SMIS)

(ITIL Service Design) A set of tools, data and information that is used to support information security management. The security management information system is part of the information security management system. *See also* service knowledge management system.

security policy

See information security policy.

separation of concerns (SoC)

An approach to designing a solution or IT service that divides the problem into pieces that can be solved independently. This approach separates what is to be done from how it is to be done.

server

(ITIL Service Operation) A computer that is connected to a network and provides software functions that are used by other computers.

service

A means of delivering value to customers by facilitating outcomes customers want to achieve without the ownership of specific costs and risks. The term 'service' is sometimes used as a synonym for core service, IT service or service package. *See also* utility; warranty.

service acceptance criteria (SAC)

(ITIL Service Transition) A set of criteria used to ensure that an IT service meets its functionality and quality requirements and that the IT service provider is ready to operate the new IT service when it has been deployed. *See also* acceptance.

service analytics

(ITIL Service Strategy) A technique used in the assessment of the business impact of incidents.

Service analytics models the dependencies between configuration items, and the dependencies of IT services on configuration items.

service asset

Any resource or capability of a service provider. *See also* asset.

service asset and configuration management (SACM)

(ITIL Service Transition) The process responsible for ensuring that the assets required to deliver services are properly controlled, and that accurate and reliable information about those assets is available when and where it is needed. This information includes details of how the assets have been configured and the relationships between assets. *See also* configuration management system.

service capacity management (SCM)

(ITIL Continual Service Improvement) (ITIL Service Design) The sub-process of capacity management responsible for understanding the performance and capacity of IT services. Information on the resources used by each IT service and the pattern of usage over time are collected, recorded and analysed for use in the capacity plan. *See also* business capacity management; component capacity management.

service catalogue

(ITIL Service Design) (ITIL Service Strategy) A database or structured document with information about all live IT services, including those available for deployment. The service catalogue is part of the service portfolio and contains information about two types of IT service: customer-facing services that are visible to the business; and supporting services required by the service provider to deliver customer-facing services. *See also* customer agreement portfolio; service catalogue management.

service catalogue management

(ITIL Service Design) The process responsible for providing and maintaining the service catalogue and for ensuring that it is available to those who are authorized to access it.

service change

See change.

service charter

(ITIL Service Design) (ITIL Service Strategy) A document that contains details of a new or changed service. New service introductions and significant service changes are documented in a charter and authorized by service portfolio management. Service charters are passed to the service design lifecycle stage where a new or modified service design package will be created. The term charter is also used to describe the act of authorizing the work required by each stage of the service lifecycle with respect to the new or changed service. *See also* change proposal; service portfolio; service catalogue.

service continuity management

See IT service continuity management.

service contract

(ITIL Service Strategy) A contract to deliver one or more IT services. The term is also used to mean any agreement to deliver IT services, whether this is a legal contract or a service level agreement. *See also* customer agreement portfolio.

service culture

A customer-oriented culture. The major objectives of a service culture are customer satisfaction and helping customers to achieve their business objectives.

service design

(ITIL Service Design) A stage in the lifecycle of a service. Service design includes the design of the services, governing practices, processes and policies required to realize the service provider's strategy and to facilitate the introduction of services into supported environments. Service design includes the following processes: design coordination, service catalogue management, service level management, availability management, capacity management, IT service continuity management, information security management, and supplier management. Although these processes are associated with service design, most processes have activities that take place across multiple stages of the service lifecycle. *See also* design.

service design package (SDP)

(ITIL Service Design) Document(s) defining all aspects of an IT service and its requirements through each stage of its lifecycle. A service design package is produced for each new IT service, major change or IT service retirement.

service desk

(ITIL Service Operation) The single point of contact between the service provider and the users. A typical service desk manages incidents and service requests, and also handles communication with the users.

service failure analysis (SFA)

(ITIL Service Design) A technique that identifies underlying causes of one or more IT service interruptions. Service failure analysis identifies opportunities to improve the IT service provider's processes and tools, and not just the IT infrastructure. It is a time-constrained, project-like activity, rather than an ongoing process of analysis.

service hours

(ITIL Service Design) An agreed time period when a particular IT service should be available. For example, 'Monday–Friday 08:00 to 17:00 except public holidays'. Service hours should be defined in a service level agreement.

service improvement plan (SIP)

(ITIL Continual Service Improvement) A formal plan to implement improvements to a process or IT service.

service knowledge management system (SKMS)

(ITIL Service Transition) A set of tools and databases that is used to manage knowledge, information and data. The service knowledge management system includes the configuration management system, as well as other databases and information systems. The service knowledge management system includes tools for collecting, storing, managing, updating, analysing and presenting all the knowledge, information and data that an IT service provider will need to manage the full lifecycle of IT services. *See also* knowledge management.

service level

Measured and reported achievement against one or more service level targets. The term is sometimes used informally to mean service level target.

service level agreement (SLA)

(ITIL Continual Service Improvement) (ITIL Service Design) An agreement between an IT service provider and a customer. A service level agreement describes the IT service, documents service level targets, and specifies the responsibilities of the IT service provider and the customer. A single agreement may cover multiple IT services or multiple customers. *See also* operational level agreement.

service level management (SLM)

(ITIL Service Design) The process responsible for negotiating achievable service level agreements and ensuring that these are met. It is responsible for ensuring that all IT service management processes, operational level agreements and underpinning contracts are appropriate for the agreed service level targets. Service level management monitors and reports on service levels, holds regular service reviews with customers, and identifies required improvements.

service level package (SLP)

See service option.

service level requirement (SLR)

(ITIL Continual Service Improvement) (ITIL Service Design) A customer requirement for an aspect of an IT service. Service level requirements are based on business objectives and used to negotiate agreed service level targets.

service level target

(ITIL Continual Service Improvement) (ITIL Service Design) A commitment that is documented in a service level agreement. Service level targets are based on service level requirements, and are needed to ensure that the IT service is able to meet business objectives. They should be SMART, and are usually based on key performance indicators.

service lifecycle

An approach to IT service management that emphasizes the importance of coordination and control across the various functions, processes and systems necessary to manage the full lifecycle of IT services. The service lifecycle approach considers the strategy, design, transition, operation and continual improvement of IT services. Also known as service management lifecycle.

service maintenance objective (SMO)

(ITIL Service Operation) The expected time that a configuration item will be unavailable due to planned maintenance activity.

service management

A set of specialized organizational capabilities for providing value to customers in the form of services.

service management lifecycle

See service lifecycle.

service manager

A generic term for any manager within the service provider. Most commonly used to refer to a business relationship manager, a process manager or a senior manager with responsibility for IT services overall.

service model

(ITIL Service Strategy) A model that shows how service assets interact with customer assets to create value. Service models describe the structure of a service (how the configuration items fit together) and the dynamics of the service (activities, flow of resources and interactions). A service model can be used as a template or blueprint for multiple services.

service operation

(ITIL Service Operation) A stage in the lifecycle of a service. Service operation coordinates and carries out the activities and processes required to deliver and manage services at agreed levels to business users and customers. Service operation also manages the technology that is used to deliver and support services. Service operation includes the following processes: event management, incident management, request fulfilment, problem management, and access management. Service operation also includes the following functions: service desk, technical management, IT operations management, and application management. Although

these processes and functions are associated with service operation, most processes and functions have activities that take place across multiple stages of the service lifecycle. *See also* operation.

service option

(ITIL Service Design) (ITIL Service Strategy) A choice of utility and warranty offered to customers by a core service or service package. Service options are sometimes referred to as service level packages.

service owner

(ITIL Service Strategy) A role responsible for managing one or more services throughout their entire lifecycle. Service owners are instrumental in the development of service strategy and are responsible for the content of the service portfolio. *See also* business relationship management.

service package

(ITIL Service Strategy) Two or more services that have been combined to offer a solution to a specific type of customer need or to underpin specific business outcomes. A service package can consist of a combination of core services, enabling services and enhancing services. A service package provides a specific level of utility and warranty. Customers may be offered a choice of utility and warranty through one or more service options. *See also* IT service.

service pipeline

(ITIL Service Strategy) A database or structured document listing all IT services that are under consideration or development, but are not yet available to customers. The service pipeline provides a business view of possible future IT services and is part of the service portfolio that is not normally published to customers.

service portfolio

(ITIL Service Strategy) The complete set of services that is managed by a service provider. The service portfolio is used to manage the entire lifecycle of all services, and includes three categories: service pipeline (proposed or in development), service catalogue (live or available for deployment), and retired services. *See also* customer agreement portfolio; service portfolio management.

service portfolio management (SPM)

(ITIL Service Strategy) The process responsible for managing the service portfolio. Service portfolio management ensures that the service provider has the right mix of services to meet required business outcomes at an appropriate level of investment. Service portfolio management considers services in terms of the business value that they provide.

service potential

(ITIL Service Strategy) The total possible value of the overall capabilities and resources of the IT service provider.

service provider

(ITIL Service Strategy) An organization supplying services to one or more internal customers or external customers. Service provider is often used as an abbreviation for IT service provider. *See also* Type I service provider; Type II service provider; Type III service provider.

service provider interface (SPI)

(ITIL Service Strategy) An interface between the IT service provider and a user, customer, business process or supplier. Analysis of service provider interfaces helps to coordinate end-to-end management of IT services.

service reporting

(ITIL Continual Service Improvement) Activities that produce and deliver reports of achievement and trends

against service levels. The format, content and frequency of reports should be agreed with customers.

service request

(ITIL Service Operation) A formal request from a user for something to be provided – for example, a request for information or advice; to reset a password; or to install a workstation for a new user. Service requests are managed by the request fulfilment process, usually in conjunction with the service desk. Service requests may be linked to a request for change as part of fulfilling the request.

service sourcing

(ITIL Service Strategy) The strategy and approach for deciding whether to provide a service internally, to outsource it to an external service provider, or to combine the two approaches. Service sourcing also means the execution of this strategy. *See also* insourcing; internal service provider; outsourcing.

service strategy

(ITIL Service Strategy) A stage in the lifecycle of a service. Service strategy defines the perspective, position, plans and patterns that a service provider needs to execute to meet an organization's business outcomes. Service strategy includes the following processes: strategy management for IT services, service portfolio management, financial management for IT services, demand management, and business relationship management. Although these processes are associated with service strategy, most processes have activities that take place across multiple stages of the service lifecycle.

service transition

(ITIL Service Transition) A stage in the lifecycle of a service. Service transition ensures that new, modified or retired services meet the expectations of the business as documented in the service strategy and service design stages of the lifecycle. Service transition includes the following processes: transition planning and support,

change management, service asset and configuration management, release and deployment management, service validation and testing, change evaluation, and knowledge management. Although these processes are associated with service transition, most processes have activities that take place across multiple stages of the service lifecycle. *See also* transition.

service validation and testing

(ITIL Service Transition) The process responsible for validation and testing of a new or changed IT service. Service validation and testing ensures that the IT service matches its design specification and will meet the needs of the business.

service valuation

(ITIL Service Strategy) A measurement of the total cost of delivering an IT service, and the total value to the business of that IT service. Service valuation is used to help the business and the IT service provider agree on the value of the IT service.

serviceability

(ITIL Continual Service Improvement) (ITIL Service Design) The ability of a third-party supplier to meet the terms of its contract. This contract will include agreed levels of reliability, maintainability and availability for a configuration item.

seven-step improvement process

(ITIL Continual Service Improvement) The process responsible for defining and managing the steps needed to identify, define, gather, process, analyse, present and implement improvements. The performance of the IT service provider is continually measured by this process and improvements are made to processes, IT services and IT infrastructure in order to increase efficiency, effectiveness and cost effectiveness. Opportunities for improvement are recorded and managed in the CSI register.

shared service unit

See Type II service provider.

shift

(ITIL Service Operation) A group or team of people who carry out a specific role for a fixed period of time. For example, there could be four shifts of IT operations control personnel to support an IT service that is used 24 hours a day.

simulation modelling

(ITIL Continual Service Improvement) (ITIL Service Design) A technique that creates a detailed model to predict the behaviour of an IT service or other configuration item. A simulation model is often created by using the actual configuration items that are being modelled with artificial workloads or transactions. They are used in capacity management when accurate results are important. A simulation model is sometimes called a performance benchmark. *See also* analytical modelling; modelling.

single point of contact

(ITIL Service Operation) Providing a single consistent way to communicate with an organization or business unit. For example, a single point of contact for an IT service provider is usually called a service desk.

single point of failure (SPOF)

(ITIL Service Design) Any configuration item that can cause an incident when it fails, and for which a countermeasure has not been implemented. A single point of failure may be a person or a step in a process or activity, as well as a component of the IT infrastructure. *See also* failure.

SLAM chart

(ITIL Continual Service Improvement) A service level agreement monitoring chart is used to help monitor and report achievements against service level targets.

A SLAM chart is typically colour-coded to show whether each agreed service level target has been met, missed or nearly missed during each of the previous 12 months.

SMART

(ITIL Continual Service Improvement) (ITIL Service Design) An acronym for helping to remember that targets in service level agreements and project plans should be specific, measurable, achievable, relevant and time-bound.

snapshot

(ITIL Continual Service Improvement) (ITIL Service Transition) The current state of a configuration item, process or any other set of data recorded at a specific point in time. Snapshots can be captured by discovery tools or by manual techniques such as an assessment. *See also* baseline; benchmark.

software asset management (SAM)

(ITIL Service Transition) The process responsible for tracking and reporting the use and ownership of software assets throughout their lifecycle. Software asset management is part of an overall service asset and configuration management process. This process is not described in detail within the core ITIL publications.

source

See service sourcing.

specification

A formal definition of requirements. A specification may be used to define technical or operational requirements, and may be internal or external. Many public standards consist of a code of practice and a specification. The specification defines the standard against which an organization can be audited.

stakeholder

A person who has an interest in an organization, project, IT service etc. Stakeholders may be interested in the activities, targets, resources or deliverables. Stakeholders may include customers, partners, employees, shareholders, owners etc. *See also* RACI.

standard

A mandatory requirement. Examples include ISO/IEC 20000 (an international standard), an internal security standard for Unix configuration, or a government standard for how financial records should be maintained. The term is also used to refer to a code of practice or specification published by a standards organization such as ISO or BSI. *See also* guideline.

standard change

(ITIL Service Transition) A pre-authorized change that is low risk, relatively common and follows a procedure or work instruction – for example, a password reset or provision of standard equipment to a new employee. Requests for change are not required to implement a standard change, and they are logged and tracked using a different mechanism, such as a service request. *See also* change model.

standard operating procedures (SOP)

(ITIL Service Operation) Procedures used by IT operations management.

standby

(ITIL Service Design) Used to refer to resources that are not required to deliver the live IT services, but are available to support IT service continuity plans. For example, a standby data centre may be maintained to support hot standby, warm standby or cold standby arrangements.

statement of requirements (SOR)

(ITIL Service Design) A document containing all requirements for a product purchase, or a new or changed IT service. *See also* terms of reference.

status

The name of a required field in many types of record. It shows the current stage in the lifecycle of the associated configuration item, incident, problem etc.

status accounting

(ITIL Service Transition) The activity responsible for recording and reporting the lifecycle of each configuration item.

storage management

(ITIL Service Operation) The process responsible for managing the storage and maintenance of data throughout its lifecycle.

strategic

(ITIL Service Strategy) The highest of three levels of planning and delivery (strategic, tactical, operational). Strategic activities include objective setting and long-term planning to achieve the overall vision.

strategic asset

(ITIL Service Strategy) Any asset that provides the basis for core competence, distinctive performance or sustainable competitive advantage, or which allows a business unit to participate in business opportunities. Part of service strategy is to identify how IT can be viewed as a strategic asset rather than an internal administrative function.

strategy

(ITIL Service Strategy) A strategic plan designed to achieve defined objectives.

strategy management for IT services

(ITIL Service Strategy) The process responsible for defining and maintaining an organization's perspective, position, plans and patterns with regard to its services and the management of those services. Once the strategy has been defined, strategy management for IT services is also responsible for ensuring that it achieves its intended business outcomes.

super user

(ITIL Service Operation) A user who helps other users, and assists in communication with the service desk or other parts of the IT service provider. Super users are often experts in the business processes supported by an IT service and will provide support for minor incidents and training.

supplier

(ITIL Service Design) (ITIL Service Strategy) A third party responsible for supplying goods or services that are required to deliver IT services. Examples of suppliers include commodity hardware and software vendors, network and telecom providers, and outsourcing organizations. *See also* supply chain; underpinning contract.

supplier and contract management information system (SCMIS)

(ITIL Service Design) A set of tools, data and information that is used to support supplier management. *See also* service knowledge management system.

supplier management

(ITIL Service Design) The process responsible for obtaining value for money from suppliers, ensuring that all contracts and agreements with suppliers support the needs of the business, and that all suppliers meet their contractual commitments. *See also* supplier and contract management information system.

supply chain

(ITIL Service Strategy) The activities in a value chain carried out by suppliers. A supply chain typically involves multiple suppliers, each adding value to the product or service. *See also* value network.

support group

(ITIL Service Operation) A group of people with technical skills. Support groups provide the technical support needed by all of the IT service management processes. *See also* technical management.

support hours

(ITIL Service Design) (ITIL Service Operation) The times or hours when support is available to the users. Typically, these are the hours when the service desk is available. Support hours should be defined in a service level agreement, and may be different from service hours. For example, service hours may be 24 hours a day, but the support hours may be 07:00 to 19:00.

supporting service

(ITIL Service Design) An IT service that is not directly used by the business, but is required by the IT service provider to deliver customer-facing services (for example, a directory service or a backup service). Supporting services may also include IT services only used by the IT service provider. All live supporting services, including those available for deployment, are recorded in the service catalogue along with information about their relationships to customer-facing services and other CIs.

SWOT analysis

(ITIL Continual Service Improvement) A technique that reviews and analyses the internal strengths and weaknesses of an organization and the external opportunities and threats that it faces. SWOT stands for strengths, weaknesses, opportunities and threats.

system

A number of related things that work together to achieve an overall objective. For example:

- A computer system including hardware, software and applications
- A management system, including the framework of policy, processes, functions, standards, guidelines and tools that are planned and managed together – for example, a quality management system
- A database management system or operating system that includes many software modules which are designed to perform a set of related functions.

system management

The part of IT service management that focuses on the management of IT infrastructure rather than process.

tactical

The middle of three levels of planning and delivery (strategic, tactical, operational). Tactical activities include the medium-term plans required to achieve specific objectives, typically over a period of weeks to months.

technical management

(ITIL Service Operation) The function responsible for providing technical skills in support of IT services and management of the IT infrastructure. Technical management defines the roles of support groups, as well as the tools, processes and procedures required.

technical observation (TO)

(ITIL Continual Service Improvement) (ITIL Service Operation) A technique used in service improvement, problem investigation and availability management. Technical support staff meet to monitor the behaviour and performance of an IT service and make recommendations for improvement.

technical support

See technical management.

tension metrics

(ITIL Continual Service Improvement) A set of related metrics, in which improvements to one metric have a negative effect on another. Tension metrics are designed to ensure that an appropriate balance is achieved.

terms of reference (TOR)

(ITIL Service Design) A document specifying the requirements, scope, deliverables, resources and schedule for a project or activity.

test

(ITIL Service Transition) An activity that verifies that a configuration item, IT service, process etc. meets its specification or agreed requirements. *See also* acceptance; service validation and testing.

test environment

(ITIL Service Transition) A controlled environment used to test configuration items, releases, IT services, processes etc.

third party

A person, organization or other entity that is not part of the service provider's own organization and is not a customer – for example, a software supplier or a hardware maintenance company. Requirements for third parties are typically specified in contracts that underpin service level agreements. *See also* underpinning contract.

third-line support

(ITIL Service Operation) The third level in a hierarchy of support groups involved in the resolution of incidents and investigation of problems. Each level contains more specialist skills, or is allocated more time or other resources.

threat

A threat is anything that might exploit a vulnerability. Any potential cause of an incident can be considered a threat. For example, a fire is a threat that could exploit the vulnerability of flammable floor coverings. This term is commonly used in information security management and IT service continuity management, but also applies to other areas such as problem and availability management.

threshold

The value of a metric that should cause an alert to be generated or management action to be taken. For example, 'Priority 1 incident not solved within four hours', 'More than five soft disk errors in an hour', or 'More than 10 failed changes in a month'.

throughput

(ITIL Service Design) A measure of the number of transactions or other operations performed in a fixed time – for example, 5,000 emails sent per hour, or 200 disk I/Os per second.

total cost of ownership (TCO)

(ITIL Service Strategy) A methodology used to help make investment decisions. It assesses the full lifecycle cost of owning a configuration item, not just the initial cost or purchase price. See also total cost of utilization.

total cost of utilization (TCU)

(ITIL Service Strategy) A methodology used to help make investment and service sourcing decisions. Total cost of utilization assesses the full lifecycle cost to the customer of using an IT service. See also total cost of ownership.

total quality management (TQM)

(ITIL Continual Service Improvement) A methodology for managing continual improvement by using a quality management system. Total quality management establishes a culture involving all people in the organization in a process of continual monitoring and improvement.

transaction

A discrete function performed by an IT service – for example, transferring money from one bank account to another. A single transaction may involve numerous additions, deletions and modifications of data. Either all of these are completed successfully or none of them is carried out.

transfer cost

(ITIL Service Strategy) A cost type which records expenditure made on behalf of another part of the organization. For example, the IT service provider may pay for an external consultant to be used by the finance department and transfer the cost to them. The IT service provider would record this as a transfer cost.

transition

(ITIL Service Transition) A change in state, corresponding to a movement of an IT service or other configuration item from one lifecycle status to the next.

transition planning and support

(ITIL Service Transition) The process responsible for planning all service transition processes and coordinating the resources that they require.

trend analysis

(ITIL Continual Service Improvement) Analysis of data to identify time-related patterns. Trend analysis is used in problem management to identify common failures or fragile configuration items, and in capacity management as a modelling tool to predict future behaviour. It is also used as a management tool for identifying deficiencies in IT service management processes.

tuning

The activity responsible for planning changes to make the most efficient use of resources. Tuning is most commonly used in the context of IT services and components. Tuning is part of capacity management, which also includes performance monitoring and implementation of the required changes. Tuning is also called optimization, particularly in the context of processes and other non-technical resources.

Type I service provider

(ITIL Service Strategy) An internal service provider that is embedded within a business unit. There may be several Type I service providers within an organization.

Type II service provider

(ITIL Service Strategy) An internal service provider that provides shared IT services to more than one business unit. Type II service providers are also known as shared service units.

Type III service provider

(ITIL Service Strategy) A service provider that provides IT services to external customers.

underpinning contract (UC)

(ITIL Service Design) A contract between an IT service provider and a third party. The third party provides goods or services that support delivery of an IT service to a customer. The underpinning contract defines targets and responsibilities that are required to meet agreed service level targets in one or more service level agreements.

unit cost

(ITIL Service Strategy) The cost to the IT service provider of providing a single component of an IT service. For example, the cost of a single desktop PC, or of a single transaction.

urgency

(ITIL Service Design) (ITIL Service Transition) A measure of how long it will be until an incident, problem or change has a significant impact on the business. For example, a high-impact incident may have low urgency if the impact will not affect the business until the end of the financial year. Impact and urgency are used to assign priority.

usability

(ITIL Service Design) The ease with which an application, product or IT service can be used. Usability requirements are often included in a statement of requirements.

use case

(ITIL Service Design) A technique used to define required functionality and objectives, and to design tests. Use cases define realistic scenarios that describe interactions between users and an IT service or other system.

user

A person who uses the IT service on a day-to-day basis. Users are distinct from customers, as some customers do not use the IT service directly.

user profile (UP)

(ITIL Service Strategy) A pattern of user demand for IT services. Each user profile includes one or more patterns of business activity.

utility

(ITIL Service Strategy) The functionality offered by a product or service to meet a particular need. Utility can be summarized as 'what the service does', and can be used to determine whether a service is able to meet its required outcomes, or is 'fit for purpose'. The business value of an IT service is created by the combination of utility and warranty. *See also* service validation and testing.

validation

(ITIL Service Transition) An activity that ensures a new or changed IT service, process, plan or other deliverable meets the needs of the business. Validation ensures that business requirements are met even though these may have changed since the original design. *See also* acceptance; qualification; service validation and testing; verification.

value chain

(ITIL Service Strategy) A sequence of processes that creates a product or service that is of value to a customer. Each step of the sequence builds on the previous steps and contributes to the overall product or service. *See also* value network.

value for money

An informal measure of cost effectiveness. Value for money is often based on a comparison with the cost of alternatives. *See also* cost benefit analysis.

value network

(ITIL Service Strategy) A complex set of relationships between two or more groups or organizations. Value is generated through exchange of knowledge, information, goods or services. *See also* partnership; value chain.

value on investment (VOI)

(ITIL Continual Service Improvement) A measurement of the expected benefit of an investment. Value on investment considers both financial and intangible benefits. *See also* return on investment.

variable cost

(ITIL Service Strategy) A cost that depends on how much the IT service is used, how many products are produced, the number and type of users, or something else that cannot be fixed in advance.

variance

The difference between a planned value and the actual measured value. Commonly used in financial management, capacity management and service level management, but could apply in any area where plans are in place.

verification

(ITIL Service Transition) An activity that ensures that a new or changed IT service, process, plan or other deliverable is complete, accurate, reliable and matches its design specification. *See also* acceptance; validation; service validation and testing.

verification and audit

(ITIL Service Transition) The activities responsible for ensuring that information in the configuration management system is accurate and that all configuration items have been identified and recorded. Verification includes routine checks that are part of other processes – for example, verifying the serial number of a desktop PC when a user logs an incident. Audit is a periodic, formal check.

version

(ITIL Service Transition) A version is used to identify a specific baseline of a configuration item. Versions typically use a naming convention that enables the sequence or date of each baseline to be identified. For example, payroll application version 3 contains updated functionality from version 2.

vision

A description of what the organization intends to become in the future. A vision is created by senior management and is used to help influence culture and strategic planning. *See also* mission.

vital business function (VBF)

(ITIL Service Design) Part of a business process that is critical to the success of the business. Vital business functions are an important consideration of business continuity management, IT service continuity management and availability management.

vulnerability

A weakness that could be exploited by a threat – for example, an open firewall port, a password that is never changed, or a flammable carpet. A missing control is also considered to be a vulnerability.

warm standby

See intermediate recovery.

warranty

(ITIL Service Strategy) Assurance that a product or service will meet agreed requirements. This may be a formal agreement such as a service level agreement or contract, or it may be a marketing message or brand image. Warranty refers to the ability of a service to be available when needed, to provide the required capacity, and to provide the required reliability in terms of continuity and security. Warranty can be summarized as 'how the service is delivered', and can be used to determine whether a service is 'fit for use'. The business value of an IT service is created by the combination of utility and warranty. *See also* service validation and testing.

work in progress (WIP)

A status that means activities have started but are not yet complete. It is commonly used as a status for incidents, problems, changes etc.

work instruction

A document containing detailed instructions that specify exactly what steps to follow to carry out an activity. A work instruction contains much more detail than a procedure and is only created if very detailed instructions are needed.

work order

A formal request to carry out a defined activity. Work orders are often used by change management and by release and deployment management to pass requests to technical management and application management functions.

workaround

(ITIL Service Operation) Reducing or eliminating the impact of an incident or problem for which a full resolution is not yet available – for example, by restarting a failed configuration item. Workarounds for problems are documented in known error records. Workarounds for incidents that do not have associated problem records are documented in the incident record.

workload

The resources required to deliver an identifiable part of an IT service. Workloads may be categorized by users, groups of users, or functions within the IT service. This is used to assist in analysing and managing the capacity, performance and utilization of configuration items and IT services. The term is sometimes used as a synonym for throughput.

Index

Index